Why Things Matter

D1594742

In this book, David M. Black asks questions such as 'why do we care?' and 'what gives our values power?' using ideas from psychoanalysis and its adjacent sciences such as neuroscience and evolutionary biology in order to do so.

Why Things Matter explores how the comparatively new scientific discipline of consciousness studies requires us to recognise that subjectivity is as irreducible a feature of the world as matter and energy. Necessarily inter-disciplinary, this book draws on science, philosophy and the history of religion to argue that there can be influential values which are not based exclusively on biological need or capricious life-style choices. It suggests that many recent scientific critics of religion, including Freud, have failed to see clearly the issues at stake.

This book will be key reading for psychoanalysts and psychotherapists as well as counsellors with an interest in the basis of religious feeling and in moral and aesthetic values. The book will also be of interest to scholars of psychoanalysis, philosophy and religion.

David M. Black is a Fellow of the British Psychoanalytic Society/Institute of Psychoanalysis and a founder member of the Foundation for Psycho-therapy and Counselling (WPF). He works in London. He has written and lectured widely on science, religion and consciousness studies and is the editor of *Psychoanalysis and Religion in the 21st Century: Competitors or Collaborators?* (Routledge, 2006).

Why Things Matter

The place of values in science, psychoanalysis and religion

David M. Black

Library
Quest University Canada
3200 University Boulevard
Squamish, BC V8B 0N8

Routledge
Taylor & Francis Group

LONDON AND NEW YORK

First published 2011
by Routledge
27 Church Road, Hove, East Sussex BN3 2FA

Simultaneously published in the USA and Canada
by Routledge
711 Third Avenue, New York NY 10017

Routledge is an imprint of the Taylor & Francis Group, an Informa business

© 2011 David M. Black

All rights reserved. No part of this book may be reprinted or reproduced or
utilised in any form or by any electronic, mechanical, or other means, now
known or hereafter invented, including photocopying and recording, or in
any information storage or retrieval system, without permission in writing
from the publishers.

Trademark notice: Product or corporate names may be trademarks or
registered trademarks, and are used only for identification and explanation
without intent to infringe.

British Library Cataloguing in Publication Data
A catalogue record for this book is available from the British Library

Library of Congress Cataloging in Publication Data
Black, David M.
  Why things matter : the place of values in science, psychoanalysis and
religion / David M. Black.
      p. cm.
  Includes bibliographical references and index.
  ISBN 978-0-415-49370-3 (hbk.) – ISBN 978-0-415-49371-0 (pbk.) 1.
Values. 2. Psychoanalysis and philosophy. 3. Philosophy and religion. I. Title.
  BF778.B59 2011
  121'.8–dc22
                                                              2010047769

ISBN: 978-0-415-49370-3 (hbk)
ISBN: 978-0-415-49371-0 (pbk)
ISBN: 978-0-203-80874-0 (ebk)

Typeset in Times by Garfield Morgan, Swansea, West Glamorgan
Printed and bound in Great Britain by TJ International Ltd, Padstow, Cornwall
Paperback cover design by Andrew Ward

Contents

Preface

This book has been two years in the writing, and about fifteen in the incubating. It consists of a series of chapters, or linked essays, broadly on the theme of values and how they can be thought about in an age when science, often described as 'value-free', has such great and well-deserved prestige. Most of these chapters began life as lectures in professional settings, then as papers in journals or, in two cases, chapters in edited books, but all have been revised, some very extensively, to become chapters in this book. They have been written in the interstices of a busy professional life, and although I hope they do not fall down on scholarship, I have envied academic colleagues who have more time for wider reading.

Papers 'incubated' over such a long span of time inevitably contain many inconsistencies: some for good reasons (one's thought has developed over this long period), some stylistic (one is no longer the same person as fifteen years ago), some for bad reasons (one has come to be high-handed with distinctions or important points one was earlier sensitive to). I have attempted in the reworking phase to diminish these inconsistencies as much as possible, but some will undoubtedly remain. Similarly, I have tried to eliminate repetitions as far as possible.

I owe many debts in connection with this book, and many of the most important are to early figures and influences that steered me, long before I encountered psychoanalysis, to a concern with issues of science, sympathy, cruelty and injustice, and a fear of a possible future in which 'gentle hearts', as W.H. Auden once put it, might become 'extinct like Hegelian Bishops'. Such a future still threatens, though the remarkable recent developments in science, in particular the new interest in consciousness, seem now to awaken new possibilities, and propel the issue of values to the forefront of our concerns. My psychoanalytic debts will be readily recognisable to my professional colleagues: I have avoided technicalities as far as possible (except in Chapter 7 where they became inevitable), but broadly the line that leads from Freud through Melanie Klein to the British post-Kleinians has given me most of my theoretical psychoanalytic landmarks. Even where, in places, I disagree with mainstream Kleinian theory, I am grateful to it for its clarity and intellectual integrity. With regard to neuroscience, evolutionary biology and philosophy, I have attempted to guide myself by recognised authorities, helped by the fact that several psychoanalysts, in particular Mark Solms, are also neuroscientists, and several, including Jonathan Lear, are philosophers. In our understanding of early development, the major recent advances have no longer come from within psychoanalysis; I have been influenced especially by the work of Colwyn Trevarthen and his associates in Edinburgh; one major root of that work is in attachment theory, which derives from the psychoanalytic tradition of John Bowlby and Daniel Stern.

Beyond my professional home territory, my reading has been extensive but I am sure, to specialists, very shallow. Michael Polanyi I mention only occasionally, but his example, as a scientist who ventured to follow the true breadth of the philosophical issues that opened up in front of him, has been a constant inspiration to me. I would say something similar of William James, a wonderfully daring and humane thinker, who figures nowhere in the psychoanalytic curriculum but who undoubtedly deserves to be read alongside Freud as one of the great pioneers in understanding psychological dynamics. I discovered the physiologist Charles Sherrington only when most of this book was in draft form, but I felt when I did so that I was meeting a kindred spirit: the challenge to the scientific vision of 'values' was his concern also, many years before it was remotely fashionable. It is notable that these impressively broad thinkers – to whom one might add Albert Einstein, Arthur Eddington, and several of the originators of quantum physics – all belong to a much earlier generation. I suspect more recent scientists have often had to work too hard to achieve their professional eminence to be able to embody the depth of seriousness and wider culture that make a William James, a Freud, a Charles Sherrington, an Erwin Shrödinger, so exhilarating and so enriching to the reader.

On a more personal front, I have discussed these ideas with many friends and colleagues over the years, and am grateful to all of them. A psychoanalyst lives in a world of continual serious conversations, with patients, with students, and also with colleagues, and my thinking, 'like the dyer's hand', has been deeply coloured by many years in this professional context. More particularly I am grateful to many people who made specific comments on some of the earlier versions of these chapters, among them Robert Chandler, Francis Grier, John Herdman, Martha Kapos, Martha Papadakis and Richard Rusbridger. I owe an altogether special debt to David Pugmire, who read the entire manuscript in draft, and with whom I have discussed many points in it along the way: the result would be a great deal more philosophically naive if I had not had the benefit of his input.

On a yet more personal front, I owe a great debt to Juliet, my wife, who, though often disapproving of my sympathy with religion, has been generously willing to discuss all these topics and to comment on many stages of the drafts. She has also endured with good humour my many hours of preoccupation, and 'absence' in all senses of the word. And finally, my parents, the one a scientist, the other a Christian, both stand behind this book. In many ways, it represents the conversation they never had together. I dedicate it to their memory.

Acknowledgements

Many of the chapters in this book have a history in previously published papers. I am grateful to the referees and editors of the *British Journal of Psychotherapy*, the *International Journal of Psychoanalysis*, the *Journal of Consciousness Studies*, and *Mental Health Religion and Culture,* who published the papers ancestral to Chapters 2 and 7, Chapter 4, Chapter 6 and Chapter 5 respectively. Jean Arundale, then editor of the *British Journal of Psychotherapy*, first asked me to write a paper on Freud's death drive (part of an exchange with Joseph Schwartz) which became Chapter 7 here. Chapter 3 had its origins in a chapter entitled 'The challenge of evolution and the place of sympathy' that appeared in *Ten Lectures on Psychotherapy and Spirituality*, edited by Nathan Field, Trudy Harvey and Belinda Sharp (Karnac, 2005) and Chapter 8 derives from a chapter in my own edited book, *Psychoanalysis and Religion in the 21st Century: Competitors or Collaborators?* (Routledge, 2006). All these papers have been adapted, some very extensively, to convert them into 'chapters'.

Permissions

Chapter 2 based on Black, D.M. (2004) 'A fact without parallel': Consciousness as an emergent property. *British Journal of Psychotherapy* 21(1), 69–82. Reprinted with permission from Wiley-Blackwell.

Chapter 3 based on a chapter by D.M. Black (2005) in *Ten Lectures on Psychotherapy and Spirituality* edited by Nathan Field, Belinda Sharp and Trudy Harvey, reprinted with kind permission of Karnac Books.

Chapter 4, based on Black, D.M. (2004b) Sympathy reconfigured: Some reflections on sympathy, empathy and the discovery of values. *International Journal of Psychoanalysis* 85, 579–96. Reprinted with permission from Wiley-Blackwell.

Chapter 5 based on Black, D.M. (2000) The functioning of religions from a modern psychoanalytic perspective. *Mental Health Religion and Culture* 3(1), 13–26. Reprinted with permission from Routledge. http://www.informaworld.com.

Chapter 6 based on Black, D. M. (2008) Reflections on the ownership of consciousness. *Journal of Consciousness Studies* 15(7), 5–27. Reprinted with permission.

Also in Chapter 6: Excerpt from "In the Waiting Room" from *The Complete Poems* 1927–1979 by Elizabeth Bishop. Copyright © 1979, 1983 by Alice Helen Methfessel. Reprinted by permission of Farrar, Straus and Giroux, LLC.

Chapter 7 based on Black, D.M. (2001) Mapping a detour: Why did Freud speak of a death drive? *British Journal of Psychotherapy* 18(2), 185–98. Reprinted with permission from Wiley-Blackwell.

In Chapter 10: Epigraph taken from Polanyi, M. (1958/1962) *Personal Knowledge: Towards a Post-critical Philosophy*. Reprinted with permission from Routledge (UK) and University of Chicago Press (US).

Chapter 1

Introduction

Science and values

Intellectual productions, however lofty their pretensions, ultimately stem from rather simple motives. That is certainly the case with the present book. One root from which it springs is the shock I remember feeling, as a young man at the time of the Vietnam War, hearing of a research chemist in California who was working to improve the adhesion of napalm to human flesh. We were daily seeing news from the war, including pictures of people on fire with the inextinguishable flames of napalm – how did this man feel, I wondered, about the work he was doing? What was in his mind when he went home in the evening and embraced the (presumably) undamaged bodies of his wife and children?

The philosopher Michael Polanyi, a background influence in much of my thinking, abandoned his first career as a biochemist when he watched his colleagues in 1933 Berlin transfer their expertise to the service of the new Nazi authorities, seemingly without self-questioning or qualms of conscience. How was it possible, he asked himself, that people who were professionally dedicated to an ideal, to the pursuit of scientific truth, could be so indifferent to considerations of morality? The question led Polanyi into his profound study (Polanyi 1958) of the personal implications of a commitment to scientific research. In order to study it, he enlarged his thinking to include psychology and philosophy, and he came to comment acutely on the arts, on the psychology of creativity and on religion. I can make no claim to Polanyi's breadth or profundity, but I have also found it necessary, attempting to address these questions of science and its relation to values, to broaden out from my home discipline (psychoanalysis in my case) to look at adjacent disciplines such as neuroscience and evolutionary theory, and also at philosophy. In fact, for me personally, the fifteen years or so over which these chapters have been meditated has been a time in which my great admiration for science has gradually moderated to make room for a recognition that science, at least as we have known it since the time of Galileo, and more especially since the time of Charles Darwin and Hermann Helmholtz, has become dangerously unbalanced. It stands in need of rebalancing, especially by philosophers who understand, better than scientists as a rule, the nature of the traps into which our use of specialised languages perpetually lures us. This need is seen most acutely in relation to values. How can values have force for us if they fail to show up in the landscape of 'fact'? – and yet, at any rate on a naive reading of science, 'value-free' scientific materialism appears to have cornered the market in declaring what is to be considered factual.

The requirement for breadth of understanding is bound to be a problem for anyone wishing to think or write about science and values. The issues exist in a space among or between many recognised disciplines, each of which calls for specialist knowledge – developmental psychology and psychoanalysis, cognitive science and neuroscience, evolutionary biology and the relatively new discipline of consciousness studies; all these need to be put in relation to the philosophy of values, of selves, and of 'reality' (that so familiar and deceitful word); they need to be examined too in relation to the history of our metaphors and to the ongoing dialogue between religion, 'atheism' (which I think of as a form of religion) and secularism. It would be helpful too to know some physics. Nobody is going to meet these requirements in full, and in a sense it becomes more difficult to do so, as time goes on, because the knowledge within each specialism grows vaster and the time required to keep up with it becomes greater. Those who are most expert in any one discipline are often the least flexible when thinking more generally. Even within my own field, which by comparison with psychology for example is quite small, no one can keep abreast of all that is published, year after year, in the (serious, peer-reviewed) psychoanalytic journals. And if you read the journals, you do not read the books, in which much of the more developed arguments are made. The same is true in all the fields I have mentioned.

Nevertheless, the issue of science and its relation to values is not going to disappear. Perhaps until the nineteenth century it seemed to most thinkers as if it could be dealt with by keeping the two topics separate: science could deal with the natural world, religion with values and 'spiritual' matters. The disengaged 'I' of Descartes, able to exist as nothing but the subject of the verb *to think*, was defined not by coincidence in the seventeenth century just as Galileo and Francis Bacon were launching what would become the Scientific Revolution; it occupied a virtual space altogether separate from the entirely mechanical universe it looked out on. A hundred years later, the pure rational subject of Kantian moral action was still different in kind from the world of phenomena in which it operated, the world constrained by time and space that science was now beginning to grasp with ever-increasing effectiveness. But such separations became harder and harder to hold on to, and the mid-nineteenth century put a lasting end to them. With Helmholtz's conservation of energy, and Darwin's evolution of all species including humankind, it became necessary to imagine a new, unified universe, in which everything to do with life, including our own mental experience and our highest values, had all emerged within the history of the solar system and from the stuff of our unique, extraordinary planet. There was no longer any point of entry for anything 'supernatural' or spiritual to act effectively in the world. If one wants to speak of the 'triumphs' of scientific thinking, that moment marks its supreme achievement. It eliminated, perhaps for ever, the idea that had haunted philosophers certainly since the time of Plato, that there could a dualism, an efficacious realm of 'spirit' alongside or superior to the ordinary visible realm of 'matter'. Since the mid-nineteenth century, science, and the thought of educated people more generally, has increasingly come to accept that 'there's just one thing here' – monism, not dualism.

Many scientists still speak of this picture as 'materialism', and I shall do so myself from time to time. But of course the word materialism is itself a hangover from the time of dualism, when 'matter' – inert, mechanical, 'base' – was contrasted with vital and creative 'spirit'. If dualism disappears, so too, necessarily, do the twin terms that compose it. The stuff of the new monism is no more 'matter' than it is 'spirit': in fact we still have no proper word for it, although physics, at the start of the twentieth century, would also radically reconceive the nature of its subject-matter and show that what had been thought to be inert and mechanical – the old-fashioned indivisible, bullet-like 'atoms' – was in reality a construction of energies, mostly empty space, impossible to pin down, and eluding all definitions. Speaking in 1927, the astronomer and physicist Arthur Eddington summarised the new quantum mechanics: 'Something unknown is doing we don't know what' (Eddington 1929: 291). (He added that nevertheless we can know a great deal about this obscure realm, because we can introduce numbers into it.) As physicists described the quantum, physiologists also increasingly discovered the astounding energy of 'life' that caused cells and minute organisms to propagate themselves at astonishing speed and in thousands of millions. Psychologists and neuroscientists, concerned with larger, multi-cellular organisms, tried for a time not to notice that, with increased complexity, these organisms also possessed or acquired another puzzling characteristic, namely, 'consciousness'. This characteristic was so puzzling and so scandalous that behaviourist psychologists like J.B. Watson tried initially to define it out of existence, or declared it a mere 'epiphenomenon', a sort of meaningless excrescence that played no causal role in the universe. Even now, in the early years of the twenty-first century, there are many philosophers and neuroscientists who claim that consciousness is entirely inefficacious: the world, they believe, would be exactly as it is even if there were no consciousness. (I shall look at some of these current theories of consciousness in Chapter 2.)

One of the difficult problems in an interdisciplinary field is to keep track of the different meanings that the same small repertory of words has for thinkers with different backgrounds. If we describe the new philosophical view as 'materialism', we will quickly be misled by our language into speaking of the world as made of 'matter', with the old implication of lifeless and inert; in this view, life and consciousness become problems demanding reductive explanation. I shall try instead, as a rule, to use the word monism, often qualifying it, in an attempt to get at the richness of the new conception, by speaking of 'multi-level monism'. But monism is also not a very satisfactory word, and neither is 'level'. The one is too abstract, the other a metaphor with too many implications. The psychoanalyst Donald Winnicott, trying to get behind another dualism our language imposes on us, the division of a person into a mind and a body, used to speak of 'the psychosomatic unit'. One of the challenges we are up against, at the present stage of our thinking, is how to overcome these suggestive and simplistic dichotomies that are built so deeply into ordinary language. However much we try to be alert, our ordinary language exerts a constant strain on our thinking, tugging it back towards traditional conceptions even while we claim to be stepping beyond them.

As consciousness appears to have emerged in more than one evolutionary line, I shall assume that it does play an efficacious role (how otherwise would it have been selected?) and therefore shall assume that the question that should most concern us is not whether it has a role but what that role is. (I shall discuss this question in particular in Chapter 6.) Looking from this perspective, among the many issues that arise is the issue of values. Values (I shall argue) come into existence with the emergence of life, and the underlying question throughout this book (I think of my scientist 'improving' the adhesion of napalm) is: what gives values power in our lives? At the most primitive levels of life, what has value is very simply what enables survival and continuation of the species; there are many questions one might ask, but the function of those early values is probably not mysterious. By the time we get to human beings, however, values have become enormously complicated. We are bound to assume that our values are the heir to the sort of values that influenced the earliest life-forms, but the attempt to derive the values of civilised human beings from the imperatives of evolution is still very speculative and uncertain. It falls foul of the fact that human beings in different societies, despite having much the same DNA, have extremely different values; and even the same human being, at different moments in his or her life, is governed by very different values.

In this book, I keep returning to one of the great historical moments of change in human values, the one that started in the seventeenth century and is generally described as the Enlightenment or the birth of the Scientific Revolution. Previously, in religious Europe, approved values could be given a very secure base: they represented God's will. It was God's will that you obeyed your feudal lord, that you were faithful to your spouse, that you did not practise witchcraft or murder the neighbour you happened to dislike or envy. And because God was the object of strong emotions of love, fear, worship and so on, God's will was important to you – you wanted to please him, or you feared displeasing him. But now, as rationality gradually displaced religious teaching as the central source of authority, the question of what attached you to your values became increasingly urgent. What constrained you? Did anything constrain you? A couple of decades after Darwin published *The Origin of Species*, Nietzsche put the issue into words with classic simplicity: 'God is dead,' he said, 'all is permitted'. It is hard not to think that the scale of violence in the twentieth century, incomparably greater than that of the eighteenth or nineteenth centuries, bears some relation to the moral shift that Nietzsche so promptly intuited.

On a less theoretical plane, this violence was also the product of the continuing advance of science. Kant in the eighteenth century had already foreseen that humankind's weapons might in the future become so terrifying that only the threat of total mutual destruction would prevent their use; the Cold War in the second half of the twentieth century proved his prescience. Those who want to speak of the triumphs of science should remember that those triumphs have come at a terrible cost, and it would be (to put it mildly) optimistic to imagine that all the bills have yet been paid. My Californian chemist, improving the adhesion of napalm, was a mere foot-soldier in the great army of scientists, working in academic or industrial settings, who appear to believe that they live professionally in a value-free world – an attitude they no doubt justify to themselves by believing that it too is 'scientific'. Many scientists, including some of the most distinguished such as Einstein and Heisenberg, have as they got older addressed this issue with increasing urgency, but these discussions remain curiously outside the scientific mainstream; they retain a certain air of eccentricity, and they seem, at any rate so far, to provide no generally recognised reference points.

The reason is, I think, that the radical ontological implications of the mid-nineteenth century development (that associated with Helmholtz and Darwin) – another historical landmark to which I shall repeatedly refer – have not been easy for those concerned about values to fully understand and digest. It has often seemed safest, for those who wanted to conserve values, to return to religious stances that were no longer compatible with the new scientific picture. I have no intention, in saying this, of sounding patronising. There is a very genuine difficulty here, and the hasty pursuit of intellectual consistency is not the highest value. It is often more honest to hold on to apparently incompatible insights, with all the accompanying discomfort, in the hope that some deeper resolution may be achieved in the future. Much of my own writing takes place in that kind of uncomfortable position.

In this context, psychoanalysis has played an interesting part. When Freud started his career as a laboratory scientist, he worked as a neuro-anatomist under the physiologist Martin Brücke; Brücke in turn was one of

Hermann Helmholz's circle, dedicated to a strict philosophical materialism. (The word, dedicated, is no exaggeration: Brücke as a young man had 'sworn a solemn oath', though to what divinity is not recorded, to accept no explanations that were not reducible to the basic terms of physics and chemistry (Sulloway 1979: 14).) Freud probably never explicitly repudiated this philosophical stance. However, when he left neuroanatomical research in the early 1890s, and started to develop psychoanalysis, the neurological knowledge of his time was too rudimentary and inflexible to support him. (I shall examine this transition in more detail in Chapter 7, when I look at what led him to his theory of a death drive.) In Freud's famous change of mind in 1897, when he realised that the stories of parental sexual abuse that he was hearing from his patients could not in all cases be true, and suspected therefore that what he was being told was 'phantasy' rather than reality, he allowed himself to make a crucial move. He allowed himself to think that 'phantasy', like 'reality', could have effects in the real world. From this move has flowed most of the broad stream of psychoanalytic conceptions: transference, splitting of the mind, many sorts of defence mechanism, psychic retreats, the importance of maternal reverie and emotional containment. It is common in psychoanalytic circles to hear reference to 'psychic reality', a strong term intended to convey that the effects of phantasy are not always slight and easily set aside as the ordinary-language term, 'fantasy', might suggest. (British analysts from the 1930s onward increasingly adopted Melanie Klein's Germanic spelling of the word phantasy, to indicate that they were speaking, not of something trivial, but of something that might be deeply unconscious and deeply influential, as the baby's phantasies about the mother's breast and body were held to be.) 'Deep unconscious phantasy' was held to structure the mind, and to influence the way the world was affectively perceived, even by the most realistic of adults.

Freud never quite gave up his hope that a developed neuroscience would eventually give concrete support for all these ideas, and as I shall suggest in later chapters, the ideas of Gerald Edelman (1992), and other more recent neuroscientists, have to a significant extent begun now to fulfil some of that hope. The degree to which the brain develops its detailed structure in response to early emotional experience, now a commonplace, makes a striking parallel to the psychoanalytic account of the early development of the 'mind' in response to the baby's relationship experience, and it has strongly confirmed the psychoanalytic belief in the importance of early relationships with care-givers. The psychoanalyst Mark Solms and others have begun to develop a neuropsychoanalysis in which the structure of dreaming, for example, seems to confirm many elements in Freud's account (Solms and Turnbull 2002). In that sense, one could say that Freud's psychoanalysis has served, to use one of his own favourite words, as a 'detour' that may eventually bring us back onto the better signposted path of neurology. However, in the process, psychoanalysis has also introduced a very different conception: it now seems that, just as the phenomena of consciousness can be influenced by physical events – very obviously in the case of such events as strokes and physical brain-damage – and new consciousnesses come into being as a result of a physical act, namely sexual intercourse, so too physical things, such as brains, can be influenced by mental events such as phantasies and transference-based construals of reality. It seems that the flows of causation can travel in both directions.

You will notice that I am already offending against my principles, and when I say 'travel in both directions' I am using a dualistic picture of the person. I am afraid that will often be unavoidable. But it also follows from the development of psychoanalysis, and the more recent discoveries in neuroscience, that the adoption of monistic 'materialism' does not have to conflict with a recognition of the extreme sensitivity and subtlety of our mental life. Perhaps much of the prejudice that people have felt against materialism springs from this cause: 'materialism' (in the philosophical sense) has seemed a diminishing thing, and has got mixed up too with 'materialism' in the consumer-society sense, a greedy and simplistic preoccupation with things and other people as objects of consumption and use, including sexual use. The history of the Communist regimes of the twentieth century, self-described as followers of Marxist philosophical 'materialism', has also contributed to a sort of reflex dislike and fear of the implications of materialism. But as already said, 'materialism' is no longer properly the correct word for the modern scientific understanding, and whether these fears are well or ill founded will largely depend on what place in a 'monistic' picture can still be found for values. For the purposes of this book, I shall adopt as best I can, despite the slipperiness of language, the perspective of 'multi-level monism'. That is, I think, the philosophical stance most compatible with the position of the modern sciences (including psychoanalysis). This stance seems to me unmistakably preferable to the more reductive monisms (such as behaviourist psychology or 'physicalism' in consciousness studies), which are one set of alternatives to it. Whether the other traditional alternatives of dualism or pluralism can still be supported I shall not consider here; scientific language is not, I think, capable of giving such theories a fair hearing: they necessarily depend on faith.

That then in extremely broad terms is the historical and conceptual framework in which I shall try to think about values in the present book. When I started writing on these themes, in the mid-1990s, I felt as though I was rather on my own with them; since then, many more people have written about them, and I have also discovered intelligent thinkers who have addressed similar problems, and arrived at recognisably similar solutions, right back to the time of Darwin. What I shall be saying was anticipated by William James in the 1890s, by Arthur Eddington in the 1920s, by Michael Polanyi in the 1950s, and by Mary Midgley in the 1990s (and many more). All of these thinkers appreciated the immense value of science as the source of knowledge about the natural world, but all of them also recognised the dangers and the poverty of an exclusively scientific take on the world. All of them recognised that an effective commitment to values calls for other sorts of knowledge, and other ways of thinking, and all of them, while maintaining their commitment to rationality, found positive things to say about the importance of religion, the arts, and humanity's heritage of moral and imaginative intuitions.

I should warn the reader that the questions to do with values are not easy to think about, or certainly I have not found them so, and the chapters that follow are more in the nature of linked essays, turning around different possibilities, than they are a coherent argument building to an overall definite, recommendable conclusion. My main hope for them is that they may contribute to an ongoing discussion, and may stimulate more people to address these issues who will bring to bear much greater knowledge and philosophical skill than I can command. Nevertheless, I like to think that the various arguments do make some progress; there are some positions, for example the 'physicalist' account of consciousness espoused by Francis Crick, or the claim advanced by many thinkers that consciousness plays no causal role in the world, which in my view are, on consideration, simply not viable: they achieve their plausibility, I think, because they are looked at from excessively specialised viewpoints, and they call attention to the necessity for more competent work in the interdisciplinary area. Over against such views, my positive thesis is that values are, in the metaphor I shall recurrently use, 'fountains of causation'; that is to say, to have a value causes effects in the world which would not have resulted in the absence of the value; this is so especially in the case of human beings who hold values in a vertical structure which is not intelligible when reduced to its constituents, whether the constituents are construed in terms of neuronal activity or of 'sub-personal' elements such as psychoanalytic internal objects.

Outline of the chapters

I shall now give a few initial pointers to the shape of the book. In Chapter 2 I begin with a broad survey of current theories of consciousness, a some-what new scientific territory and one that is still rather fascinating because of its impressive absence of consensus. It remains at present a sort of Burgess shale of possibilities. The need for an input from philosophy is nowhere more apparent than in the attempt to think about consciousness.

Chapter 3 is more historical. I try, in rather more detail than in this introduction, to locate where we have come from to reach the present state of the argument. I am at pains in this chapter, as elsewhere in the book, to emphasise how the 'cognitive' cast of mind, no doubt unsurprisingly dominant in scientists and many philosophers, tends to downplay and often to overlook entirely the 'affective' or emotional component of consciousness which must have played the largest part, initially, in its selection by the evolutionary process. One aspect of this, the role of sympathy, becomes the theme of Chapter 4. I suggest that we are not going to understand the power of values in our lives unless we recognise the huge importance of the capacity correctly called sympathy (which I distinguish from 'empathy' – we need both words, and have lost something important when we collapse them into one).

In Chapter 5 I shall look at the role of religion in promoting personal development, and compare what religions do with what psychoanalysis does. The reader may be surprised that, as a psychoanalyst, I am as sympathetic as I am, in this chapter and elsewhere, to religion. This is because, despite the abuses and intellectual confusion of much Western religion historically, religions have nevertheless been in the past the containers and purveyors of profoundly important values, and have also provided a context in which thought about these values has been vivified, charged with energy and therefore enabled to develop. It is not mere coincidence that it was out of a Judaeo-Christian culture that, eighteen hundred years or so after the crucifixion of Jesus, legislation was finally enacted condemning the institutions of slavery, torture and capital punishment, and attempts were made to formulate laws asserting universal human rights. Values emerge into efficacious action in a complex climate of feeling, reflection, social conditions and individual conscience, and religious traditions have often been the storehouses of such values and of the seeds of future values. They deserve some credit for this function.

I follow this with the first of two summary chapters, in which I attempt to give an overview of where this thinking is taking us. I speak in Chapter 6 of the importance of 'subjectivity', and suggest that it is often a better word in these discussions than 'consciousness' because it says more clearly what it is that the new scientific picture is being called on to integrate. I also suggest that the issue of values will be properly comprehensible only when we can be more clear about the issues of subjectivity which have traditionally been excluded from scientific discourse. If we are serious about monism, however, it closes down our freedom to make exclusions of this sort.

After this summary chapter, I start by looking at two more specialised topics. The first (Chapter 7) is the history of Freud's curious but remarkably fruitful idea of a 'death drive', which led to major advances in psychoanalytic understanding of destructiveness. Freud's theory is not in itself satisfactory, but it opened up for reflection the issue of the human capacity to delight in destruction – seen on the normal scale, so to speak, in what one might call ordinary cruelty, malice, envy, murderousness, and so on, but now able to manifest itself on a different scale altogether thanks to modern technology and methods of warfare. These developments now put at risk everything that human beings most deeply value, and we need to become as clear as we can about destructive motives and what values *they* represent. I regret that this chapter is rather specialised and will be of interest, probably, mainly to psychoanalytic readers; those without a specialist interest in psychoanalysis may prefer to skip or skim it.

The second specialised topic (in Chapter 8) picks up some of the themes of Chapter 4 and is an attempt to look at the idea of 'transcendence' from a psychoanalytic point of view. In one way or another, the idea of transcendence is present in most religious thinking, and distinguishes it rather firmly from science; can a 'monistic' scientific thinker find any meaning for it or does it simply have to be discarded? I suggest that the psychoanalytic idea of a psychic 'position', which we owe to Melanie Klein, gives a comprehensible way to conceive a hierarchy of values without bringing in any notion of the supernatural.

Chapter 9 discusses a wider issue: that of the self, and whether we can speak of a 'true self' over against other versions of the self, including the Buddhist idea, independently arrived at by David Hume, that ultimately there is no such thing as the self. I also consider the idea of a 'false self', which was put forward by Donald Winnicott. The notion of seriously held values presupposes that there will be a stable self to recognise and espouse the value, and yet on enquiry the self is hard to find. I think there are good reasons for this: selves are prone to splitting and dissolution, and a reasonably reliable self is a considerable psychological achievement. I conclude the chapter with a brief digression on the role of the 'avatar' in much traditional religion. I see it as a recognition of the weakness of the self, and the need of the self for help in maintaining its stability and its values despite overwhelming experience.

Chapter 10 is the second summary. In this final chapter, I seek to build on these ideas to consider what makes responsible commitment a possibility. What is perceived as a value calls on the self for action; responsible action, if it is to be possible at all, requires a stable self and values that can be relied on to have some duration. How is this possible if values are wholly based on subjective feeling? I address this question by discussing what Charles Taylor (1989) has called the 'ontological horizon' of moral choices. I conclude that there must be such a horizon, and it requires values to have, in some sense, a degree of objective reality. We are left with a paradox, for the objectivity we discover is not, like the objectivities of physics, one that is demonstrable to all; the 'cynic' may remain closed to it. For this reason, responsible commitment, even within a monistic scientific picture, can never finally avoid the challenge of faith.

Let us go on now to a brief overview of some of the current theories of consciousness.

Chapter 2

Consciousness

'A fact without parallel'

Introduction

The topic of consciousness offers a fascinating reminder of the power of fashion in scientific thought. Early in the twentieth century, the behaviourist psychologist J.B. Watson attempted to define it out of existence: so-called consciousness was merely behaviour, measurable and controllable like any other physical event. The neuroscientist Antonio Damasio (2000) tells us that, as recently as the 1970s, ambitious neuroscientists who were curious about consciousness were well advised to keep their thoughts to themselves: they would quickly have been dismissed as flaky. And yet, since the 1980s, consciousness has become one of the hottest topics around, eagerly studied by neuroscientists, cognitive scientists and evolutionary biologists, and the object of innumerable books, academic papers and competing theories.

The topic of the present book is values, but since values would be meaningless in the absence of consciousness to suffer their competing pushes and pulls, I shall begin with a summary survey of some of the current theories that attempt to account for consciousness. In doing so, I hope to point out one or two implications of the existence of consciousness which are sometimes overlooked.

We all know what consciousness is, and yet to try to speak of it is challenging. Psychoanalysts use the word consciousness so frequently that one might imagine that we, at least, understand it; but when we look more closely we find that psychoanalysis sheds no light on its essential nature. And in fact psychoanalysis tends to use the word consciousness differently from the other sciences: its interest, most often, is in consciousness as differentiated from 'unconsciousness'. Together, for psychoanalysis, conscious and unconscious elements make up a dynamic, causally interactive system called 'the mind' (in James Strachey's English translation; Freud's word was 'the soul' (*die Seele*)). As we said in Chapter 1, Freud was a materialist, a follower of Helmholtz, in his underlying philosophy, and he did not set out to create a dualistic picture, but the language available to him at the end of the nineteenth century carried him unavoidably in that direction. Despite Freud's theoretical materialism, we see him repeatedly struggling with those familiar problems of dualists, the 'mind-body frontier', and how events 'in the mind' can influence events 'in the body' and vice versa.

Now that consciousness has come back onto the scientific scene, since the 1940s in cognitive science and only since the 1980s in neuroscience and evolutionary biology, the word tends to be used rather differently. It refers to the mental component of experience, known to all of us subjectively because we have extremely sophisticated minds ourselves, but assumed by most of us to be also objectively present in other people, and generally imagined to be present in less sophisticated form in at least some non-human species. The interest here is not so much in the difference between conscious and unconscious mental processes – an extremely volatile difference in the processes we have subjective access to – but in the difference between mental experience and physical events, in particular the sort of measurable physical events modern neuroscience is well equipped to deal with. Because of the cognitive bias of most scientists, mental experiences are often cashed as 'thoughts' or 'logical operations' or 'information-processing', but in their more primitive and fundamental forms mental experiences are probably better conceived as affective, having to do with feelings, or impulsive, having to do with fears or desires that impel to action. In speaking of these matters, I shall sometimes use the word 'experiencing' as a term of art, in an attempt to name a sort of mental event more primitive in evolutionary terms than the sort of sophisticated operations which are familiar to us, in which thought, feeling and impulse are at least to some extent differentiated.

The language of 'embodiment', developed in the later decades of the twentieth century by some cognitive scientists (e.g. Varela et al. 1993) and some philosophers and linguists (e.g. Lakoff and Johnson 1999), gives us nowadays a much more flexible way of talking about these issues than was available in Freud's day. Nevertheless, addressing the subject of consciousness, all these many thinkers still encounter much the same difficulty that psychoanalysis meets: they discover it very hard to speak of consciousness directly. The new language can help us to understand the conditions in which consciousness arises, or the functions it may fulfil which have caused evolution to select and enhance it, but it can say surprisingly little that helps us to understand what it is in itself. I shall argue that this is not because they just have not happened to stumble yet on the correct hypothesis, but that it is intrinsic to the nature of consciousness that it can only remain ungraspable by Galilean science, the science which has made such prodigious advances in the past four hundred years.

I am not sure that Freud would have said quite what I am saying, but I think he might have done. As he got older, he seemed to become more and more aware of the extraordinariness of consciousness (and more aware of it too, perhaps, in its modern sense). In *The Outline of Psychoanalysis*, written at the very end of his life just after he had escaped from Vienna and come to London, he speaks of consciousness as 'a fact without parallel, which defies all explanation or description' (Freud 1940: 157). I think he clearly implies there that consciousness is irreducible and beyond understanding.

But I am getting ahead of my argument. Let me go back now and look at some of the theories that are currently on offer.

Panpsychism, physicalism, functionalism

The psychologist Max Velmans (2000) has put forward an interesting theory to account for the presence of consciousness. He looks at the evolutionary story, and argues that we have no reason to claim any particular point on the evolutionary scale as the point at which consciousness makes its appearance. We know consciousness exists because we have it ourselves; we feel confident in attributing it to other human beings, and most people, unless they are fundamentalist Cartesians, have little doubt that dogs and chimpanzees have a sort of consciousness; but why should we stop there? Why not frogs, why not worms, why not all life? Brain-cells, after all, are only cells that have become specialised because of their location. If, in an embryo, you transplant a skin-cell into the brain, it changes its nature and become a perfectly good brain-cell. If you think brain-cells give rise to consciousness, what threshold do you discern, between the cell in the skin and the cell in the brain, at which consciousness comes on the scene?

And if you grant that – so Velmans's argument goes – what frontier do you see between the inorganic and the organic at which consciousness might suddenly insert itself? Since consciousness is so completely *sui generis*, we cannot map its arrival onto any material event – perhaps it pervades the entire natural world. He suggests that consciousness, no doubt in some immensely attenuated form, permeates the universe; it is a 'primary quality' of matter, but plays no part in the familiar causal stories of cosmology and physics. If it did not exist, our universe would be exactly as it is; but, he adds, 'the lights would be out' (Velmans 2000: 259), there would be no 'point' to any of it. We live in a reflexive universe, not in a mechanical one.

This view is not wholly original to Velmans. Something like it has been suggested by Charles Sherrington (1940) and Arthur Eddington (1929), and more recently by thinkers like Teilhard de Chardin (1959), Thomas Nagel (1979b) and Galen Strawson (2006). (Nagel (1979b: 193) described it as 'hopelessly unacceptable', but he did not feel it could be dismissed out of hand.) Technically, it is called panpsychism, or one could call it a sort of radical animism. If the *psyche* in *panpsychism* implies pan-consciousness, I think this argument is hard to sustain, but I start with these thinkers because I believe they are right to be so astonished by the fact of consciousness – so profoundly impressed by it that it leads them to reimagine the whole world that positivistic science has presented to us. I want to join them in their astonishment, and I too think that science as we have known it since Galileo will have to be reconceived if we are to take into account the 'fact without parallel', the fact of consciousness.

(The sort of arguments this book deals with recurrently approach the threshold of panpsychism, which a surprising number of recent thinkers have been willing to cross. I shall regularly turn back from it. The alternative to panpsychism is some picture of *emergence*, and the claim that new arrangements of matter can generate wholly novel properties. I shall discuss this issue at several points, and in particular in Chapter 7 when I talk about the 'ownership' of consciousness. But in general, my answer will be that we are bound to accept emergence (difficult as that is to understand) because the panpsychist alternative is unintelligible. I think it is unintelligible because it creates the impossible question of who or what could be the subject, the 'I', of a panpsychic consciousness. But this is one of several points in these arguments, probably the most acute one, where it's safest to say that no really satisfactory theory is yet on offer.)

At the other extreme from Velmans stands a philosopher like J.J.C. Smart, or a neuroscientist like Francis Crick. Crick also, as it happens, uses the word *astonishing*, but he does not use it of consciousness: he uses it of his own theory. In his book, *The Astonishing Hypothesis*, Crick (1994) claims that consciousness can be wholly reduced to physical events in the brain. As he puts it: 'You, your joys and your sorrows, your memories and your ambitions, your sense of personal identity and free will, are, in fact, no more than the behaviour of a vast assembly of nerve cells and their associated molecules' (Crick 1994: 3). To Francis Crick, and to many other neuroscientists and some philosophers such as J.J.C. Smart (1962) or Patricia Churchland (1986), brain events not only are the correlates of conscious experience, but also they are identical with conscious experience. Once we have described the electrochemical transactions in the brain, they believe, there will be no more questions to ask. Theories of this sort represent a position known as physicalism; they hold that consciousness is identical with brain-states.

A variant of physicalism, particularly popular in recent years, is what is called functionalism, represented by many cognitive scientists and such philosophers as Hillary Putnam (1960), David Lewis (1972) and Daniel Dennett (1991). Functionalists also believe that mental states are physical states, but 'they are defined as "mental" not because of their physical constitution but because of their causal relations' (Searle 1997). Functionalism has been heavily influenced by the development of computer science and artificial intelligence, and the notion that information can be carried by a physical system, not because of the physical stuff it is made of, but because of the causal sequences into which that stuff can be put. Depending on its programming, the same computer hardware can perform a vast range of operations; analogously, the brain, according to this theory, is essentially an information-processing system, responsive to 'experience' and with a huge capacity for adaptation and self-modification (Wegman 1985; Edelman 1992). What we call conscious mental states, therefore, are nothing additional to physical matter that arranges itself in symbolically coded sequences in response to selected features of the environment.

Since, in this picture, the essential function of the mind is computation, 'consciousness' once again assumes a subordinate position: the 'computations' on which mind depends are performed by non-conscious physical subsystems working at great speed, with which conscious functioning could only interfere. (The meaning of 'non-conscious' processes in cognitive science is quite unlike the meaning of 'unconscious processes' in psychoanalysis (Varela et al. 1993: 47–50). An unconscious mental process in psychoanalysis is potentially conscious, at any rate in principle; there is nothing of this sort in computer science.)

These physicalist and functionalist theories have certain important strengths, which have made them persuasive to many thinkers. For one thing, they do not conflict with the immensely successful paradigm of post-Galilean science. And in many ways, they are eminently compatible with what we see. A human organism, including its brain, develops from the event of conception, responds hugely to affective experience and education, and is impaired in characteristic ways by drugs, malnutrition, physical brain-damage, and so on. Gerald Edelman (1992) has shown that the structure of the brain is only to a limited extent determined by the genes; the fabulously complex pattern of synaptic connections (a thousand million million of them, 10 to the power of 15, by the end of the first year of life) is fine-tuned and changes continually in response to the affective environment in which the baby or child find themselves. This demonstrates (to me, though not presumably to the physicalist) that the causal sequence can run from conscious experience to brain-structure. And of course the scientific literature is full of examples such as the effect of strokes, Alzheimer's, brain-tumours, lobotomies, CJD and so forth which show the causal story flowing in the other direction, when traumatic changes to brain-structure alter conscious experience. There are also weird phenomena such as 'blindsight' (in which people who are consciously 'blind' behave in ways which clearly show they are, in some sense, able to 'see' – for example, when asked to point at a particular object, they do so reliably, although they believe they are only making an inspired guess). These phenomena are very extraordinary, and become comprehensible only when you know in detail the pattern of the brain-damage the individual has suffered. Antonio Damasio (2003) has presented a detailed evolutionary explanation of how conscious feeling states may have developed; he suggests that they have accrued on the back of processes in the brain leading to the formation of 'maps' that keep track of the micro-second to micro-second changes in overall body-state.

Fascinating and impressive as they are, however, the physicalist and functionalist arguments fail to prove their point. What they show very convincingly is that states of human consciousness are caused by, or perhaps they only correlate with, brain-states, but they do not show, and cannot show, that states of consciousness are identical with brain-states. This is shown by the fact that you can know as much as you like about a brain-state, but the only way to find out what state of consciousness connects with it is to ask the 'owner' of the brain. Similarly, you can know a great deal about a state of consciousness, as Shakespeare knew a lot about ambition, without having the first idea about the brain-state that accompanies it. Whatever else these two sorts of state may be – and no scientist doubts that they are connected in crucial ways – they are not identical.

The history of psychoanalysis is interesting in this regard. It began when Freud, whose initial training was as a neurologist, realised that his physical science was too primitive to allow him to understand what was happening to his neurotic patients. In the course of the 1890s, he crossed the gap, and began to allow himself to speak of mental events in terms of mental causes, discoverable by introspection. For the next seventy or eighty years, psychoanalysis made huge advances, guided by gifted intuitive clinicians like Melanie Klein and Wilfred Bion. But because introspection is subject to so many uncontrollable influences, and its vocabulary loses an essential flexibility when one ties it down by definitions, psychoanalytic theory evolved very differently in different places, and different theories now can no longer really be mapped onto each other, either to confirm or to disconfirm them. (No one quite knows how compatible the theories of Klein, Winnicott, Lacan, Kohut and others may be; individual psychoanalysts tend to be at home in one or two vocabularies but not in others.) It may well be that a developed neuroscience will come to our rescue, as Freud always thought it eventually would, by clarifying our vocabulary and showing us more precisely what we mean by the words we use. Something of this sort has already happened in the new differentiation by neuroscience of various sorts of memory – short term, implicit, semantic, procedural and episodic – which can be distinguished because they are all stored in different locations in the brain. Or – another example – we now know that recognition of faces is performed by a different part of the brain from the recognition of inanimate 'things'. Neuroscience confirms our intuitive sense that faces are something very special for us (Turnbull and Solms 2003: 73–74).

These immensely valuable discoveries follow from the careful work of neuroanatomists such as Gerald Edelman and Francis Crick. There can be little doubt that in coming years, our understanding of infantile development, of the effects of traumas such as separation and abuse, of the positive influence of well-attuned parents and committed educators, and of the action of the different sorts of psychotherapy, including cognitive behavioural therapy and psychoanalysis, will all be transformed and put on a far more solid and convincing foundation as a result of neuroscientific discoveries (see for example Gabbard and Westen 2003). Chronically controversial topics in psychoanalysis such as the death drive, which I shall discuss in detail in Chapter 7, and 'primary narcissism', a self-focused state which according to Freud precedes the baby's relating to others, may at last be laid to rest, or, more accurately, we may become able to discern what that is true is being aimed at in these intriguing but unsatisfactory formulas. In what I am going to say about consciousness, I want to go beyond what neuroscience can tell us, but this is in no way to underestimate the huge contribution that neuroscience still has to make to the project of understanding the mind.

The danger for neuroscience, as for psychoanalysis in the past, is that its impressive successes blind its practitioners to its limitations. The question that preoccupies many neuroscientists – How does consciousness derive from the brain? – is not only a hard question, but also an act of imperialism. It is claiming ontological primacy for the subject of neuroscience; it is claiming that, if we want to understand consciousness, the brain is the thing we have to get to grips with. This is by no means self-evident. In fact, if what we are concerned with is the link between brain and consciousness, that is precisely something which will not appear in the brain, which is itself one term in the relation we are seeking to examine. The philosopher Colin McGinn (1989), in an important article, argued on these grounds that what he calls the 'mind-body problem' will always remain unsolvable. Because of the nature of our cognitive capacities, we are on either one side of the divide or the other, we are either introspecting or doing neuroscience: the link is systematically inaccessible to us. (McGinn was not saying it did not exist, and he suggested that it might even be quite unremarkable; his point was that it is our own cognitive nature that may make the link a matter of 'terminal perplexity' for us.)

The psychoanalyst Mark Solms (1997), who is also a neuroscientist, discussed the subject of consciousness in the light of a striking metaphor used by Freud. Consciousness, said Freud (1900: 615–616), is 'a sense organ for the perception of psychic qualities'. Just as our ordinary sense organs, sight, for example, give us a certain take on the world, and we see it as coloured, extended, composed of different 'things' which exclude one another in three-dimensional space – whereas another sense organ, hearing for example, gives us a quite different take on it and we perceive a world made up of sounds of varying volume, pitch, timbre and duration, spread out in time and only rather obscurely in space – in the same sort of way, the 'sense organ' of consciousness gives us access to another world, one of thoughts, affects, desires, fantasies and so on. By bringing together the deliverances of these different sense modalities, we constitute what we think of as the ordinary comprehensible world of trees and people and books, related to one another in space, linked by causality and enduring in time. But in reality, the world is vastly more complex than what our sense organs perceive, and there are whole decks of reality, such as quantum events and dark matter, that we have no capacity to perceive at all. And the electromagnetic spectrum itself stretches out above and below the rather narrow bands our senses discern.

Kant in the eighteenth century claimed that the objects of experience tell us nothing of things as they are in themselves. Solms's argument is an extension of this. He says that, just as vision tells us of visible things (including neurons), so consciousness tells us of psychic things, and neither tells us the whole truth about a third, unknown, objective reality, 'the mental apparatus and its functions'. He concludes: 'The supposedly mysterious distinction between mind and brain thus dissolves into a simple distinction between different perceptual modalities, facing in different directions' (Solms 1997: 691, 700), mind facing inward, so to speak, and vision, hearing and so on facing outward.

This argument, however, stops too soon. Solms has taken Freud's metaphor, of consciousness as a sense organ, literally, and we need to ask further questions. With other sense modalities, (to use Solms's own example) with seeing and hearing that both tell of a 'third thing' which manifests as lightning in one modality, and thunder in the other, science can give us an intelligible account of how these different experiences originate. We can understand that our sense organs are affected by two different sorts of wave motion, both activated by a single event. With consciousness and the physical senses we can give no such account. We cannot even imagine the language in which such an account could be made.

Moreover, what is it that faces inward, or outward? We notice that Solms has changed from speaking of consciousness to speaking of 'mind', the word favoured by Freud's translator and by English-speaking psychoanalysts. Mind can be conscious, but it can also be unconscious, and Freud's so-called 'discovery' of the unconscious came about because he realised that mental processes, like physical processes, occur in continuous causal chains and are understandable, but our awareness of these causal chains, our consciousness of them, is intermittent. Consciousness does not only face 'inward', reflexively; at least as much it faces outward, and tells us, or it seems to tell us, of mind-independent realities such as stars, birds and other people. Consciously or unconsciously, the mind receives the deliverances both of the external senses and of whatever metaphorical 'sense organ' – if there needs to be such a thing – that perceives psychical qualities.

In a later restatement of these themes, in the book he co-wrote with Oliver Turnbull, Solms writes: 'The mind itself is unconscious, but we perceive it consciously by looking inwards. It is this capacity for "looking inwards" (for introspection or self-awareness) that is the most essential property of a mind' (Solms and Turnbull 2002: 76–77). The problem here has become one of too many entities: there is a mind, consciousness, and also an unaccounted-for 'we' who, like the mind, 'look inwards'. I think what we are seeing is something that continually bedevils discussions of consciousness: the difficulty of talking about subjectivity objectively. We have to do this, and yet when we do, subjectivity too readily becomes just another objective thing to be accounted for, and loses its distinctive difference. Yet how can we give it primacy, when 'the mind' is unmistakeably subject to damage as a result of physical events? I shall come back to all this, and try not to fall into all the same potholes, when I talk about the ownership of consciousness in Chapter 6.

At all events, the attractive simplicity of Solms's conclusion is not sustainable, I think. Consciousness is not just a sensory modality like the others, and perhaps Freud realised this when he later called it a 'fact without parallel': he meant that no generic term applies to it (Freud 1940: 157). But in order to call it something, let's call it, not very accurately, the realisation of a capacity. Consciousness is the realisation of a capacity which brings attention both to the deliverances of the senses and to what is going on in our mind. Valuably from an evolutionary point of view, it is what allows us to bring attention to what we are 'consciously doing', that is our main action, as opposed to our many unconscious actions and the many processes, such as digestion and the operation of the immune system, that go on in us 'non-consciously' – without even the possibility of becoming conscious. Consciousness is also of immense importance to a social species that depends for survival on the emotional connections among its members. It exists necessarily at a higher logical level than the sense organs, whose deliverances it receives. Moreover, we have to distinguish different grades of consciousness: there is a 'raw sensory consciousness' and a 'reflexive consciousness' (in Nicholas Humphrey's (1997) terms), or a 'core' consciousness and an 'extended autobiographical' consciousness (Damasio 2000). And two grades is almost certainly too few. We are forever 'seeing things' without 'seeing what they mean', and this happens at successive levels: we saw the little fish, and we saw the bigger fish that was about to eat it; that was a drama in itself, but we didn't see the even bigger fish that was about to eat them both . . . and so on.

Consciousness is owned by subjects

Thinking like this takes us in a very radical direction indeed. But I see no alternative to it. The sciences, including quantum physics, psychoanalysis, neuroscience, and so on, are all highly sophisticated extensions of our capacity to perceive and to reflect. Our ordinary sense organs have been vastly extended by our technical equipment – microscopes, PET and fMRI scans, particle accelerators, the carefully constructed instrument of the psychoanalytic hour, and so on – and our ordinary capacity to reflect has been hugely expanded by learning the traditions of science and philosophy, and by receiving the comments and criticisms of our colleagues, but, essentially, what is going on in science is sense observation and reflection. In particular, in relation to our topic, what neuroscience talks about, the brain and nervous system, the axons, dendrites, transmitter molecules and so forth, are all presented to us as if they were things that might in principle be visible and tangible. But it is not vision or the sense of touch that knows of them: it is consciousness. Consciousness is, so to speak, at the logical high point of all our experience, and it is from what the psychoanalyst Wilfred Bion would have called the vertex of consciousness that all the sciences have the particular reality they have. There is therefore no way that science can explain consciousness, because consciousness is what knows science; consciousness is logically anterior to science.

To say this is to reach a certain sort of boundary. Perhaps there is no way to be an 'expert' on consciousness, because consciousness is prior to our expertise. I speak from a psychoanalytic perspective, and psychoanalysis can claim a degree of knowledge about mental mechanisms which limit consciousness, or distort its access to certain sorts of impulse or affect; we can also see many of its uses, for example, in deciding what we will regard as reality – what we believe or, on reflection, do not believe (Britton 1998) – in learning new skills and negotiating new situations, and in arriving at decisions about action. Our pleasure in play and interaction with conscious others is a delight and excitement at shared consciousness which profoundly influences, perhaps even makes possible, our whole existence as social animals. I shall discuss all these things in more detail in later chapters, but it is clear that they are hugely important from an instrumental and evolutionary point of view. By the time we reach animals as complex as ourselves, there is no feature of our lives which has not been crucially shaped by play and conscious decision, either by ourselves or by others, in the present or in the past.

The point I want to focus on here, however, is something different. It is the fact that consciousness is always owned by a subject.[1] Psychoanalysis has often been reproached for the fact that it refers to other people as 'objects', an unfortunate usage for which there are in fact good historical reasons. The interest of early psychoanalysis was primarily in others as the 'objects' of our infantile desires and anxieties, love and hate, envy and gratitude, and the 'subject' of these motives is always ego. But when we think about

---

1 David Hume famously denied this (Hume 1739: Book 1, Part 4, Section 6). But his denial was of a 'self' that somehow has a separate existence from its experience – perhaps a bit like a Christian soul that can survive the death of the body. My use of 'subject' is not intended to imply such a thing-like 'self', but merely to claim that it is not possible to conceive of experience without conceiving a subject who experiences it.

consciousness, we become aware of something very different. It is that consciousness is always owned by a subject. To reflect on consciousness is to recognise the ubiquity of subjectivity. This does not, of course, annihilate the existence of 'objectivity', though it does reveal it to be dependent on intersubjective agreement on how language is to be used. Given that agreement, there are plenty of 'objective' facts which are perfectly solid. Belgium did not invade Germany in 1914: Germany invaded Belgium. Acid plus base gives salt plus water. Facts of this sort are not under threat, and, given a reasonable degree of agreement about the language we are speaking, there is no reason why they should not be called objective.

But when we think that consciousness is owned by *subjects*, and not by *objects*, areas of thought become accessible that have hitherto been problematic for psychoanalysis. Empathy, a word much favoured in psychoanalysis, gives us access to the mental world of another by 'trial identification'; essentially, it treats *his* mental world as an object for *my* understanding, and I, ego, continue to be the subject. Sympathy, a word disfavoured in psychoanalysis, experiences the other as subject, and can do this so powerfully that the welfare of ego is disregarded. Friendship, the pleasure of knowing another as a subject, and justice, the quality that recognises others as subjects deserving equal consideration with the self – these things cannot, I think, be properly understood when others are considered only as objects. Love itself, that deeply and necessarily ambiguous feeling, is not adequately understood in terms of desire, gratitude, meeting of needs, etc., only, as scientific psychological thinkers often wish to believe; it involves also a recognition of the other as a subject, capable of consciousness and suffering like the self.

When we think like this, we realise that subjectivity occupies a higher logical level than objectivity. It is parallel to consciousness in relation to science. We can be objective about subjectivity only up to a point, because subjectivity keeps reinserting itself above our (new) objectivity; we cannot solve the mystery of consciousness by science, because consciousness will always be doing the solving. (I shall argue in Chapter 10 that we can only finally base ourselves in these matters on a necessary circularity.) The philosophical pact that science has made with its adherents, ever since Galileo and John Locke in the seventeenth century defined the primary qualities of matter as those that were present in the object whether or not it was perceived by anyone, was designed to exclude subjectivity from the world. That was a brilliant and hugely productive 'fiction'; it constructed a model of the world which could be grasped by measurement and therefore described by mathematics, and therefore in the long run it allowed a control of the world that neither of these men could remotely have foreseen. That control is still extending, now into the subatomic realms and the genetic material of human and other living beings; it is responsible too, of course, for the neuroscientific advances we have been discussing.

(I shall discuss all these themes in much more detail in future chapters, sympathy in particular in Chapter 4, the ownership of consciousness and the role of Galileo and Locke's model of primary qualities in Chapters 3 and 6.)

Consciousness as an emergent property

At the start of this chapter I quoted Max Velmans (2000) and his pan-psychic vision of a universe in which some precursor of consciousness is present even in inorganic matter. I think this goes beyond what the evidence requires, and I am not even sure that it is fully intelligible. We certainly need to account for the presence of consciousness in many life-forms, and I think this is most convincingly done if we think of consciousness as an 'emergent property' which accrues upon some of the attributes of living organisms – complex arrays of neurons being one such attribute though perhaps not the only one. Having emerged, it becomes something on which natural selection can act, and if it offers advantages it is likely, like any other advantageous development, to be selected for and to contribute further to the continuing history of evolution.

Emergent properties are properties that develop when constituents at one level of structural organisation are united in a particular way to form a new level of structure. New properties may then 'emerge' which are wholly unpredictable from the lower level of organisation. One striking example is life itself. There is no way, from the properties of inorganic matter, that you could predict the property of life, and the striving of all living beings to keep themselves in a state of life, to avoid pain and damage, and to reproduce. (Many biologists disagree; we will look at some views that contradict this in Chapter 3.) There are many such thresholds. Another is the threshold between quantum particles, governed by laws that we can encompass only by paradoxical statement, and atoms which can take part in physical and chemical interactions that we feel we understand. (They allow us to have what William James (1882) called 'the sentiment of rationality'.) Arthur Koestler (1982) used the word *holarchy* to describe the resulting hierarchical picture, holarchy deriving from *holon*, a word meaning something which is *whole* when viewed on its own structural level. An atom is a whole when viewed from the level of atoms, but a part when viewed from the level of molecular structures; a molecule is a whole when viewed from the level of molecules, but a part when considered from the level of the biological cell.

The American Buddhist thinker Ken Wilber, expounding Koestler, gives a rather simple rule for discerning levels within this holarchy.

> If you destroy any particular type of holon, then all of the higher holons are also destroyed, because they depend in part on the lower

holons for their own components. But the lower holons can get along perfectly well without the higher: atoms can exist just fine without molecules, but molecules cannot exist without atoms.

(Wilber 1996: 32)

If we apply this rule to human consciousness and the brain, we can see clearly how things stand. Functioning neurons can exist without consciousness, such as in sleep, anaesthesia or coma, but consciousness cannot exist (so far as we know) without functioning neurons. Consciousness therefore is an emergent property, dependent on Crick's vast assembly of neurons, but emerging at a higher level than them and not reducible to them.

This is a different sort of view from Velmans's, and in my opinion more plausible because more comprehensible. Like Velmans's view, however, it requires a radical change in the way we conceive what is ordinarily called *matter*. Matter shows itself to be much more extraordinary than the mere 'moving particles' of traditional philosophical materialism. Quantum physics has already disturbed that picture by showing that 'particles' can equally be conceived as systems of energy. If we add in the implications of consciousness, then reductive, single-level monisms, or the various sorts of dualism, are replaced by a multi-level monism. I prefer the phrase 'multi-level monism' to the more familiar dual-aspect monism for two reasons: first, because it implies an indefinite number of causally interacting 'levels', not just two; and second, because it implies that these levels exist in a logical hierarchy, created by the different decks of emergence. There is no reason, in such a picture, to privilege one deck of the multi-level system as 'more real' than any other: quarks are not more real than atoms, atoms are not more real than molecules, and neurons are not more real than subjects of consciousness.

To speak in this way of consciousness as an emergent property of matter may seem a kind of whimsical idea, a piece of fanciful ontology without consequences. But this is not the case. I spell out two possible consequences of this idea, both of which I shall enlarge on in subsequent chapters: first, consciousness has its own laws, and second, we discover a world of necessary (not contingent) uniqueness.

Consciousness has its own laws

First, emergent properties, being natural properties, are governed by natural laws which belong to their particular ontological levels. The laws that govern the behaviour of atoms are not the laws that govern quantum particles, but they are equally definite and can be discovered – discovered not invented, to make an important distinction. Living cells, such as neurons, also obey their own laws, which are different again. If consciousness is best understood as an emergent property, we would expect to find that there are laws to do with consciousness – What keeps it clear? What represents its healthy functioning? What enables it to be used for the greatest benefit of its possessors? – which are unique to its level, and can be discovered from observation only at the level of consciousness, not from some lower level such as neurons. Concepts to do with morality are of particular interest here, because they show very clearly that selves, the central units in which human consciousness occurs, can be unitary and enduring and are not discoverable when reduced to lower levels in the hierarchy. Responsibility, for example, the determination to be answerable for one's actions, is a notion that has a powerful meaning at the level of human consciousness, but no meaning at the level of neurons. Responsible moral agency is by its nature the property of an 'integrated' subjectivity, which cannot be translated without remainder into a well-functioning neuronal system without losing precisely what gives it its moral character.

What is meant by 'observation at the level of consciousness'? It implies a reflexive process, that consciousness can observe consciousness, and there is something paradoxical here: consciousness is ordinarily, as we say, *of* something, and we never catch ourselves being conscious but conscious only of consciousness. We never come upon consciousness in a pure state, so to speak. (I believe some Buddhists would dispute this.)

There are no agreed answers to these questions; one can indicate only a few pointers. Psychoanalysis gives a model of one person consciously attending to the communications of another, and attempting by 'interpretations' to unite and extend the conscious world, in particular the affective world, of the other. We become aware that consciousness is something that can be guided, withheld, split off, broken up and muddied, and so on, and we know nowadays that in recognising and interpreting these events psychoanalysis is influencing neuronal activity. It does not, however, focus on issues to do with consciousness as such. It is like someone who attends to the lamp and the lamp-stand, but not to the light in and for itself.

In religious traditions, meditation also attempts to act on consciousness. There are many forms of meditation, some of which involve imaginative or contemplative exercises. The spiritual exercises of Ignatius Loyola require the practitioner to imagine a scene, often an episode from the Christian story, in great detail. The intention is to generate and reinforce particular emotions and a deeper commitment to a specific belief. In Tibetan Buddhism, there are visualisation exercises which are intended to be used at the moment of death, to facilitate the transition to the next stage in the cycle of rebirth. Such techniques use the power of imagination in an essentially instrumental way, and their focus, in so far as I can understand it, is on the content of consciousness, not on consciousness itself. Other Tibetan techniques, however, known as *shamatha*, attempt to go beyond content altogether, and to contemplate the underlying 'consciousness' in and as itself; in the technique known as Dzogchen it is claimed that a yet deeper, 'primordial', 'clear-light' consciousness can be attained that reorients the meditator's whole perception of the world he lives in. Such claims are currently being investigated by Western neuroscientists (Dalai Lama 1999; Wallace 2007, 2009).

Other meditation techniques are not concerned with the content of consciousness, though they do not attempt to eliminate it. They deal with the unavoidable fact that there always *is* a content of consciousness by depriving it of excitement; they focus on something neutral and repetitive. Attention is directed to the recurrent movement of the breath or abdomen, or to some repeated phrase or syllable. The classic statement of the goal of such practices, in the Yoga-sutras of Patanjali, is 'the cessation of the spontaneous activity of the mind-stuff' (*yogah citta-vrtti nirodhah*, cited in Eliade 1958). The word for spontaneous activity, *vrtti*, also carries the meaning of waves: the image is of rough or choppy waters calming to mirror-like stillness.

In the Christian tradition there is also the distinction between two sorts of life, the active and the contemplative, with the implication that active life, the fulfilment of desires and duties, is incomplete without something else, called contemplation. Contemplation by quietening the mind allows a deeper perception of reality; presumably it bears some relation to Patanjali's 'stilling of the activity of the mind-stuff'.

The interest of all this in our present context is that these techniques point to areas of experience and motivation that science has as yet only very partially incorporated into its understanding. There is an important motive which might be described as a desire to contemplate life, as well as to live it. The preoccupation of recent psychoanalytic thinkers with the notion of a 'third position' from which relating may be seen and thought about points to an integrated version of these dual motives. For example, in a paper on the ego, the psychoanalyst Ronald Britton (2003b: 100) writes, 'In optimum development and function, we move seamlessly from self-subjective to self-objective positions', and he emphasises that these positions are both versions of the ego, the 'I', not of the superego. Some meditation practices perhaps aim to separate off and develop this 'third' element which Britton describes as able to view the self objectively. We may need to take further Melanie Klein's ideas of a healthy splitting of the ego, to enable certain developments to take place, and speak of an ego of contemplation as well as an ego of activity. (In her picture, the baby needs to 'split' its earliest experience of the mother into good and bad, so that a strong capacity for love can be built up before the baby has to cope with the reality, that the mother not only is lovable but also has limitations, has other concerns, is sometimes in a bad temper or mentally unavailable, etc.) Health here implies that the splitting takes place in such a way that there can be a manageable transition to and from different versions of the ego (different 'selves', so to speak: see Chapter 9). If one of these alternative selves is an ego of contemplation, it may be conceived as a different 'subject' from the one governed by motives of desire and aversion, or by what Freud called the reality principle; we can then understand that the poignancy of loss and death is to do with not only the cessation of a certain stream of activities and relationships, but also a unique awareness of the world.

A world of necessary (not contingent) uniqueness

Connected with this, and a second consequence of seeing consciousness as an emergent property, is the issue of the ownership of consciousness. The fact that consciousness is always 'owned' or carried by subjects is to my mind what gives rise to the truly hard problems in this area. There are many local conundrums to do with the relation of consciousness to particular physical brain-states, but they are as nothing to the mystery that the consciousness relating to *that* brain belongs to you, the consciousness relating to *this* brain belongs to me. (As I have said, one problem with the 'panpsychic' account of consciousness is to know who or what could be the subject of a panpsychic consciousness.) If I am interested to know what you are conscious of, you have to tell me: I have no other means of access, however much I may perform PET or fMRI scans, or however much I observe you on the analytic couch. And if you refuse to speak, or if you tell me a lie, I can be shut out. The specific data of consciousness cannot be reached by any merely objective method. We have to approach subjects, who can tell us, not objects, from whom or from which we can deduce things.

And to take seriously the existence of subjects is to discover a world of uniqueness. The world of Lockean primary qualities, the world of conventional science, is a world of uniformity, in which things are potentially substitutable. In it, we have accounted for things in full when we know a large enough number of causal stories. Even if there is a singularity, as in the case of the Big Bang, it is only contingently unique: in principle, there could be other Big Bangs and other universes (indeed many physicists believe this to be the case). Given the valencies of oxygen and hydrogen atoms, and given suitable conditions, water will follow. It is not important in any way: it just happens. Chaos theory is sometimes thought to disrupt this picture, but in fact chaos theory merely recognises the limitations of our measuring apparatus. The world known to physics is a just-so story; it has no poignancy.

A world of unique subjects is an entirely different matter. It is unimaginable from the standpoint of physics. This I think is what Freud (1940) meant when he spoke of consciousness as a 'fact without parallel'. As best I understand the matter, for conventional science, 'normal science' as Thomas Kuhn (1962) called it, to take issues of consciousness seriously is to make an extremely bold and risky step: the paradigm which has been so successful for the past four hundred years cannot contain subjectivity, though thinkers like Francis Crick and Daniel Dennett may still fight an impressive rearguard action to make it seem that it can, that subjectivity is not really something unparalleled. But the natural world contains us, and therefore it contains subjectivity; therefore it cannot be adequately described in the language of primary qualities which was devised, precisely, to exclude subjectivity. So much is obvious, in my view. So to attend to these realities of consciousness and subjectivity is to require science to take a major stride into a new paradigm: we cannot yet see where that stride will land us. In particular, we cannot see whether the outcome will be a transformed science, in which matter is redescribed and subjectivity finds a place in an enlarged hierarchical picture that includes primary qualities such as mass, velocity or dimension, or whether it will be that science has to refuse, finally, to take that step, and will accept a frontier, beyond which it has no authority, and some other form of knowledge has to be allowed to exist. Stephen Jay Gould (2001), shortly before his death, proposed that religion should be regarded as a realm totally separate in this way, but religions make claims about the world on too many fronts to be separated off so completely. The realm of subjectivity and consciousness, however, may prove to be a domain of this sort.

I shall try to explore all these themes in more detail in the chapters that follow.

Chapter 3

Value-free science?

Galileo and Darwin

Introduction

At the end of Chapter 2, I mentioned Stephen Jay Gould, who late in life published a book entitled *Rocks of Ages*, in which he argued that science and religion need in no way be in conflict (Gould 2001). Science and religion, he said, are two entirely separate domains of intellectual authority, two non-overlapping magisteria as he majestically put it, and the religionist and the scientist are each free to go about their business without in any way having to glance over their shoulder to look what the other is up to.

There is an attractive simplicity to this idea, but it is hard to sustain. Religions are bound to make reality-claims – indeed, perhaps the pro-foundest of all reality-claims – and therefore, like sciences, they are bound to be interested in all the questions to do with our knowledge of reality: such questions as, how do we know what we know? What persuades us that something is true? What do we regard as evidence? How can we tell – and can we tell – what is delusion and what is truth-telling? (All the questions, in short, known by philosophers under the heading of epistemology.)

In the past four hundred years, these philosophical questions have been formative. They have shaped the disciplines of modern science and they have brought pressure to bear on religious thinkers to re-examine their fundamental assumptions. In coming chapters I shall suggest that religious traditions contain intuitive understandings about values that we should not dismiss merely because, like T.H. Huxley in Darwin's day or Richard Dawkins more recently, we can no longer take literally the mythological forms (the 'metaphors') in which religious vision has hitherto presented itself. Questions about values cannot be properly addressed unless we are prepared to listen to and take seriously our evaluative intuitions, the 'moral horizons', to use Charles Taylor's (1989) phrase, in which we spontaneously find ourselves living. It is these which have in the past appeared to receive support from the mythological claims of religion, which they in turn have reciprocally supported, and to take these moral horizons seriously today, when we are epistemologically so much more sophisticated, requires us to appraise them carefully, but not dismissively, in the light of scientific understanding.

The relation between religion and science over the past four hundred years has been extremely complex. The historian John Hedley Brooke (1991) has shown how at different times religious believers have used science to support their own arguments, and similarly many scientists have been devoted adherents of religion. The great pioneering physicists of the twentieth century, Einstein and the quantum physicists, developed in many cases remarkably mystical ways of understanding the world (I shall speak at some length in Chapter 6 of Erwin Schrödinger's views). But the fundamental challenges that an increasingly scientific frame of mind has presented to religion have sprung from two great scientific 'successes': first, from the extraordinary success of scientific explanation in accounting for the physical world without requiring any additional input from a supernatural realm – this is the argument from the conservation of energy – and second, from the success of Darwin's evolutionary theory in accounting for biological realities. Psychology may be fitted into this picture as a branch of biology. The first of these successes stems from the move Galileo made, at the beginning of the seventeenth century, to distinguish what would later be called by John Locke the 'primary qualities' of matter from the secondary.

Galileo and the 'primary qualities' of matter

In June 1633, Pope Urban VIII ordered the 'rigorous examination' of Galileo by the Inquisition. Galileo was 69; he had already been twice examined by the Inquisition, he was under 'vehement suspicion of heresy' and he knew that 'rigorous examination' involved torture, with the threat of burning alive if he was found guilty.

If you want to claim any one man as the originator of the modern scientific mind, Galileo would probably be the plausible choice. To this day, if you read his account of discovering that the moon has mountains and valleys, like the earth, and is not the perfect smooth sphere required by Ptolemaic astronomy, or if you read of his realisation that the small specks beside Jupiter could not be fixed stars far beyond Jupiter, as would fit with the Ptolemaic view, but were four moons in orbit around the planet, you sense that most impressive and admirable quality of modern science, the absolute attention to the facts of observation, and the patient process of considering what hypothesis would best account for them. The outcome of such observation and consideration, 'discovery', can give the scientist a sense of revelation not unlike a religious experience.

When you hear that he was threatened with being burned alive, you may recall that Galileo had already given thought to the nature of heat. In 'The Assayer' (1623), he had suggested that heat is one of those qualities which have no real existence except in us, and outside ourselves are 'mere names'. He wrote:

> Those materials which produce heat in us, and make us feel warmth, which are known by the general name of 'fire', would then be a multitude of minute particles having certain shapes and moving with certain velocities. Meeting with our bodies, they penetrate by means of their extreme subtlety, and their touch as felt by us when they pass through our substance is the sensation we call 'heat'. This is pleasant or unpleasant according to the greater or smaller speed of these particles as they go pricking and penetrating; pleasant when this assists our necessary transpiration, and obnoxious when it causes too great a separation and dissolution of our substance.
>
> (Galileo 1623: 277)

Galileo was wrong about the primary qualities of fire, as it happens, but he was right about one of its secondary qualities: he was right about its obnoxiousness. Confronted with the threat of torture, he renounced his views, at any rate in public, and he lived for the remainder of his life under house arrest in Florence.

But what Galileo was getting at in his account of heat was the distinction which was taken up and named by John Locke (1689) and which would determine the approach of science for the next four centuries. This was the distinction between the 'primary' qualities of matter, which are the objectively measurable qualities such as dimension, mass, velocity or temperature, and the 'secondary' qualities, which depend on the nature of our sense organs and include such things as heat, colour, smell, sound or sweetness. A 'quality' for Locke was a technical term and it meant the 'power' something has to produce an 'idea' in our minds: a snowball, for example, produces in our mind the ideas of white, cold and round. Some of these qualities, he said, are present in the object 'whether they are perceived or no' (Locke 1924: 72): these include bulk, figure, number, situation and the state of motion or rest. These are the 'primary and real' qualities of the object, and they create in our minds ideas which manage to resemble the qualities themselves: 'their patterns', as Locke (1924: 69) put it, 'do really exist in the bodies themselves'. Ideas produced by other qualities, however, are secondary. That means they are like nothing in the bodies themselves, but are caused by the action of primary qualities on our sense organs.

> Let not the eyes see light or colours, nor the ears hear sounds; let the palate not taste, nor the nose smell; and all colours, tastes, odours, and sounds, as they are such particular ideas, vanish and cease, and are reduced to their causes, i.e. bulk, figure, and motion of parts.
>
> (Locke 1924: 70)

These statements by Locke became the founding document, so to speak, of the enormously influential distinction between primary and secondary qualities on which the approach of modern science is based. This distinction is so simple, so profound, and so familiar, that it is still startling to realise how vast its effects would be. One principal effect was that the world, conceived in terms of primary qualities, could be measured, modelled mechanically, and grasped with extreme accuracy by mathematics. So much was obvious immediately. Another less obvious implication, which took more time to have its effect, lay in Locke's use of the word 'real': the primary qualities were not only 'primary', but also real, and the secondary qualities, apparently, were not real, or not exactly.

The 'scholastic' world-view

What was the intellectual picture that preceded this model, and that Galileo, soon to be supported by major thinkers like Francis Bacon and Descartes, was disturbing? It was the impressive synthesis of Christian theology and classical Greek thought put together by Thomas Aquinas in the thirteenth century, and which despite the rise of humanism and Protestantism still dominated Europe's universities four centuries later. It is usually called Aristotelian scholasticism. It was a system characterised above all by strong vertical hierarchies. God was above his Creation, humans were above the beasts, rulers were above their subjects, men were above women, parents were above children, and the Ancients were above the moderns. Spirit was above matter. Spirit was the stuff of which spiritual beings like God, souls and angels were made; matter was the stuff of which material things like earth and the human body were made. The individual human suffered, because he was torn between his soul, which aspired upward, and his flesh, which dragged him down into base earthly desires. The upward aspiration of the soul was entirely literal: it desired to return to its home above the stars, which were fixed in their places on the eighth crystalline sphere of the Ptolemaic heavens.

Given that this entire intellectual structure was essentially built of words, a 'fiction', it offered no definite standard of factual truth by which other fictions could be recognised as such and rejected. In what follows, I shall for particular reasons be critical of Galileo's distinction between primary and secondary qualities, but we can see that at the time it was an enormous step forward: it must have seemed like opening the windows in an extremely stuffy room. Suddenly there were statements of measurable fact that were definite and could be relied on. As Charles Sherrington (1940) showed, writing about the sixteenth century physician Jean Fernel, in the mid-1500s, only a generation or so before Galileo, it was impossible for even the most rational and vigorous mind to separate out facts from the many layers of theological, Ptolemaic, astrological, alchemical, magical, superstitious and in general preternatural obscurations in which the natural world had become wrapped. This tangle was so confusing that it was not properly sorted out even by the time of Newton, who still engaged in alchemical research.

One of the ways in which the Aristotelian scholastic system seems most strange to us now is that the past had authority over the present. If you wanted to know what you should believe, you did not rely on your own experience or your own judgement; you turned to the proper Authority, which in the first place was Scripture, the Word of God, which was always correct if sometimes difficult to understand, and second to the other designated authorities, the Church Fathers, or to certain great pagan philosophers, in particular Plato and Aristotle. The proper use of reason was to 'deduce' from Authority what was the case; it was not to 'induce', to use the technical word, what was the case from the facts around you.

This attitude is so unlike the way we think nowadays that it is easy to mock it. In reality, it is far from extinct, and it deserves some respect. Even today, responsible scientists think many times before departing from major authorities, and venturing to rely on their own independent thinking. This conservatism is a necessary condition of Thomas Kuhn's (1962) 'normal science'. A few years ago, the respected *Journal of the American Psychoanalytic Association* published an early article by the psychoanalyst Robert Stoller, describing apparently telepathic dreams relating to his patients; Stoller had written it in the 1960s, but he took the advice of his supervisor, Ralph Greenson, and buried the paper for forty years in a desk drawer. He did not fear being burned at the stake, but he did fear, in the climate of American psychoanalysis at the time, that such a paper could destroy his career (Mayer 2001). We have seen that rather similarly Antonio Damasio, when he started out as a young neuroscientist in the 1970s, felt it important to conceal his interest in consciousness. Even now most responsible psychologists would still, like Stoller, conceal any curiosity they might feel about telepathy, clairvoyance and the 'paranormal'.

Part of the scholastic world-view was the Ptolemaic astronomical picture. The heavenly bodies, being higher than the earth, were more perfect than the earth, and part of their perfection was that they moved in perfectly circular orbits and were themselves perfectly smooth spheres. When Galileo built his telescope, and saw for the first time that the shadows of mountains on the moon were longer at dawn, and shorter at noon, exactly like the shadows of mountains on earth, it was suddenly clear that scholastic theory was vulnerable to empirical attack. When he went on to declare that the primary qualities of the world were those that could be measured, and all others were secondary, he inverted the entire diagram of Aristotelian scholasticism: suddenly the Authorities of the past were only people like us, who had looked at the world like us, and who had very possibly made mistakes like us as well. In fact, they had certainly done so, more especially because they had not recognised the importance of comparing their speculations with observation. Francis Bacon, Galileo's contemporary, came to refer dismissively to Aristotle and the Church Fathers as Idols of the Theatre (meaning the lecture theatre).

In the course of the seventeenth century, Bacon, Descartes, Locke, Newton and many others built on these revolutionary insights. Intellectually, it was a hugely exciting time: in many ways the Scientific Revolution was the most innovative moment in human history since the start of agriculture, and the founding of the first civilisations, approximately ten thousand years earlier. The Pope and the Catholic church tend to figure in this story as the villains, but it is possible to have some sympathy with their concern. The ebullient Galileo was attempting something without precedent in Christian Europe, to examine and understand the world while excluding all the elements that make it precious or meaningful to us. The 'shining tents of Israel', as William Blake would later put it, were to be transformed as a result of Galileo's vision into 'Newton's particles of light'.

The Scientific Revolution also gradually transformed the attitude of responsible thinkers to knowledge. Any responsible thinker today is bound to have a primarily scientific attitude to knowledge. That does not commit him to any particular scientific theory, but it does commit him to certain methods of argument and to certain basic rules about the role of evidence and about what constitutes good reason to believe in the truth or falsity of his assertions. (It implies a certain epistemology.) Freud (1933b) once discussed the question of whether psychoanalysis requires a distinctive world-view (*Weltanschauung*) of its own. He concluded that it did not: its world-view is the ordinary scientific one. I think that is correct. There is a scientific world-view, which is essentially to do with refusing to claim final certainty, and recognising that theory is only deserving of respect if it is supported by appropriate evidence (evidence, that is to say, of a sort appropriate to the subject-matter) and can survive comparison with possible alternative explanations. This essentially scientific attitude to knowledge is not confined to designated 'sciences'; it applies equally, for example, to the writing of modern history or biography.

But this scientific attitude did not need to exclude alternative ways of reflecting on the world, and on experience, and it is only in the past two centuries that some scientists have started to arrogate to themselves certainties in a way reminiscent, ironically, of the medieval Catholic church. Galileo himself, like Stephen Jay Gould, saw no problem with having two visions of the world, and, prior to the terrifying involvement of the Inquisition, he had stated his position with characteristic energy and clarity. The Holy Scriptures and the phenomena of nature proceed alike, he said, from the divine Word. The Holy Spirit is not concerned to teach us whether the heavens move or stand still; his goal is our salvation, which is the truly important thing. However, if we choose to take an interest in such lesser matters as the behaviour of the planets, then we can do so by reading in God's other book, the Book of Nature, in which truths can also be found. Truths could not contradict one another, he said, and so there could be no danger that the discoveries of science would overthrow 'the dignity and majesty of Scripture' (Galileo 1615).

In many ways, it was Descartes who took the crucial intellectual step which opened the way to a science that would be unimpeded by theological concerns, although he himself always kept an important place for God. The split which Descartes insisted on, between a thinking subject, *res cogitans*, and a purely mechanical world of extended 'stuff', *res extensa* – which has of course a significant similarity to Locke's world of primary qualities – was paralleled by another split, between the thinking subject and God. Charles Taylor (1989) has compared Descartes's thought to that of St Augustine, from whom Descartes derived many of his key ideas (including the *cogito* argument). In Augustine, however, God works in the depth of the soul and is increasingly found there by the devout seeker. In Descartes, God's existence is proved by the clarity and distinctness with which the thinker sees that God *must* exist, and on the strength of this fact he can be confident that his science is veridical. But in this process, the centre of gravity, as Taylor puts it, has shifted: the most interesting thing now is no longer God, but my mind, or rather, the disengaged 'I' who knows, and can in principle master the world by knowledge.

The intoxicating ambition of the new science was stated clearly and rather chillingly in 1637 by Descartes in his *Discourse on the Method*:

> instead of that speculative philosophy which is taught in the schools [i.e. Aristotelian scholasticism], we may find a practical philosophy by means of which, knowing the force and the action of fire, water, air, the stars, heavens and all other bodies that environ us, as distinctly as we know the different crafts of our artisans, we can in the same way employ them in all those uses to which they are adapted, and thus render ourselves the masters and possessors of Nature.
>
> (Descartes 1637: 111)

Descartes's philosophy stands at a cusp. As the seventeenth century proceeded, and Newton astonished Europe by discovering 'Nature's laws' and the mathematical formulae that expressed them, the prestige of this new way of thinking exploded among educated people. The spectacular advances that these understandable, rational, down-to-earth attitudes made possible began to be applied to the Bible itself. In the eighteenth century, the factual inconsistencies in the Gospels (which people had no doubt always noticed and felt they had to keep quiet about) began to be discussed, as did the moral inconsistency between God's teaching and his apparent government of the world (Kors 1990). The story of the mass murderer and adulterer King David, for example, seemed to show God's government in a particularly dubious light. If God favoured King David, then perhaps human moral standards might be better than God's. Witty, irreverent thinkers like David Hume and Voltaire suggested that if God needed to intervene in his universe, it was presumably because he had made a botch of designing it in the first place. The 1755 Lisbon earthquake, an 'act of God' which caused the deaths of more than thirty thousand people, became in Voltaire's *Candide* the archetypical example of God's indifference to human welfare. It was an argument hard to refute. Rational thinkers began to move towards Deism, which kept a place for God as initiator of the universe, but downplayed the messy particulars, as they increasingly came to seem, of the Christian narrative. 'Atheism' and 'materialism', though still generally feared and greatly disapproved of, increasingly became thinkable possibilities.

But for a long time the mental world of humans remained outside science's scope. The world of matter and the world of mind, *res extensa* and *res cogitans* as Descartes called them, seemed clearly distinct, and as long as that was the case it was possible to think that humankind was somehow a separate creation from the rest of the world, subject to different laws and intended for a different, higher purpose. In the first two and a half centuries after Galileo, spirituality retained a place, essentially because no one could wholly connect the world of humans with the world of nature. And there was always a counter-current of hostility to the onward march of Galilean science. I have already quoted Blake. At the end of the eighteenth century, Goethe also passionately opposed Newton's account of light. His objections were based on a misunderstanding, but he too was deeply worried by the elimination of human subjectivity from the scientific account of the world. Goethean science, which in the 1990s was the object of renewed interest (Bortoft 1996), was essentially an attempt to include a place for the subjective elements of experience, the disparaged 'secondary qualities'.

The challenge of evolution

By the end of the eighteenth century, many thinkers were foreseeing the inevitability of making the connection between humans and nature. Goethe, Darwin's grandfather Erasmus, Lamarck, Schopenhauer, all put forward theories of evolution around the turn of the nineteenth century. But none of them could quite work out a convincing mechanism to account for the links they were glimpsing. Lamarck's version of evolution is described by one disapproving modern commentator as 'downright spiritual; it featured an inexorable tendency toward greater organic complexity and more highly conscious life' (R. Wright 1994: 232). Its most notorious feature, the inheritance of acquired characteristics, has remained controversial right up to the present. Darwin did not entirely repudiate it; Freud accepted it (to the embarrassment of many of his followers). The inexorable tendency to greater complexity would reappear in Teilhard de Chardin's (1959) notion of 'complexification' as one of the characteristics of evolution.

Every historian of evolution discusses the reasons for 'Darwin's delay' – the twenty years that Darwin waited before publishing in 1859 his theory of the origin of species by natural selection. But the probable reasons are not hard to understand. Darwin no longer had to fear the fires of the Inquisition, but he was a gentle and cautious man with a hugely bold and tenacious mind, and he saw very clearly what the implication of his theory was. At a stroke, by revealing a natural mechanism to account for the origin of all species including humankind, he was annihilating the entire objective basis of belief in God's creation of the universe, and in humankind's divinely ordained place and purpose within it. The belief that we were dealing with two things, body and soul in Aristotelian scholasticism, or body and thinking mind in Descartes's more modern variant, was conclusively contradicted by evolution, which affirmed that everything about the human being had emerged in a single process out of the ordinary matter of the Earth and solar system, and the comprehensible motivations of creatures needing to survive and reproduce. The argument between dualism and monism, powerful in Western thought since the time of Plato, seemed at last to have been empirically settled, and in favour of monistic materialism.

Darwin delayed a further twelve years, after publishing *The Origin of Species*, before publishing *The Descent of Man* (1871). There, he shows his very clear perception that henceforth we shall have to account for the spiritual qualities of human beings, the capacities for justice, for loyalty, for the pursuit of knowledge, and so forth, by discovering an origin for them in factors that link with the evolutionary imperatives of survival and reproduction. This was now the inescapable condition for all the characteristics of living beings. In his *Autobiography* (1887), Darwin suggested, somewhat anticipating Freud, that moral beliefs were inculcated in the first years of life and then 'took on the character of an instinct, meaning that they were followed independently of reason' (Brooke 1991: 281). The historian John Hedley Brooke tells a poignant story of Darwin's wife excising from the *Autobiography* a sentence in which Darwin compared a child's belief in God with a monkey's fear of a snake. 'There is perhaps no more piquant expression of the Darwinian challenge than that Emma Darwin should confide in her son Frank that "where this sentence comes in, it gives one a sort of shock"' (Brooke 1991: 281).

That then is the evolutionary challenge, and with Darwin we are generally felt to arrive at the sharp point of the attack made by 'materialism' upon 'spirituality', by 'science' upon 'religion'. However values are to be conceived, they will in future have to be compatible with a world-view in which species emerge, and develop their characteristics, by the processes of evolutionary selection. The penalty for failure was extinction. In Tennyson's words, written shortly before the publication of *The Origin of Species*, 'from scarpèd cliff and quarried stone' the evidence of countless extinctions was already clearly recognised, and was deeply worrying.

As if all this were not disturbing enough for Christians raised with a belief that God cares for every sparrow, further reflection revealed an even more alarming implication of Darwin's theory. If our physical brains, and all our capacities, have been shaped by the inexorable requirements of survival and reproduction, surely that must apply equally to our emotions and our thinking processes. Far from being created to give us access to the truth, the meaning of life, or the recognition of the Good, they have emerged for one reason only, namely because in the ancestral evolutionary environment, these emotions and mental processes enabled our predecessors to cope better with predators and competitors in the search for food and mating opportunities. If, for example, it has been in the reproductive interests of a man to be able to persuade a woman, at a moment of sexual seduction, that he loves her deeply and forever, then the capacity of men, at such moments, to genuinely believe that they feel such love will have been strongly selected for; and, presumably, if it has been in their genetic interest subsequently to be able, with equal sincerity, to have the same conviction in relation to a second woman, and to put their earlier declarations out of mind, then that capacity too will be part of men's innate endowment.

More recently, individual genes, discoverable as sequences within the DNA molecule, have come to be seen as the units in which evolution deals (rather than whole organisms). The geneticist Richard Dawkins has described this modern version of Darwinism with great clarity. As he puts it, 'we are all survival machines for the same kinds of replicator – molecules called DNA'; these replicators 'created us, body and mind' (Dawkins 1976: 21, 20). Organisms, says Dawkins, are nothing but machines designed by complex molecules which happen to have the curious property of self-replication. If so, anything that might be called idealism, morality, truth and so on can only be a veil of illusion and self-deception thrown over our acts, not by reprehensible hypocrisy, of which one might be critical, but by our genes, to which moral judgement is beside the point.

The question posed by evolution to the moralist now emerges clearly. If we, like the giraffe and the albatross, exist solely because natural selection in its infinite and meaningless vicissitudes has produced us – and that includes our thinking, our emotions, our senses and all our capacities for experience, including our sense of morality and values – what weight can we put on any of it? Perhaps, to make the sort of argument beloved of sociobiologists, to have a mystical experience is just a smart move in status-seeking, if you happen to live in a religious society. Or perhaps, if a man is faithful to his wife, he is just being bamboozled by her DNA, whose interests will be best served if he sticks around to protect its next embodiment. On the other hand, if he is unfaithful, perhaps he is equally being bamboozled by his own DNA, whose interest is quite independent of hers, and in fact quite independent of his own interests as a whole organism. Such arguments can seem to box us in on all sides, and be an invitation to cynicism.

The use and abuse of metaphor

However, this sort of thinking is itself a bit of an elephant trap. It has imperial ambitions, to dominate the entire world of argument, and we need to get a handle on how it sets out to do so. It led Dawkins himself, a geneticist, to extend his thinking to the realm of religion, on which he has made a ferocious onslaught (Dawkins 2006). Locke's linguistic decision, not only to distinguish the primary qualities of matter from the secondary ones – in itself a perfectly legitimate and important distinction – but also to privilege the primary as 'real' over against the secondary, gives us I think an important clue to an underlying confusion in this thinking. It assumes that some one language is the language in which truth is correctly told.

We may start by considering the use of metaphor. The metaphor that Richard Dawkins has popularised, the 'selfish gene', nicely dramatises his point, but, as many people have felt intuitively, it does more work than should be demanded of a teaching aid. A gene is a molecular sequence within the more complex long strand that is the DNA molecule. As such, it is not the sort of thing that is able to be selfish or to have purposes. Similarly, organisms, though in many respects they resemble machines, and their functions are regularly described as mechanical, can be called machines only in a metaphorical sense. A machine is something built by a machine-maker to fulfil a certain purpose (of the maker, not of the machine); organisms come into existence on a different basis, and not to fulfil any purpose. (Occasionally there are exceptions, in the human world, when a baby is conceived in order to secure an inheritance, or pigs or salmon are farmed purely in order to be used as meat.) If a gene that becomes replicated is described as 'successful' (with the implication that it has achieved its purpose), that is a value projected by the biologist onto the molecular event; it may be a value that we (being the organisms we are) cannot help holding, but it comes from the universe of secondary qualities and with an implicit aura of subjectivity and personal possession (*my* progeny, *my* DNA – or, presumably, if 'I' am a DNA molecule, 'copies of *me*'). In a world of primary qualities, notions of this sort are unintelligible, and in a metaphor-free language of primary qualities, if such a thing were possible, there would be no way of saying them.

Part of the point here is captured in the old biology joke: 'What's the definition of a hen?' Answer: 'An egg's way of making another egg'. The comedy of this is that one is left for a moment stumped by it: it says something that is true at one level (there cannot be an egg without an antecedent hen), but in language appropriate to a different level (to have a 'way of making' implies conscious intention, which eggs do not have).

It is not that there is anything wrong with metaphor. All communication depends on metaphors, and there is no way we can avoid them. As Lakoff and Johnson (1999) have demonstrated, even our most abstract thought employs metaphors derived from our bodily experience, so deeply imprinted in us that we no longer recognise them as such. Metaphors too can be extremely useful as teaching aids, but they are bound to be misleading if they are used without a recognition of the boundaries of their implications. Dawkins's metaphor of the selfish gene, which appears to invite us to admire the gene and despise or pity the deceived organism, plays with an idea of exploitation: it deprives organisms of their rightful place as initiators of action, and puts them in the position of dupes. Because the secondary qualities – which are essential if we are to think in terms of success, selfishness, exploitation, and so forth – are denied any rightful place in Dawkins's picture, when they are brought in as metaphors they are applied incomprehensibly.

The point here is a paradoxical one. It is that by using an anthropo-morphic metaphor, Dawkins brings in an inappropriate subjective lan-guage, disguising as he does so, no doubt without noticing it, the fact that what he is describing requires an *appropriately* subjective language. The fact that there is no such language, no appropriate language for 'subjective' elements at the level of molecules, creates a void which the anthropo-morphising metaphor exuberantly vaults over. If we venture to try to say more fully and non-metaphorically what needs to be said, we would have to tell a story not only about self-replicating molecules, but also about the birth of 'desire' in the universe; that however we imagine the nature of those earliest virus-like life-forms, it will have to include in the lightest way conceivable some 'subjective impulse' that causes them to move in one direction rather than another. Once we speak of life, we are telling a story which can no longer be told completely in the language of primary quali-ties. (To speak of 'self-replicating molecules' is an attempt to speak of life without acknowledging it.)

To restate this more fully, but continuing to use the language of primary and secondary qualities: as soon as we speak of life, and of entities that act in the world as well as respond to physical events, we have to bring 'secondary qualities' into the picture. To these entities, the world has become in certain aspects 'attractive' or 'repulsive'. These are secondary qualities and they point to new values and a new level of reality. (The word 'level' too is a metaphor, a teaching aid, meaning that it facilitates or even enables think-ing; but as a metaphor it also will carry unintended implications against which we will need to defend ourselves.) What it means to say that secon-dary qualities describe a new level of reality is that they can no longer be reduced to the primary ones (they are 'emergent' from primary ones).

The fears that Blake and Goethe, and many others more recently, have felt about the brilliant and triumphant progress of modern science are in touch with the danger that to privilege primary qualities may downgrade or fail to recognise the crucial importance of other important things that are secretly stigmatised or marginalised when they are called secondary. What Galileo successfully showed was that systems of primary qualities are best understood if we think only in terms of primary qualities. That is a very important truth, with huge practical implications, but it is of limited relevance to other systems, and it becomes very seriously misleading when we continue to employ it as we approach the enormously complex systems that biology deals with, which include of course human beings and human societies.

Brief digression on science and rhetoric

There is an interesting issue here which deserves a little more space. It is the role of rhetoric in scientific writing. When Dawkins speaks of a 'Replicator', a self-replicating molecule, and avoids any reference to 'life', he is engaged in a rhetorical strategy that is going to minimise the role of the organism. He is deciding an issue which is, as he in fact acknowledges (Dawkins 1976: 18), intrinsically ambiguous. The organism is the agent, and many influences, including undoubtedly its genes, play a part in determining its action. But some genetic potentials, for example, are activated only when the organism has certain sorts of experience; and what sorts of experience it has will in large part be determined by the environment, by geographical and climatic factors, by the availability of food and mating opportunities, and so on. At what point in the scale of life issues of learning also enter the picture we do not know; perhaps very early. We do know, for example, that a flatworm can be taught by conditioning to turn left or right in a Y-labyrinth. With learning comes a degree of individual difference: not every worm with a given repertory of genes would turn left at this juncture, but this one does. It seems excessively anthropomorphic to use words such as *choice* and *foresight* when speaking of worms, but in the capacity for conditioned learning we can glimpse their precursors. Dawkins's emphatic rhetoric breaks through the delicate network of interactive balances that allows an organism to live, and a species to survive, in a continually changing ecosystem.

In 1940, the Nobel Prize-winning physiologist, Sir Charles Sherrington, discussed at length the role of 'life'. He was writing of course before the discovery of DNA, but like Dawkins he was concerned with the ambiguity of the inorganic/organic boundary. He wrote:

> Instead of a specific principle which is life, life is an example of the way in which an energy-system in its give and take with the energy-system around it can continue to maintain itself for a period as a self-centred,

so to say, self-balanced unity. Perhaps the most striking feature of it is that it acts as though it 'desired' to maintain itself. But we do not say of the spinning of a heavy top which resists being upset that it 'desires' to go on spinning. The very constitution of the living-system may compel it to increase; thus a self-fermenting protein-system, granted its conditions, *must* increase. Broadly taken however there is in 'living' nothing fundamentally other than is going forward in all the various grades of energy-systems which we know, though in some less rapidly and less balancedly than in others. Whether atom, molecule, colloidal complex or what not, whether virus or cell or plant or animal compounded of cells, each is a system of motion in commerce with its surround, and there is a dynamic reaction between it and the surround. The behaviour of the living body is an example of this, and we call it 'living'. The behaviour of the atom is an example of this and we do not call it living. The behaviour of . . . 'viruses' is an example of this and there is hesitation whether or not to call it 'living'. There is between them all no essential difference.

(Sherrington 1940: 84–85, original emphasis)

A little later he writes: 'Chemistry and physics refuse to define life: they eschew the word' (Sherrington 1940: 86). Sherrington is going beyond rhetoric: he is presenting a detailed argument for his position. But it is a curious one. In the eyes of physics and chemistry, *everything* is an energy-system: there is nothing else for it to be, unless it is a vacuum, and even that is questionable. A living cell, virus, plant and so on are therefore bound to show up in physics and chemistry as energy-systems. That does not prove there is nothing distinctive about life. You might make an analogy: a joke in a Christmas cracker, a declaration of war, and a novel are all ink-lines on white paper, therefore there is no essential difference between them. To an autistic person, or an illiterate one, this might seem a persuasive argument. But to the person who can understand their significance, the difference between them is huge.

Similarly, the idea that a living being is *merely* an energy-system, just like a rock or a spinning-top or an eddy in a water-channel, is 'true' only to the person who surveys it without sympathy. (We will come to sympathy in Chapter 4.) This is not to deny that there are many ways in which living organisms are influenced and directed by forces over which they have no control or of which (in the case of humans) they are scarcely or not at all conscious. But sympathy gives us access to the subjective aspect of a living organism, and unless we wish to say that it is always delusive (as undoubtedly it sometimes is), then it reveals a decisive difference from non-living systems such as spinning-tops and eddies in channels.

When organic chemists entered biology, they made huge advances in understanding the cell. Sherrington in his vivid way describes their arrival:

'it was an audacity which reaped a great harvest in new knowledge. Their mush of unrecognisably disintegrated cells, obtained by freezings, mincings, crushings, grindings, squeezings, yielded to chemical analysis secret after secret of cell-life' (Sherrington 1940). Sherrington, despite the argument I have just quoted, loved and was moved to astonishment by the intricate precisions of the biological cell; he reveals I think his true sympathy when he lists that extraordinary schedule of violent procedures. Perhaps it could be carried out only by scientists whose sympathies had first been anaesthetised by the rhetoric of primary qualities.

No 'theory of everything'

The measurement of 'primary qualities' probably gets about as near to non-metaphorical science as is possible, but even that depends on certain fundamental metaphors (to borrow examples from Lakoff and Johnson (1999), the perception of time as 'passing', or the perception of one number as 'higher' than another) which can never be wholly eliminated. The world of primary qualities is a 'model', a sort of abstract diagram of the universe it purports to describe. The branching tree of Darwinian evolution is equally conceived in metaphor. Many people have suggested that Darwin's picture of the 'struggle for existence' is modelled unconsciously on the ruthless world of nineteenth century capitalism (just as the vertical hierarchies of scholasticism are sometimes said to model the feudal system). Without such models and metaphors we could never grasp whole systems, but the fact that we cannot help using them means that the system we are grasping is always to an indeterminable extent distorted.

Recognition of the shaping power of language and its rhetoric and implicit metaphors is one of the useful contributions of postmodern thinking. It allows us to say with confidence that there can never be one 'Theory of Everything', the dream of a certain sort of physicist. The world will always be more complex than any explanatory theory can encompass. It follows, to return to our starting-point in this chapter, that the arguments between scientific languages, or the debate between science and values, can only be conclusively decided if the person challenged accepts to use the same language as the challenger. The Christian claim that God made the world in six days can be refuted by science because it is, at any rate on the face of it, a claim about the formation of planet Earth and the length of time that process took. These terms have the same meaning to both parties,[2] and the

---

2 Some religious thinkers have attempted to undercut this argument by altering the meaning of one of the terms and suggesting that by 'days' the authors of Genesis were referring to geological epochs. In doing this they stumble into making the same mistake as their opponents and assume that a story told on a mythic level is attempting to state empirical fact on a scientific level.

story told by science accounts for the evidence in a way that the biblical story does not. But the fact of 'emergence' means that the full story of the world can never be accurately told in the language of any one level. The language that describes the first seconds after the Big Bang with miraculous precision will be unhelpful if we wish to describe the origins of the Second World War, or the remarkable life of Picasso.

Similarly, a moral claim, that human life is meaningful, or that we should not casually kill other humans, is not refutable (nor verifiable) by a biologist, because modern 'normal' science has no place for concepts of meaningfulness or moral values. But this does not mean that moral concepts are without importance. The effect of moral values in human life is incalculable. (Consider the difference, merely in tangible consequences, between a US President who sees nothing wrong with authorising the use of torture, and one who does see something wrong and forbids it. Abraham Lincoln's shift in moral judgement, from thinking that slavery should be tolerated, albeit with distaste, to thinking that it was a disgrace to a civilised nation and must be abolished, has had incalculably vast consequences, which still reverberate a hundred and fifty years later.) Moral values recognisably have consequences in the shared real world, and if we are to tell a story to account for them it will need to be a story different from that of positivist science; it will need to be a story that makes a place for the distinctive specialness of moral feeling. We may ask on what simpler feelings moral feeling is based – how has it emerged in an evolving species? – but we may not dismantle it into mere 'delusion' because that would make incomprehensible its unique presence in our experience and the unique power and persuasiveness to others of its functioning.

In the individual, moral feeling (examples would include outrage against injustice, or compassion for those who suffer helplessly) is often sufficiently powerful and impelling to override other motives which are more easily comprehensible in evolutionary terms (sexual desire, self-protection, etc.). Sympathy is a crucial element in such cases. Developed morality, however, requires very much more than sympathy: it requires the capacity to reflect about different affective reactions and to choose among them. The psycho-analytic account of morality has often gone little further than a description of internalised judgements by parents and others (the 'superego'), and such an account is plainly insufficient because it overlooks the important self-assertion of the person him- or herself ('ego') when significant moral decisions are made. Nevertheless, the idea of an internalised judging figure can give a model in theory, and may give a basis in fact, for a 'superior', higher-level faculty that is able to debate and choose among affective responses.

It is also clear that moral feeling, including what is felt to be the range of applicability of notions such as justice and compassion, varies greatly between societies, and has a changing history within a given society. These variations will also have to be accounted for. Though moral values can have great power, that power is highly variable in different individuals, and is strongly influenced, even in the same individual, by subjective or socially contingent features. We cannot ascribe our moral values wholly to the adaptive strategies recognised by evolutionary biology: their variation is clearly affected by social history, by fashion, by individual learning and relationships, and also by that powerful and unpredictable force, the individual conscience, which on occasion can act compellingly and in apparent defiance of self-interest and even of the interest of genetic kin.

Before we can approach all this, however, we need to look at the elementary factors, recognisable to biology and evolutionary science, which more deeply underlie our sense of values. One such factor is our elementary capacity for sympathy, both with humans and with other animals, and to this we will now turn.

Chapter 4

Sympathy is different from empathy

Introduction

Because psychoanalytic theory started out from Freud's early one-body neurologically based picture, and then in Freud's later work and the work of subsequent analysts tried to reach out from there to give an account of the irreducibly social nature of human psychology, psychoanalysts can sometimes find themselves confused about the order and logical hierarchy of their concepts. We catch ourselves trying to explain simple notions by more complex ones. We have a lot of specialised concepts, with names like intersubjectivity, alpha-function, projective identification, and mentalisation, but have often overlooked or, more accurately, have failed to recognise, an elementary building-block on which all these concepts depend. The ordinary name in English for this building-block is *sympathy*, but to use this word nowadays can be problematic.

First, *sympathy* is a word many people – not only psychoanalysts – spontaneously avoid. If psychoanalysts use it inadvertently, they will often 'correct' it and say 'empathy' instead. *Empathy*, by contrast, is a word we use with pride. We feel that by *empathy* we make a trial identification with the other, without losing our secure stance in ourself, and as a result of empathic contact we can relate our interpretations accurately to the patient's internal state. In the mid-1980s the psychoanalyst Harvey Kelman spoke of 'the current universal approbation accorded to empathy' (Kelman 1987: 111).

The word *sympathy* has also suffered from a belief that it implies a wish to help (which is often disparaged in phrases like 'tea and sympathy'). Psychoanalysts are trained to be wary of their wish to help, and this wariness has created an air of tough-mindedness, in some parts of the profession, which has also made it hard to use the word *sympathy* without shame at its apparent softness and lack of direction. Freud (1912: 115) explicitly recommended psychoanalysts 'to model themselves . . . on the surgeon, who puts aside all his feelings, even his human sympathy'.

Such a fundamental notion, however, has inevitably been a silent presence in psychoanalysis, particularly in our attempts to understand what happens in babyhood. Wilfred Bion (1962: 35–36) gave a central place to 'maternal reverie', which clearly implies the existence of sympathy, but the word *reverie*, appearing to describe something taking place entirely within the mother, does not help us to understand the complex communication which reverie can sometimes arrive at. I shall give an example in a moment of the sort of communication that can occur as a result of 'reverie' in a psycho-analytic session. In recent years, psychoanalysts have joined with develop-mental psychologists in trying to observe as accurately as possible what goes on between mothers and babies. In Britain, such observation is now a standard part of psychoanalytic training. 'Affect attunement' (Stern 1985) between mother and baby is recognised as crucial to the baby's healthy development, and is inconceivable without the existence of sympathy.

One of the clearest accounts in the psychoanalytic literature of what I shall call the primary meaning of the word sympathy appears in a discussion by the psychoanalyst, Joseph Sandler (1993). Sandler described walking in a crowded street, and seeing someone walking ahead of him stumble. Sandler instantly corrected an impulse in himself to stumble. He spoke of this as an example of 'recurrent primary identification' or 'unconscious temporary mirroring', and suggested it is pervasive in our communications. Interest-ingly, he quoted the pioneer psychologist William McDougall, who in 1909 described the same phenomenon and called it 'primitive passive sympathy' (quoted in Sandler 1993: 1101). But for his own account, Sandler preferred the more technical phrases.

When we find the word *sympathy* used without embarrassment, it is often in its adjectival or adverbial forms. The developmental psychologists Colwyn Trevarthen and Kenneth Aitken (2001), for example, defining 'primary intersubjectivity', describe experiments which 'show that the young infant has expectations of the emotional quality of the engagement and the normal contingencies of a *sympathetic* adult response'. They also speak of it in the negative: infants are traumatised if they meet '*unsym-pathetic* and inappropriately timed maternal behaviours' (Trevarthen and Aitken 2001: 9, my emphases).

A brief history of the word *sympathy*

I shall start by looking briefly at the history of the word *sympathy*. It derives from the Greek, the *sym-* being *with*, and the *pathy* coming from *pathos*, which implies suffering. The word *pathos* also stands behind such familiar words as *patient*, *passivity* and *passion*.

It is worth spending a little time on this history, because our present uneasiness with the word *sympathy* has cost us something very important, and very relevant in particular to the concern of the present book with the basis of values. The word *suffering*, interestingly, and not by coincidence, has followed a rather similar path. Its primary meaning is simply experiencing: what I do not *do* actively, I *suffer*, I experience, passively or receptively. When Goethe undertook to describe the origin of the different colours, he spoke of 'the deeds and sufferings of light' (Bortoft 1996: 46). He did not mean that light can suffer pain, as we might expect with that word now; he meant merely to describe the way light can be altered by something other than itself, for example by the thickness of the atmosphere.

Similarly, *sympathy* in its primary meaning is not to do with sharing pain, but with sharing the *passivities* of human experience. Its importance was recognised by some of the major thinkers of the eighteenth century Scottish Enlightenment, and then by Romantic poets such as Wordsworth and Coleridge, but disappeared soon after because, I think, of the difficulty of holding on to its primary and fundamental meaning. It was described very clearly, however, by David Hume. In his major philosophical work, *A Treatise of Human Nature* (1739), he writes:

> We may begin with considering anew the nature and force of *sympathy*. The minds of all men are similar in their feelings and operations; nor can any one be actuated by any affection, of which all others are not, in some degree, susceptible. As in strings equally wound up, the motion of one communicates itself to the rest; so all the affections readily pass from one person to another, and beget correspondent movements in every human creature.
>
> (Hume 1739: 368)

You will notice that this definition makes no reference to pain, and Hume certainly does not intend his definition to relate to any particular subdivision of human feeling. I shall take the liberty now of quoting him at more length, because he is here defining something fundamental. He writes:

> No quality of human nature is more remarkable, both in itself and in its consequences, than that propensity we have to sympathise with others, and to receive by communication their inclinations and senti-ments, however different from, or even contrary to our own. This is not only conspicuous in children, who implicitly embrace every opinion propos'd to them; but also in men of the greatest judgement and understanding, who find it very difficult to follow their own reason or inclination, in opposition to that of their friends and daily companions. To this principle we ought to ascribe the great uniformity we may observe in the humours and turn of thinking of those of the same nation; and 'tis much more probable, that this resemblance arises from sympathy, than from any influence of the soil or climate, which, tho' they continue invariably the same, are not able to preserve the char-acter of a nation the same for a century together. A good-natur'd man finds himself in an instant of the same humour with his company; and

even the proudest and most surly take a tincture from their countrymen and acquaintance. A chearful countenance infuses a sensible complacency and serenity into my mind; as an angry or sorrowful one throws a sudden damp upon me. Hatred, resentment, esteem, love, courage, mirth and melancholy; all these passions I feel more from communication than from my own natural temper and disposition. So remarkable a phaenomenon merits our attention, and must be trac'd up to its first principles.

(Hume 1739: 206)

One point to notice in this account is that sympathy, in Hume's sense, is not a feeling. It is a 'propensity', a spontaneous capacity, to pick up the feelings of others. Hume has been criticised by modern philosophers, for example John Rawls, who says this is not an account of sympathy 'as we normally understand it', but rather an account of 'imparted feeling' (Rawls 2000: 86). But this I think is a mistaken projection backward of our modern linguistic usage. Hume is using the word *sympathy* more, not less, accurately than our modern idiom, and our loss of his precise meaning leaves us floundering in the welter of technical terms (intersubjectivity, recurrent primary identification, mirroring), and lacking a general term to fulfil the elementary role that Hume's *sympathy* occupies.

It is curious how hard it has turned out to be to hold onto this account of sympathy as a capacity, a propensity, quite distinct from the emotional feeling of compassion that is often given the same name. In Hume's later writings he seemed to lose hold of the distinction himself, preferring the even more ambiguous term 'fellow feeling', and his follower Adam Smith, the founder of the science of economics, although he famously based his whole understanding of what he called the 'moral sentiments' on sympathy, meant by sympathy something markedly different from the capacity (Smith 1759). Smith's concern was with 'mutual sympathy', the basis in his view of honest friendship and social approval; we strive to achieve such sympathy with others, he says, and where it cannot be reached the painful emotions of disapproval are activated (Phillipson 1983). Because Smith's account of sympathy has been widely quoted, it has tended to push Hume's earlier version into the background.

Interestingly enough, over a century after Hume wrote his *Treatise*, when Darwin came to think about the development of the distinctive human characteristics, he too put what he called 'the all-important emotion of sympathy' (Darwin 1871: 106) squarely in the centre of the picture. He saw sympathy as widely present in the higher animals (he mentions dogs, monkeys and elephants) and also in certain birds, including pelicans and crows. Darwin was a good amateur psychologist, and many of his formulations remain very suggestive. For example, he writes:

Even when we are quite alone, how often do we think with pleasure or pain of what others think of us – of their imagined approbation or disapprobation; and this all follows from *sympathy*, a fundamental element of the social instincts. A man who possessed no trace of such instincts would be an unnatural monster.

(Darwin 1871: 112, my emphasis)

And again:

Many a civilised man, or even boy, who never before risked his life for another, but full of courage and *sympathy*, has disregarded the instinct of self-preservation, and plunged at once into a torrent to save a drowning man, tho' a stranger . . . Such actions . . . appear to be the simple result of the greater strength of the social or maternal instincts than that of any other instinct or motive.

(Darwin 1871: 110, my emphasis)

In these passages, Darwin interestingly links the motive of sympathy with the 'maternal instincts', and, although he does not spell out how boys or men might act from maternal instincts, we can glimpse behind his writing some shadowy notions of internalisation and transference. In the first of these quotations, we can see the importance of sympathy in the formation of 'internal objects', a notion not available to Darwin but clearly anticipated by him here.

Darwin, however, was not a philosopher and his use of language lacks Hume's precision. Much of the time his word *sympathy* has Hume's meaning, and he even quotes Hume at one point (Darwin 1871: 109n), but often, as in the passages quoted, it gets mixed up with the more modern meaning, of an emotion of compassion or warm concern, and he does not distinguish between these two usages.

Sympathy is different from empathy

The recognition of sympathy in animals, or pre-verbal infants, is of particular importance because it allows the differentiation of sympathy from empathy to be made rather clearly. *Empathy* is a modern word, which appeared first in 1909 used by the American psychologist Edward Bremner Titchener as a translation of the German *Einfühlung*. The psychoanalyst George Pigman (1995) has written an excellent summary of the history of *Einfühlung*, which I draw on in my next few paragraphs.

In 1909, *Einfühlung* was itself quite a new term in German, having first been used in 1873 by the art historian Robert Vischer. It arose out of a long history of discussion by German thinkers of the way in which we can be moved by aesthetic perceptions. In 1774, for example, Goethe's friend

Herder had urged those wishing to understand the world of the Ancients to *'fühle dich in alles hinein'*, feel yourself into everything.

Theodor Lipps (1851–1914), a philosopher admired by Freud, gave a central place to Vischer's concept. (Lipps was wryly quoted by Freud in his correspondence with Wilhelm Fliess as having anticipated many of Freud's own discoveries.) Writing in 1903, Lipps spoke of 'an arrangement of my nature which is not further describable' which causes me both to have an impulse to mimic the facial expression of someone in front of me, and to tend to experience the affective state, the feeling, represented by that expression. This 'arrangement', though described in more detail, is very close to Hume's account of sympathy as a spontaneously acting capacity. According to Lipps, when I 'feel myself into' the resulting psychic experience, I achieve *Einfühlung*. Lipps believed *Einfühlung* should be extended from its initial aesthetic application and become a fundamental concept in psychology and sociology – that *Einfühlung* 'is what enables us to realise that we have selves and that other selves exist' (Pigman 1995: 242).

Freud is often thought to have given little place to *empathy*. This, however, is a confusion caused by James Strachey's English translation. *Einfühlung* and its related forms were in fact used on quite a number of occasions by Freud – some twenty in all – but were not consistently translated by Strachey in the *Standard Edition* of Freud's works. (Strachey may have disliked the words *empathy* and *empathise* on aesthetic grounds.) One occasion when Freud used *Einfühlung* is in a famous passage in his 1913 paper 'On beginning the treatment': 'It is certainly possible to forfeit this first success if from the start one takes up any standpoint other than that of sympathetic understanding, such as a moralising one' (Freud 1913: 140).

'Sympathetic understanding' in the German is *Einfühlung*, and the translation is doubly misleading, as Pigman (1995) points out, both because it fails to reveal Freud's positive valuation of empathy, and because it fails to make a clear distinction from *sympathy* in the sense of 'sympathising'. Pigman also points out that for Freud, unlike Lipps, *empathy* had a strongly intellectual flavour, and relates to the process of putting oneself, consciously or unconsciously, into someone else's position in order to understand him. This brings Freud closer than Lipps to the prevailing modern usage of the word *empathy*.

Since Freud, many psychoanalysts have used the term, with greater or less concern for these shades of meaning. I want to keep psychoanalytic technical language, of which there is far too much, to a minimum, but need now to refer to one technical concept, projective identification. This term was first used by Melanie Klein (1946) to mean a state of phantasy in which parts of the self are perceived, not in the self, but outside in someone else. By communicative methods which are often invisible, this phantasied perception often comes to be apparently supported by reality. A relatively simple example would be the not uncommon situation in which John is angry with Janet, but doesn't fully realise this, and instead believes (i.e. has the phantasy that) Janet is angry with him. John then may take offence at something Janet says, imagining it to be hostile, and Janet is confused in turn: she doesn't think she was hostile, but – could she have been? She is no longer sure, and John's barrage of highly critical outrage has made her angry *now*, even if she wasn't before. Thus John's projection of anger *onto* her has become a projection of anger *into* her, and neither party properly knows what has happened or what the anger, now undoubtedly present, is in origin about. A lot of confusion in intimate relations has this form. A psychoanalytic way to describe it might be to say that John has 'put his anger into' Janet by projective identification, initially in the form of an 'unconscious phantasy' that she's angry, but then, by behaviour which may in the reality situation be very hard to discern – physical posture, tone of voice, pheromonal signals – has caused her to respond in a way that seems to confirm the phantasy.

This notion, that we can communicate our feelings by creating versions of them in the other, has since been used to describe many sorts of inter-action; Bion, in particular, considered that projective identification was a 'normal' sort of communication between baby and mother. If a baby is terrified, it can't say so, but it can scream in a way that causes an echoing alarm in the mother, and causes her to attend urgently to the baby's needs. Bion speaks of the trauma a baby suffers with a mother who is unable to receive projective identifications. In his *A Dictionary of Kleinian Thought* (1989), Robert Hinshelwood defined *empathy* as a form of projective identification, 'one of those benign forms of projective identification which can be included in "normal projective identification"' (Hinshelwood 1989: 295). His account of empathy states that it is a certain form, namely a benign form, of projective identification, in which one person projects his capacity for self-perception into someone else's situation in order to 'gain', as he puts it, the other person's experience. Hinshelwood (1989: 296) emphasises that in empathy there is 'no loss of reality, no confusion of identity'.

The phrase 'no confusion of identity' implies that empathy is a sophis-ticated mental operation in which the two persons involved are very clearly separate but one is consciously setting out to conceive the other's mental landscape. We might think of psychoanalyst and patient, or sales assistant and customer, and there is something analogous in chimpanzees, for example. A small chimpanzee who has spied a banana, in the presence of a larger chimpanzee who does not know it is there, will skilfully position himself between the large chimpanzee and the banana so that the large chimpanzee cannot see it; and he will nonchalantly look around and pretend to be preoccupied with other matters until the large chimpanzee goes on his way. Absent the competition, the small chimpanzee quickly grabs the banana. The mental operations involved in such a deception are quite elaborate; they include a capacity to imagine himself in the other chimpanzee's place, in a physical sense, and also to be aware, in some sense, of the other chimpanzee's desires and thinking processes, while postponing gratification and retaining a very clear contact with his own self-interest.

Sympathy is very different from this. In sympathy, self and other are not clearly distinct, and what takes place is an automatic, involuntary response to another's emotional state. Neuroscience has shown the presence of 'mirror neurons' which respond immediately to the emotional presentation of another by triggering a configuration of neuronal firings that parallels what is going on in him; we seem to meet an interesting echo here of Theodor Lipps's description of an impulse to mimic the facial expression of the other. Sympathy of this sort is a spontaneous and involuntary response; it makes empathy possible, but it operates at a quite different level of sophistication: empathy is the more sophisticated and often conscious act, which uses as a tool the elementary and inescapable propensity I, following Hume, call sympathy. Sympathy is with the other as 'subject'; empathy relates to the other as 'object'. This distinction will be crucial when we attempt to understand more clearly the basis of moral values, but it gets lost when empathy is used confusedly, as it often is, to cover both meanings.

Unfortunately, the issue is further confused by the fact that ordinary language does use the word sympathy, but uses it in two quite different ways, which need to be clearly distinguished. I shall call Hume's usage, the capacity, sympathy sense one, and the more common modern usage, the emotion of compassion, sympathy sense two. To dramatise the distinction, we might say that the professional torturer, tormenting his victim, must be very sympathetic to his victim. That is, in sense one. In sense two, of course, he is horribly unsympathetic. He knows what torture feels like, but he knows without compassion.

To summarise and draw out a few points relating to these reflections so far: first, the word *sympathy* has become disparaged among psychological professionals, though it still gets smuggled in usefully in its adjectival forms. If we look at it historically, however, we find it has two distinct and important meanings: the first meaning is a spontaneous 'propensity' to be directly affected by the feeling state of others, in a way tending to cause an identification with them. Sympathy in this sense just happens; it is not something we set out to do, or even necessarily are conscious we are doing. It is this propensity which causes us, for example, to identify instantly with what Daniel Stern (1985) called 'vitality affects', the unverbalised emotional messages carried by every detail of another person's posture, gestures, hesitations, use of eye contact, tones of voice, and so on. (Damasio (2000) has described the same phenomenon using the term 'background emotions'.) Sympathy in this sense is already present in babies and some animals. It is not an emotion: the word propensity, which I have borrowed from Hume, is a good description of it: it is rather like a perceptual capacity, telling us of the feelings in our environment as vision tells us of colour. Like vision, of course, it is not always accurate. The second meaning of sympathy is a warm concern for the feelings of others. Sympathy in this sense, also called compassion, *is* an emotion, or a range of emotions, akin to sorrow and belonging with what psychoanalysts call the depressive position group – the emotions that recognise social reality – and like other emotions it can be highly developed, repressed, split off, conscious or unconscious, mistaken, and so forth.

Second, *empathy*, although the word is often used where *sympathy* would be more accurate, has a distinct meaning of its own. It is a more complex act involving imagination, a 'trial identification' done by someone who is consciously or unconsciously attempting to understand or imagine another's mental state 'from within'.

Third, empathy, and sympathy in the sense of compassion, both depend on the elementary capacity, sympathy sense one. Like our other perceptual capacities, sympathy sense one is often remarkably accurate, though it can be mistaken or misled, for example. It is educated and developed by emotional experience, and especially by experiences of 'affect attunement' with caring others in infancy. It probably lies at the root of what is often referred to as intuition.

Fourth, the relation between sympathy (sense one), the capacity, and sympathy (sense two), the emotion, is complex, and raises questions of psychological health, normality, etc. We might caricature two extremes by saying that the charming and seductive psychopath is strong in sympathy sense one, but devoid of sympathy sense two, whereas the woman who commits what Anna Freud (1936) called altruistic surrender is so overwhelmed by sense two that she helps her friend to her own detriment.

There does not seem any intrinsic reason why the conceptual territory should be divided up between these words in the way I am recommending. The initial use of the word *Einfühlung*, by Vischer and Lipps, is as close to my *sympathy* sense one as it is to *empathy*. But given the use of sympathy by Hume and Darwin, and the subsequent history of *Einfühlung*/empathy in the hands of Freud and later psychoanalysts and psychologists, I think this distribution of the words is intelligible historically, and departs as little as possible from our ordinary usage.

The history of the words *sympathy* and *suffering* may have a wider significance. Both words, which initially had to do simply with 'experiencing', have come to convey something more related to 'experiencing pain', 'suffering' in its modern sense. It is as if passivity and receptivity, the necessary condition of having experience, has been given as time has gone on an increasingly negative reading; as if activity alone is the source of happiness. Perhaps here we make contact with a familiar theme of psychoanalysis, which we have already met in Chapter 3 when we looked at Descartes's ambition for the new scientific 'method' – a theme which Freud

(1937) summed up at the end of his life as the 'repudiation of femininity' by both sexes. It may also have a sociological significance, to do with fear in an increasingly individualistic and competitive society of finding that one has motives which do not contribute to self-assertion.

Sympathy, however, whether or not explicitly acknowledged, plays a big part in psychoanalytic interactions. It can of course in practice be very much more complex than it sounds in theory. I will illustrate its role using two case examples.

First case example: Sylvia

Sylvia was a woman in her forties who came to see me because she was depressed after a relationship with a man — the latest of a series — had broken up. She was an overweight, strongly built woman, a trained opera singer, who (I thought) used food to swallow down feelings of rage and humiliation. She had been obese as a child, and the pattern went back to infancy when she had been succeeded at the age of 12 months by the next sibling, the first and much-longed-for boy. She seemed to have experienced his arrival as her own loss of the role of lovable, desirable one; her discovery of her singing talent allowed her once again to occupy centre-stage, but failed to make up for this deeper loss. Her initial attitude to me was hesitant and deferential, somewhat incongruous in this tall woman of rather regal bearing. After some seven years, when her life situation had considerably improved, and the prospect of ending analysis began to be spoken of, she became for the first time enormously angry with me. In session after session, she would be speechless with rage — sometimes lying in silence for the entire 50 minutes — and she would experience any remark by me as intolerably provoking. She would shout at me that she hated me, she saw me as smug, and she hated me in particular for saying that she didn't want to face reality. What made me think I knew what reality was? Her reality was not mine.

I said that I thought she idealised the position of the baby. I said she thought that the truly desirable thing was to be a baby, and the thought of growing up, and developing, and of eventually leaving analysis, seemed to her a miserable second-best; if I thought it was desirable, and that it might be a good thing that we were working towards it, then I was stupid and arrogant and entirely out of touch with reality. I didn't make all these interpretations at once, but this was the tenor of my responses in many sessions. Typically, when the silence broke, and she had raged and shouted at me for most of a session, I would touch some chord in her, or she would touch some chord in herself, and she would break down in painful tears and self-reproaches. We might then have two or three sessions in a more ordinary frame of mind, and then the rageful silences would recommence.

As time went by, this pattern became increasingly hard to bear. She was coming five times a week, never missed a session, and had a powerful presence. I worried that nothing I said seemed helpful. I began to feel I had exhausted what I thought I could understand of the reasons for the pattern, and I lost interest in repeating my interpretations. I felt unjustly punished by the enormous silences, which were hard to endure, and then often shocked and disconcerted by the rage and shouting, which were sometimes frightening, and sometimes reduced me too to silence. Finally, one session, after she had again bellowed her hatred of me, we fell into what felt like an angry, silent, mutual stand-off. I thought that anything I might say, whatever its content, would be heard, and very possibly would be said, as an angry or patronising retaliation.

In the minutes that followed, I found myself relaxing. My thoughts wandered. I suddenly came to with a shock and tried to reattend to my patient, who was lying there silently. Then I remembered that wandering thoughts may be of interest, and wondered what it was I had been thinking about.

I found I had been remembering an episode from my adolescence, not consciously thought of for many years. I had been hitch-hiking in France in the late 1950s, when British teenagers were often treated with considerable contempt by the local people. One hot day, I had taken a train to a remote country area, and got off at a small station. Two or three local people got off as well, and preceded me down the dirt path to the little gate which was the exit from the station.

A girl about my own age, 17 or so, had come out to the gate to collect the tickets. I presume she was the station-master's daughter; very possibly this was the one train of the day. Ill-tempered because of the heat, and with the many pockets of the back-packer, I couldn't find my ticket, and angrily flung the things I could find – keys and cash – onto the ground. Without hesitation, she knelt down, picked them up, and politely gave them back to me. I found my ticket and handed it to her.

Thinking about this distant episode now, in the session, I felt a sudden surge of gratitude to this girl. She could easily have responded with contempt or mockery, and instead she had treated me with an entirely unexpected quality which I experienced as a straightforward, friendly acceptance of my feeling, without even needing to draw attention to it. I had been in an infantile mood, and she had shielded me from the possibly humiliating consequences.

At this point, in the session, I began to see what was happening with my patient in a new light. I felt that I had become capable, not just of making more or less intelligent interpretations to her, but of feeling sympathetically in touch with her predicament. I was able to say with genuine feeling how awful it was to feel raging and excluded, and at one and the same time to know that the feelings were unjustified, and yet be helpless to change them. I became able, so to speak, to pick up, and in the course of the ensuing work to hand back to her, important contents which belonged to her and which she needed. No single interpretation, of course, can alter patterns that are so deeply imprinted, but from then on, having remembered my French experience, I more often felt able to speak to her in a different manner. Over the next few months, the rages gradually diminished, and termination, when it finally came, felt manageable and worked-towards.

If we try to understand more deeply into what was happening in this situation, the notions of empathy and projective identification account for only parts of it. Empathising is what I was trying to do initially: I tried to make a 'trial identification' with my patient, and out of that I had formulated my various interpretations to' do with her longing for the position of the baby and the bleakness she felt at developments which might be thought of by some, perhaps including me, as progress. On reflection, I don't think these interpretations were necessarily altogether wrong, but they were counter-productive because their somewhat abstract style appeared to inhabit effortlessly the 'adult' attitudes that were being commended as appropriate to reality. They were made, apparently, by someone who was invulnerable to the 'infantile' conflicts they were describing, and as a result the patient was left feeling isolated and exposed as inadequate, rather than safely contained and understood.

Projective identification takes us further, in understanding another aspect of the interaction. The patient's rage, which reduced me to silence, can be thought of as a projective technique, intended to get rid of an intolerable feeling, a sense of inferiority and helplessness, and when I finally could find nowhere further to go with my interpretations, and I too felt helpless, the projection had taken place. The attempt to simply get rid of the feeling (psychoanalysts call this: evacuation) had no doubt failed, but more importantly a communication, the imparting of a similar feeling to the other, had been achieved. By itself, however, this led only to stalemate. What then occurred, the wandering thoughts or reverie which arrived at a piece of autobiographical narrative (belonging to me, not to her), cannot be understood as solely a projective process by the patient. My wandering thoughts had arrived at a memory of my own which reconfigured the feeling of helplessness, and reminded me of an episode in which I had 'suffered' feelings somewhat similar to my patient. This reverie also put me in touch with an 'internal object' – the remembered girl – who embodied some of the friendly understanding and non-judgemental qualities the situation was calling for.

I am suggesting that *sympathy* in the first sense, the capacity, is what guides this reverie, which is not exactly unconscious but which takes place in a state of distraction – separate, in one sense, from the tension and emotion of the encounter, but at the same time clearly affected by it and guided by it.

It is a particular trap for therapists that the necessary attempt at *empathy*, which views the patient's mental state as an 'object' for understanding, can itself become a defence against *sympathy*, which involves the much simpler acceptance of patient and therapist as both 'subjects', both ordinary human beings capable of similar sufferings. For sympathy to come on the scene, the therapist needs to be willing to 'suffer' in unanticipated ways, and probably, when there is therapeutic failure, it often has to do with the therapist's reluctance or inability to let this happen. It is like a sort of creativity: the necessary suffering cannot be done by willing it, but there needs to be an openness to letting it happen, and then to taking it seriously when it does.

Two claims for the importance of sympathy

I shall now make two large claims for sympathy in this sense (sense one, the capacity). First, that it is an ego-function (though it can be unconscious) and it makes an important contribution to our perception of reality. For example, it improves the accuracy of our social perceptions. One important fact about sympathy is that it takes time. We can imagine someone, an overworked nurse perhaps, who might wish to help but who might be too busy to have the time for sympathetic reverie. Such a person might indeed help, but less accurately than a comparable nurse who has the time and emotional openness to make room for her capacity for sympathy. There is an interesting parallel in creative scientists, such as Einstein or the plant geneticist Barbara McClintock, who both made impressive scientific discoveries which were only subsequently supported by adequate evidence. Einstein and McClintock both described the quality of attention they brought to their subject-matter as sympathetic. When Einstein described the process by which he reached his ideas, he said: 'To these elementary laws there leads no logical path, but only intuition, supported by being *sympathetically* in touch with experience' (Keller 1983: 145, my emphasis). The power of sympathy in such immensely gifted individuals can cause them to seem almost clairvoyant. However, the idea of sympathising with something inanimate, such as a beam of light or, in McClintock's case, the genetic material of maize, may be a metaphor; it awaits further consideration. (It is interesting, however, to recall that the word *Einfühlung* originated in philosophers concerned with aesthetics, such as Vischer and Lipps, before it was used by psychologists.)

If sympathy in sense one, the capacity, can enhance accuracy, sympathy sense two, the emotion, may impair it. Freud gave correct guidelines, I think, with respect to both. He said that the correct posture for the analyst was one of 'evenly suspended attention', which creates the conditions for sympathy sense one; he was critical, however, of excessive 'therapeutic ambition' (Freud 1912: 111–115), and therefore enjoined wariness of sympathy sense two.

The second large claim I want to make for sympathy sense one picks up the larger theme of this book: it is that sympathy sense one is the ultimate basis for what is objective in our perception of moral value. This argument needs to be made at greater length and I shall return to it later, when I speak about the basis of responsibility. Essentially, I again follow David Hume's argument in the *Treatise* (1739), which is carefully constructed and properly psychological. By itself, Hume says, our sympathy is prejudiced in favour of those near us, or those resembling us; properly moral values depend on an extension of sympathy by imaginative acts in which we put ourselves in fantasy close to events which in reality are far away. For example, if I am in London, and I hear of suffering caused by floods in Pakistan, I may not immediately have a reaction of concern; it is only when I identify with an imagined self, to whom the floods and the suffering people are directly present, that I have what I feel to be an appropriate reaction. Hume goes on to derive from this projected image of myself an impartial person, a 'judicious spectator' who can be imagined as present at all events, including those involving me directly, who would have appropriate and proportionate responses free from the inevitable biases of any actual person. Not just the fact, but the appeal, of justice can be understood from our sympathy with this judicious spectator.

This account of the basis of moral values has several impressive advantages. Like psychoanalytic thinking, it grounds values firmly in emotional experience, rather than in a religious revelation or in an intellectual operation such as a utilitarian calculus. But it improves on many psychoanalytic accounts by making possible a clear distinction between morality derived from the superego, that is from internalised precepts and prohibitions, and morality based on conscience, that is on the person's own capacity for sympathy, imagination and reflection. (Superego and conscience often get mixed up in psychoanalytic writings: they should be kept clearly distinct.) It makes comprehensible, too, the reality that our best values do not always determine our actions, and also that we are aware of an emotional response of guilt, ruefulness, or remorse, when this is the case. If, as Ronald Britton (2003a) has suggested, in healthy development ego needs to take over the function of judgement from superego, Hume's account offers an intelligible basis on which it could do so.

It also gives us a way of understanding the feeling we have that certain historical developments, in which the ordinary moral perceptions of a society become controversial, are criticised, at first by courageous individuals and then more widely, and eventually change, may represent 'progress' or be a backward step. I mentioned in Chapter 3 the evolution in Abraham Lincoln's thinking about slavery, which did not happen in isolation but was linked with all the issues of the American Civil War and a profound debate, in both America and Europe, about the rights and wrongs of slavery. Another example would be the abolition of capital punishment in Britain, also the outcome of a long gradual process and an increasing sense of revulsion in thoughtful people against judicial killing. When we hear of such developments, we are apt to feel (though not everyone feels) that something 'progressive' has occurred. Hume's theory gives us a way to understand that this feeling may have an objective component and not be merely dependent on subjective preference. Moral progress or regression can be assessed, at any rate to some extent, on an objective scale.

It is not possible to ground the objective component of values wholly on a mental mechanism, such as projective identification or recurrent primary identification, because these are essentially activities taking place in phantasy, and what is required is a perception, in some way, of reality. *Sympathy* in what I am calling sense one, the capacity, enables us to make a somewhat accurate appraisal of a certain sort of reality, namely another person's psychic reality as the subject of experience. I mentioned in Chapter 2 the striking metaphor that Freud (1900) employed when he described consciousness as a 'sense organ for the perception of psychic qualities'. I am tempted to use a similar image about sympathy, sense one, the capacity, and speak of it as a 'sense organ' for the perception of the affective states of other people. But to arrive at proper values requires a great deal more than merely sympathy sense one. Imagination, dialogue and conscious reflection are also required. Even then, a further step is called for, to explain why we are moved to action by what this process reveals to us. Immanuel Kant, responding to Hume, spoke of the 'respect' that we cannot help feeling when we encounter moral worth, and I shall come back to this argument in some detail in Chapter 10.

In successful psychoanalytic work, development takes place in the patient's sense of values. These developments are not explicitly aimed for, but are inevitable accompaniments of other sorts of emotional change. We often speak of these changes in terms of an enlarged capacity for intimacy, more genuine toleration of difference, an increased capacity to process emotional experience before reacting to it (a lessening of impulsiveness), and so on; or we use readily available if somewhat obscure metaphors such as a greater capacity for depth in relationships or understanding. Tolerance is a particularly important notion when we think of what we hope will be the gains from psychoanalysis. 'The criterion of all later capacity for adaptation to reality,' Melanie Klein wrote, 'is the degree in which [the child is] able to tolerate the deprivations that result from the Oedipus situation' (Klein 1926: 129). These painful Oedipal deprivations include feelings of separation, exclusion, the realisation that one is not always loved, or always lovable, and the experiences of hatred, envy and jealousy. Nowadays, we are likely to conceptualise these desirable changes as also the internalisation of more tolerant 'objects'; the 17-year-old French girl in my story of Sylvia is an example.

Changes of this kind can be seen as extensions of our capacity for sympathy, on which can be built a recognition of the reality of other people as subjects like ourself, and of ourself as not only the all-dominating peremptory 'I' of narcissism but as 'one among many'. Put like that, we can see that the general direction of the developments hoped for from psychoanalysis is also the general direction of the moral developments we call progressive in the public sphere. I shall give another brief clinical example to illustrate this.

Second case example: Sarah

Sarah came for help initially in her middle fifties, and I continued to see her until her death in her middle seventies. Her background was traumatic. She believed she had been sexually abused by her father as a small child, and in latency, aged about 8, she remembered being exposed to her parents' intercourse in grossly inappropriate ways, lying awake as they had forceful sex in the same room, and on some occasions in her bed, with her in it. At the age of 12 she witnessed her father's brutality and sarcasm towards refugee children whom the family took in for a charitable organisation. She remembered how her father refused to allow one boy, who was sick, to go to hospital, and the boy died. (This memory was so shocking that we both wondered if it was correct. By chance, it was corroborated during the therapy when one of these refugees, now a man in his sixties, made contact with her wishing to discuss his own memories of childhood.)

Sarah grew up isolated and depressed. In adolescence, her relations with boyfriends were destroyed by her compulsive jealousy, which would arise without evidence and quickly reach delusional intensity. In her early twenties she became depressed and was hospitalised on two occasions. She trained as a librarian and managed to hold down a job in a small provincial town. In her forties she was again in psychiatric hospital with depression, following a long string of brief relationships, often one-night stands.

When she came to me in her fifties, she professed extreme contempt for the ordinary values of society. No word in the language, she told me, was so ridiculous as the word *wife*. The best position for a woman was to be unmarried and hunting outside the camp. She had no wish for a loving relationship with a man, merely for transient sexual encounters.

Such things were said with a characteristic mixture of anger, a certain grandiloquence, and a kind of sad puzzlement, as if she didn't quite convince herself and yet was describing what she actually thought. Suicide often seemed an attractive option. She evoked in me a powerful feeling of compassion for the sad isolation of her life.

Despite her conscious memories of her past, her transference to me was curiously trusting. Even when, early on, she found it hard to approach the door of the consulting-room because she was besieged with images of me as a sexual abuser, she nevertheless told me of these thoughts very directly, and was calmed and relieved when she had done so, as if from somewhere she kept some belief in a good relationship that could be trusted.

She never came more than twice a week – for much of the time once a week and in the last years once a fortnight. Over the nearly twenty years of this long therapy she began to write autobiographical short stories, and in her late sixties she published a collection of them. Publication was hugely significant to her. She felt she had lived her life skulking in secret corners, and now she had come out and entered a public world. In terms of our present theme of sympathy, the idea of living in a public world, as opposed to being shut away in a secret one, is to do with living in a world enlarged by sympathetic participation with other people – a world containing other 'subjects like the self'.

The nature of her desire for men also changed. She met a vulnerable artist, very frightened of closeness, and felt very tenderly towards him. The compulsive jealousy that had always tormented her disappeared; she was able to be aware of her partner's previous relationships without becoming furious. She maintained that relationship for nearly a year, and when it ended she was sad rather than angry and contemptuous. She began to allow men an internal life of their own, including sexual feelings towards other women. She had always wanted to live in a big city; now she moved to one, and began to participate in various courses and shared activities. I began to hear of female friends for the first time. At the age of 71, she told me that for the first time in her life she sometimes had positive feelings of happiness. She linked them in particular with the fact that she had now begun to 'go towards people', and had lost her fear that good experience would always be followed by terrifying retribution. (In psychoanalytic language, her 'internal objects' had become less 'punitive'.)

I think what we glimpse in this brief history is the gradual re-establishment of the capacity for sympathy, which had been shocked into retreat by early traumatic experience. Sarah had been unable, perhaps for genetic reasons, to deal with early trauma by 'splitting', which might have led to the familiar outcome of the denial of suffering and identification with the aggressor, and perhaps to a re-enactment of an abusive cycle, the familiar pattern in which 'the abused becomes the abuser'. Indeed, versions of this had occurred in her earlier adult life, when her paranoid jealousy led to the abrupt abandonment of loving partners, with short-lived feelings of cruel triumph. But the fact that these reactions of jealousy diminished and became manageable when she came into therapy suggests that the main component of them was fear of betrayal and abandonment rather than primarily the sadistic pleasure of 'punishing a bad sexual object'. She became able to have friends, which is perhaps the profoundest key to happiness. The seeing of others as 'subjects' and not only as 'objects', the fundamental posture of morality, is an index of the presence of sympathy; its everyday manifestation is the capacity for friendship.

Conclusion

To sum up: the psychoanalyst Daniel Stern, whose research into communication and emotions in infancy has contributed greatly both to psychoanalysis and to developmental psychology, speaks of 'affect attunement' by the mother as crucial to the affective development of the baby. Babies are acutely aware of the degree to which the mother's attunement is accurate, and they may be shocked or traumatised by gross failures of accuracy (Stern 1985: 138–161). Another psychoanalyst, F. Broucek (1982), has suggested that areas in which the mother is at sea – and these might include such major departments of emotional life as aggression or sexuality – will be the areas in which she can't 'attune' with her baby, and which may later cause an otherwise competent child to suffer feelings of shame and internal collapse. Sympathy in what I am calling sense one, the capacity, is the elementary and involuntary response that makes affect attunement possible. It underlies the successful self-orientations (precursors of successful intervention) by both parents and psychoanalysts, and it allows children or patients in turn to discover their own emotional resources and to inhabit the world of emotion and relationship without excessive bewilderment. Autistic children are not able to use the capacity for sympathy, and, to whatever extent they are autistic, are frequently bewildered.

So I am making a big claim for it. It is by 'sympathy', not empathy, that we recognise that others are subjects of experience, like ourselves, and there is no other basis on which true values can be built. Sympathy is also the capacity that makes possible the more sophisticated function of empathy, and the more developed and specific affect of compassion which, confusingly, is often also given the name sympathy. It is the capacity that gives us the possibility of living in an accurately perceived emotional world where, in principle, and with the help of imagination and reflection, sound judgements of value may be made, and where a basis may be discerned for calling judgements of value sound. I shall return to this point in Chapter 10.

Chapter 5

How religions work

A comparison with psychoanalysis

Introduction

In speaking of sympathy as essential to what is objective to our sense of values, I have several times said: but it is not enough. We also need conscious reflection, imagination, judgement, and so forth.

Psychoanalysis is of course one of the formal arenas created to provide a space in which we can reflect on our experience, our values and our choices. But psychoanalysis is a comparatively recent invention. The traditional forum for such reflection has been religion. For many years, and certainly since the time of Darwin, 'religion' has been an object of suspicion for educated people, and it is not difficult to see why: not only do religions tend to affirm mythological stories which educated people increasingly find difficult or impossible to believe (or they believe them only in a separate compartment from the beliefs on which they act in most of their daily lives), but also they often do so in highly emotive ways, inducing shame or guilt, or in tones of irrational certainty which can be used to justify wars, murders, and every sort of mental and physical stupidity and cruelty. In the West, the negative valuation by Christianity of everything to do with sex, at its extreme in the nineteenth century, left behind it a legacy of misery that still reverberates on into the twenty-first century. Prejudice against homosexuality, to take just one example, is still justified by reference to Leviticus, a text dating from the sixth century BCE. Savage warfare between Shia and Sunni Muslims, or between Israeli settlers and Palestinian Arabs, is similarly justified by appeals to a mythologised past, to holy books and 'immemorial' religious loyalties.

The global case against religion, therefore, is a strong one, and it has been persuasively and repeatedly argued over the past two centuries by many thinkers including Marx, Nietzsche and Freud; more recently it has been made yet again by Richard Dawkins (2006) and Daniel Dennett (2006). Freud made the case against religion on a number of occasions, and particularly in *The Future of an Illusion* (Freud 1927b). As a psychoanalyst, he attempted in particular to understand the psychological function of religious claims. In essence, he suggested that they were defensive against many sorts of inescapable anxiety. For example, he said, we defend ourselves in the face of our anxieties about death, transience, and the uncertainty of all our decisions by supplying ourselves with a fantasy-figure, a god, who we imagine will protect us from catastrophe, and whose commandments are clear and unmistakable. Our fear of death is comforted by the belief in an afterlife; our fear that we may not be 'good' is comforted by knowing that we have obeyed the rules. If we have not obeyed the rules, we can repent and be forgiven, perhaps after accepting our well-deserved punishment. We are like children, said Freud, frightened of the dark: God is our comforting strong father. The belief in miracles, wonders, resurrections, keeps us living in a magical world in which harsh reality never has to be faced full-frontally: death will not really be final, our enemies will not really triumph over us, and even when 'in this world' they seem to, God can be relied on to put things right in the end and they will suffer for ever in an eternal Hell. All these fantasies are essentially infantile consolations and fulfil our childish wishes. Asked by Romain Rolland to comment on a more mystical sort of religion (Rolland spoke of the 'oceanic feeling'), Freud (1930) said that such religion seeks the restoration of 'primary narcissism', the safe, amorphous, boundary-less world in which Freud believed the newborn baby to live. Another sort of religious person, Freud (1907) said, protects himself by obsessional rituals and formulaic phrases, treating these essentially meaningless and ineffective behaviours as alternatives to facing up to the true, painful challenges of life.

There is undoubtedly a great deal of truth in all these criticisms. However, there is no good reason to repeat them, and for the purposes of this book I shall consider the negative case against religion to have been abundantly and convincingly made. It is more interesting now, I think, to examine what may be of positive value in religious traditions which, whatever their defects, have also been found precious over many generations, and which, delusive or otherwise, are regularly shown by researchers to give psychologically valuable benefits to their adherents. Religious people, for example, are shown to be happier than non-religious; they are likely to have more enduring marriages, with all the benefits that entails for the coming generation, and they tend to enjoy better physical health (Townsend et al. 2002). And despite the triumph of secular ways of thought in many areas (particularly in Europe, though less so in the United States), religion refuses to lie down and die. Widespread yearning for 'spirituality' inspires a whole tide of would-be religious thinking, whether in the form of regressive fundamentalism, flirtation with New Age or exotic religious traditions, or reinvented modes of observance. Psychologically, it is clear that there is a craving for something of a religious kind, which is no more suppressed by the polemics of scientific thinkers than the craving for sex was suppressed by pious Christian propaganda in favour of virginity. There continues to be something in religion that is not understood by the polemic against it.

In this chapter and the next, I shall consider how religions function, psychologically speaking, and shall suggest that, for all their deficiencies, the religious traditions hold on to intuitions concerning values that are crucially important, and that cannot be said in the language of conventional science. In this chapter I shall look in particular at the claim religions make to promote psychological change, and consider how they may do so.

Religion and psychoanalysis

Psychoanalysts have always been interested in religion. Despite his frequent robust dismissals of it, Freud kept returning to the topic, and in his 'historical novel', *Moses and Monotheism*, written at the age of 80, he found reasons for admiring Judaism and for preferring it to Christianity (Freud 1939). Jung too, coming from a Protestant Christian background and influenced by spiritualism and theosophy, was saturated in religious thought; his split from Freud, one of the great schisms in psychoanalytic history, was in part because he felt that there were positive elements in religion that Freud was failing to recognise; and despite a sort of orthodoxy of atheism that the idealisation of Freud imposed on the first two or three generations of psychoanalysts, by the 1950s Erich Fromm, Erik Erikson and many others were finding far richer and more subtle ways to speak of the religious traditions. Freud's confident separation of religion and 'science' – religion is illusion, 'our science is no illusion' (Freud 1927b: 56) – typical of his time, has been undermined from many angles: Michael Polanyi (1958) showed how the notion of scientific truth rests upon subjective and emotion-laden choices; philosophers of language have shown how the world we perceive is inescapably structured by the language in which we describe it. Theologians such as Raimon Panikkar (1989) have come to speak of the different religions as essentially different structures of language. More recently, the study of consciousness, and the difficulty of integrating it with conventional science, have shifted the whole debate onto a new terrain.

There are of course still plenty of psychoanalysts, as there are still plenty of other scientists, who speak from the same materialist philosophical base as Freud in 1907. But the new situation has made a great deal of new thinking possible, and nowadays many psychoanalysts refer to religion with respect. Since the 1980s, following a long silence on the topic, there has been a spate of psychoanalytic books and papers on religious matters, not by any means all of them hostile. I have sketched this history elsewhere (Black 2006).

This development creates a difficulty, however. As long as psychoanalysis could adopt an attitude of unquestioned superiority, there was no problem: religion could be dismissed as infantile, and therefore intellectually insignificant (even if it sometimes happened to say some things that seemed valuable, or that resonated with psychoanalytic insights); psychoanalysis, by contrast, was responsible: its approach to knowledge was the adult path of a science, and though it might of course make mistakes, in the long run the path of science was the path to truth. But if religions now deserve respect, what can they deserve respect *for*? Do they know something that psychoanalysis doesn't? Or are they just players in a wholly different ball-game, and they can be respected as one might respect poetry or Chinese opera?

Addressing these issues, the psychoanalyst Neville Symington (1994) made a useful distinction between (in his terms) 'primitive' and 'mature' religion. (The word 'primitive' is perhaps unfortunate, as it echoes the old-fashioned, ethnocentric use of the word by anthropologists. But Symington's meaning is psychoanalytic, not anthropological.) By 'primitive' religion he means a form of religion that is essentially magical, believed without proper reflection, and aiming at personal protection and survival. 'Mature' religion, by contrast, can be rational, thoughtful, nuanced, and is able to discuss important themes such as truth, love, evil and goodness. It is capable of being undogmatic and respectful towards alternative views, including secular views. As Symington (1994) says, neither Freud nor Jung fully recognised the existence of mature religion, and their positions are unsatisfactory because they relate almost entirely to 'primitive' religious attitudes.

Symington's distinction needs to be used with caution. In any lived religion, primitive and mature elements are inevitably mixed up, and it is important that 'mature' does not simply get used as a stick to beat 'primitive' with. A functioning religion not only speaks to intellectuals, but also has to find emotional and imaginatively appealing ways to convey its message, and to speak to children and young people, and to the immaturity still present in adults; moreover, the 'immature' is disconcertingly prone to reveal within it the seeds of future creative and original thinking. The 'mature' vision, however, is necessary to control the 'primitive' elements, which otherwise are vulnerable to promoting mere superstitions or to takeover by paranoid motives. Evangelical Christianity, fundamentalist Islam, extremist Judaism and the extraordinary nationalist Hindutva movement have all in recent years shown how vulnerable even major and long-established religious traditions are to such takeovers. Paradoxically, this may be in part because of the success of the polemic against religion by modern science: perhaps fewer genuinely 'mature' thinkers are now working within religious structures than was the case in the past.

If we wish to enquire about the more creative ways in which religions function, a good place to start is by looking at the question of goals. Any actual religion, in practice, is such a many-faceted social construct that to formulate an adequate account of its 'goals' would be alarmingly complicated: it would need to include social, political, economic and family perspectives, not to mention the views of theology. But looking from the perspective of psychoanalysis, and with an underlying concern with the development of values, I shall confine my comments to psychological functioning. I shall suggest that the psychological function of a religion is to be an engine of personal transformation. In some way or other, every major religion acts to transform its practitioners' view both of themselves and of the world in which they perceive themselves to be set. In the process, it necessarily affirms the importance of certain values and downgrades the importance of certain others.

As psychoanalysis in its very different way attempts to do something similar, we may get a sense of how religions work by comparing them with psychoanalysis, and considering how the two approaches achieve their effects.

Confusion about goals: psychoanalysis

To start with the goals of psychoanalysis, one of the first things that has to be dealt with here is a sort of red herring. Psychoanalysis, like every other profession, instils certain powerful slogans into its practitioners. All analysts carry in their professional superego voices which say to them, like Freud, 'renounce therapeutic ambition', or like Wilfred Bion, 'eschew memory and desire' (Bion 1970: 42–43). So powerful are these injunctions that many psychoanalysts in the past used to say that they had no desires for their patients except to analyse them.

Such an attitude is not just hard to explain to the public, who understandably want psychoanalysis to have the goal of helping its patients. It is also clearly an impossibility. Psychoanalysts are bound to have wishes for their patients; they would be inhuman if they did not. If you listen to any professional case presentation, it is easy to see the worry that analysts suffer when they feel unable to help their patients, and the corresponding relief they feel when there is a breakthrough into understanding and capacities for love, sadness, gratitude and so forth. Analysts are clearly, if guardedly, also in general pleased when they are able to report that the patient became able to marry or settle into a long-term partnership, decided to have children, or achieved success or promotion at work. From these reactions, it is clear that the desires of the analyst and the desires of the patient coincide. If they did not, psychoanalysts would be guilty of something we are sometimes accused of, namely, imposing a treatment on the patient for our own purposes rather than the patient's.

In the 1990s, Joseph Sandler and Anna Ursula Dreher (1996) looked into the whole history of 'aims' in psychoanalytic therapy. They came up with a large number of formulations. Many of the most vivid and convincing continue to be Freud's own, and in some ways it is difficult to improve on his famously downbeat early formula: 'much will be gained if we succeed in transforming your hysterical misery into common unhappiness' (Breuer and Freud 1895: 305). That dates from 1895. Forty-two years later, Freud produced a more modern-sounding formula: 'The business of the analysis is to secure the best possible psychological conditions for the functions of the ego; with that it has discharged its task' (Freud 1937: 250).

Most later analysts would agree with this latter version, but questions remained as to how these best possible conditions for the ego's functioning were achieved. Was it by modifying the archaic superego (Strachey 1934), or by making conscious the ego's defences against conflict (A. Freud 1936)? Sandler and Dreher (1996) themselves conclude, as do most more recent thinkers, with a rather modest statement of outcome goals, stressing that a desirable outcome for one patient may be very different from a desirable outcome for another. Tantalisingly, they point out that 'the formulation of aims will vary according to the value systems of the analyst and patient' (Sandler and Dreher 1996: 121).

The American psychoanalyst Jonathan Lear (2009), who is also a philosopher, has suggested that the overarching psychoanalytic goal is 'freedom', and the different schools of psychoanalysis, which often appear to be in conflict, are in reality aiming at different aspects of freedom: freedom to be different, freedom to love, freedom to think one's own thoughts, and so on. There is much to be said for attempting to state a single, abstract goal in this way, but the choice of 'freedom' is a difficult one: it falls foul of the fact that all our freedoms have to be lived within the unfreedoms of a particular society, and within the framework of physical reality and the biological facts of age and sex and the probably unshiftable effects on brain-structure of our earliest emotional experience. The goal of 'freedom' undoubtedly catches something essential about what psychoanalysis aims at, but equally true is the recognition of limitation.

But a common feature of virtually all statements of psychoanalytic goals is that, like Freud's later formulation, they are about psychic structure. The aim is to weaken the grip of the archaic superego, to strengthen the ego, to enhance the patient's psychic integration, to work through depressive anxieties, to help the patient to be somewhat free of compulsions and impulsivity, and so on – the goal is *that* sort of thing; it is not to persuade the patient that certain statements are true, or that one way of life is superior to another. Therapy is not philosophy. The hope of psychoanalytic therapy is that the patient will become more able to make his or her own decisions, on a basis of better self-knowledge and improved psychic functioning.

The goal of religions

I shall make my own formulation of the goal of psychoanalysis in a moment. But let me first go on to look at the goals of religions, bearing in mind that religions, including the two great families of highly developed religion, the Abrahamic and the Indian, are very different from one another.

Non-religious people often think that what religions are about is believing rather improbable things: virgin births, miracles, resurrections, reincarnation, the objective existence of God or gods, divine interruptions of the continuity of cause and effect, and so on. And it is true that every religion, in its popular versions at any rate, has its share of such things. This is true even of Buddhism, though the Indian religions at their best tend to show a somewhat relaxed, even humorous, attitude to the question of actual belief in these stories.

I shall take my examples mainly from two religions, Christianity and Buddhism, of which I have some personal experience. Nowadays, there is an enormous amount of cross-cultural influence, which makes it difficult to say that the goals of any one religion have developed entirely independently of those of another, but it is possible to make some tentative distinctions by looking at the earlier traditions in each case.

Even then, cross-cultural influence cannot be ruled out. When the Buddha was born, a wise old man, Asita, wept bitterly. When asked why he was weeping at such an auspicious event, Asita replied that it was for himself: he was so old that he would not live to see the Buddha's enlightenment. This has an inverse echo in the Christian story of Simeon, the old man who praised God that he had lived long enough to see the birth of Jesus, and several commentators have suggested that perhaps influence flowed, in this case, from Buddhism to Christianity (Thomas 1949). Later, the development of the ideal of the Bodhisattva, which took place in the early centuries of the Christian era, is in some respects so like the Christian ideal that it is possible that there was now influence flowing in the opposite direction. The distinctive smile of enlightenment, on the lips of the Buddha's statues, has been shown to derive from images of the Egyptian Pharaohs, brought to India by Alexander's armies. And of course Buddhism itself arose out of, and in contrast to, an older culture of Brahmanism. We are never on safe ground in claiming an uncontaminated tradition.

Nevertheless, if we look at what are likely to be the oldest elements in Buddhism, it is convincing to think that the determining preoccupation of the historical Buddha, Gautama Siddhartha, was with transience. The myth tells us that he was brought up with all the heart can desire: he was a cherished prince, had three palaces for hot, cold, and rainy seasons, lotus ponds, dancing girls, a wife, and finally, that supreme blessing, a son. In earthly terms, the myth is telling us, he wanted for nothing.

The psychoanalyst, however, is bound to notice, though the commentators mention it only in passing, that his mother died seven days after his birth. (When, centuries later, Mahayana Buddhism generated myths of many previous Buddhas, early maternal death would become a regularly repeated detail.) And at the age of 29, Gautama met the three Heavenly Messengers: he went out from his palace on three successive days, and met, respectively, an old man, a sick man, and a corpse being carried to cremation. The awareness of old age, sickness and death drained all the pleasure from his luxurious life; he left his wife, his newborn son, and his palaces, and embarked on a life of austerity.

His project, therefore, was to come to terms with these difficult realities. A colleague of mine has suggested that this was essentially to enter (in Kleinian language) the 'depressive position': the narcissistic pleasure in youth and sensuality had been undermined by the awareness of decay and transience, and a new position had to be found in the mind if he was not to be overwhelmed by terror and revulsion. The death of his mother is particularly poignant in this connection: we may imagine that the birth of his son touched on deeply buried memories of loss, too early to be laid down in any form in episodic memory. (I shall give an example from clinical work of a comparably early experience of loss in Chapter 8.)

To translate the Buddhist myth in terms of the depressive position, however, though not entirely inaccurate, is not the whole story. Gautama's solution was not, like Job's, to return at last to his family and possessions, a wiser and more sober man. His renunciation of the world of desire was final. Following his enlightenment (or in the myth's language, after he had attained Buddhahood), his teaching of the Four Noble Truths, which is almost certainly as near as we can get to the teaching of the historical Gautama himself, was of a path to a reality – or we could call it another psychic 'position' – in which there was no longer a desire for things to be one way rather than another. In psychoanalysis, the fundamental goal of working through the depressive position is to overcome splitting and establish a united ego despite the painful grief and conflict this entails. It describes, not a freedom from desire, but a capacity to maintain desire and full engagement despite frustration and anxiety. This is quite different from the goal of early Buddhism.

One may, of course, think that the Buddha's goal is an unreal fantasy. I shall argue that it is not unreal, but that it is a 'position', and like the depressive position, it can never be stably established. I shall return in a moment to the notion of a 'position'. It was not a mere historical accident that Buddhism was initially a religion specifically for those who had 'gone forth to a homeless life', that is, for celibate monks and nuns. Later, in Japan, and nowadays in the West, it has been very extensively adapted for lay people, many of whom, whether they know it or not, now see it through psychoanalytically tinted spectacles. In its essence, however, it is a very radical teaching indeed, perhaps as radical as it is possible to be.

If we think now of Christianity, we find ourselves in a quite different world, both imaginatively and doctrinally. We now know that the Gospel picture of Jesus Christ, despite its appearance of historicity, is very largely a literary creation. Even details which look like a modern concern for historical fact are delusive. For example, we are told that Jesus was born when Quirinius was Governor of Syria, and Herod was King in Judea. But it turns out that these two periods of office did not overlap (Küng 1974: 149). Many of the details of Jesus's life can be shown to derive from pious or politically motivated elaboration of Old Testament sources, and presumably have a purely literary origin. Geza Vermes (1973) has shown convincingly that Jesus can be seen as a recognisable type, a Hasid, within the framework of contemporary Judaism, but we are probably right to assume that the apparent facts we have about the historical Jesus are hardly more reliable than those we have about the historical Buddha.

Nevertheless, I think we can again make out the central initial preoccupation of the religion: not now with transience, but with the question of how we should act in the world in relation to God and to other people. The central story, of a good man who is the victim of terrible injustice because he will not betray his own vision, is a myth with universal application: love and sincerity, telling the truth as one perceives it, are constantly under threat in every human situation. The resurrection story is an enormous statement of hope, that even though crushed again and again, love and sincerity can never be finally destroyed.

In Buddhism, we see above all the function of a religion in creating a *vision*, an understanding of the world, in its practitioners. In Christianity, we see more clearly the activity of worship (the early etymology is *worth-ship*) that creates, or singles out and emphasises, particular *values*. To declare Jesus to be the Christ, who is God, the second person of the Trinity, co-equal with the Father, and so on, has made for all kinds of intellectual puzzles; but for the ordinary believer it has worked powerfully on the emotional level, to assert the supreme importance of the values of love and sincerity which the story of Jesus, at its best, embodies. Vision and values, the two creative productions of religion, cannot wholly be separated. In later chapters I shall return to these issues using a more philosophical language.

The values of Christianity, and the values of modern psychoanalysis, are in many ways remarkably close. The Kleinian emphasis on the importance of the predominance of love, its constant threat from our hatred and perversity, and the need for mourning and reparation because of our attacks on the good object, has a rather exact parallel in the Christian emphasis on love, which is damaged by sin and selfishness, and must then be reinstated by penitence and amendment of life. This is partly because Freud, Melanie Klein, and Christianity are all in their different ways the heirs of Judaism, and both Christian and psychoanalytic values stem from the Jewish world-view. But the difference is that psychoanalysis believes that these values accrue as a result of a natural process, the repeated experience of the survival of the good object despite our assaults on it (and they are at risk if the good object does *not* survive our assaults); Christianity is less optimistic, and believes that these values have to be asserted, and that even then they only acquire power in the believer's heart as a result of divine grace. The 'revelation' of Christianity is the realisation that these values are not arbitrary, certain values among others, but are supreme and have 'universal' significance (they are God's values and can therefore be said to be objective). (For a rather different take on the continuing echoes between psychoanalysis and Judaism, see Stephen Frosh (2006).)

Curious as the language of religion tends to sound to scientific thinkers today, it is worth noting that one of the difficulties of psychoanalysis is its lack of predictive power. One child, brought up in very damaging circumstances, may develop a steadiness and good temper quite beyond the reach of another, whose circumstances seem vastly more favourable. The psychoanalyst, to understand this, does not speak of 'grace' but is likely to invoke 'constitution' (i.e. genetic factors) which underlie 'unconscious phantasy', the construction the baby or small child puts on its experience. Jonathan Lear (1990) has opened up a possible bridge between the psychoanalytic understanding of love, and the Christian, by pointing out that we can come into being, psychically, only as a result of receiving the 'loving attention' of another. We cannot therefore, he says, go outside of love, to evaluate it, because our own existence, as conscious beings capable of thought and judgement, depends on it. However, the capacity of individuals to 'receive' and therefore to benefit from the loving attention available to them varies greatly, for reasons which are still not fully understood (and may be genetic).

The notion of a psychic 'position'

I want now to come back to the notion of a psychic 'position'. Melanie Klein in her earlier writings used the word rather freely. There were a manic and a feminine position, as well as the more familiar depressive and the later paranoid-schizoid ones. Nowadays, our use of the word has narrowed down essentially to these latter two.

A position is described as an ego-state: 'the characteristic posture', says Hinshelwood, 'that the ego takes up with respect to its objects', 'a constellation of anxieties, defences, object-relations and impulses' (Hinshelwood 1991: 394, 393). This sort of language is now so familiar in psychoanalytic circles, and is so useful clinically, that we can easily forget how odd it is. An abstraction, the I – ego is James Strachey's translation of Freud's *das Ich* – is being described as having a physical characteristic, a posture. How can we imagine what we are talking about?

In order to imagine it, it may be helpful to look again at neuroscience. Neuroscience is helpful to psychoanalysis for two reasons. One is because, as long as we use a solely psychological language, psychoanalysis can do very little to persuade a sceptical third party. The best attempts by psycho-analysts to describe psychic structure, whether speaking of id, ego and superego, or about internal objects and the dramas in which they par-ticipate, are essentially metaphorical. These metaphors are well established within our professional world, and they have proved invaluable in our attempts to understand clinical material, but they are frustratingly intan-gible if we want to think scientifically and communicate with people outside the linguistic community of psychoanalysis. If we assume that all our mental life has its physical correlate in observable brain events, then even if our understanding of the brain remains approximate, at least we have a foothold on a world in which public and literal statement is, in principle, a possibility.

The second reason for speaking of neuroscience is because, as described in Chapter 2, our knowledge of it has developed very rapidly in recent years. Gerald Edelman, Antonio Damasio and other neuroscientists have now given us a model, more or less comprehensible to the layperson, in which the brain develops crucial aspects of its actual physical structure in response to the person's experience, and particularly their earliest experi-ence (Edelman 1992). This is an astonishing new understanding, only clearly established since the late 1980s, which now affects our entire under-standing of what we mean by personal and psychological development.

I shall confine myself here to outlining some of Edelman's basic theory. The neurons that make up the brain are connected to one another at tiny electrochemical junctions called synapses. When information is transmitted through the brain, it travels in the form of electrical impulses, which pass along the neurons and then jump to the next neuron by way of chemical transmitters released at the synapse. The number of synaptic links in the adult human brain is astronomically huge: there are about one thousand million million of them: 10 to the power of 15. Edelman is fond of saying that the human brain is the most complex material structure in the universe.

At birth, the infant's brain has a huge number of potential synaptic links, but they have only partially been connected up. They get connected, over time, in accordance with the infant's experience. For example, a child attempts to catch a ball. If the child succeeds, the synapses that helped her catch the ball, for example those involved in hand–eye coordination, become more firmly established, and others, which might impede her in catching the ball, are weakened or deleted. The psychoanalyst will want to add, of course, that what the child regards as success is also learned, and will depend on other synaptic patterns which have previously become established, and which reflect the attitudes and responses the child has already encountered in the people around her.

This very much parallels the sort of thing that we see happening in a baby in relation to the production of sounds. The infant initially produces a very wide range of vowel and consonantal sounds, but rapidly learns to restrict himself to the sounds used in the language of the people around him. Similarly, the astounding verbal take-up of a small child, often learning new words instantly from a single hearing, rapidly hardens and, so to speak, sets; already by the age of 5 new words are becoming harder to acquire. The talent and enthusiasm of children for mimicry is also interesting in this connection: what seems like mere fun and playfulness makes a huge contribution to personal and physical development, and also to the capacity to understand what is happening, mentally, in other people. As I argued in speaking of sympathy in Chapter 4, it is likely that 'understanding' another person is a derivative of the impulse to mimic them; work by Malloch and Trevarthen (2009) and their colleagues emphasises in particular the importance of music and rhythmic elements in the early patterns of imitation and divergence that are called 'attunement'.

Edelman's theory is of especial interest to psychoanalysts, because it gives us a way of understanding the extraordinary flexibility of human beings, both psychologically within a culture, and also cross-culturally and across historical epochs. We have all marvelled at the fact that much the same genetic material can generate such impressively diverse creatures as the Dalai Lama and Mao Tse-tung, Casanova and Immanuel Kant. Edelman's theory gives us a preliminary handle on the causes of this diversity: the brains of these very diverse people have been shaped not only by their genetic inheritance, but also by their individual, emotion-laden developmental experience. We no longer have to wonder, as Freud did, how a brain formed 'in the Stone Age' is able to cope with the complexities of life in modern Vienna. The brain of a Stone Age person would have been profoundly different from the brain of a modern Viennese, despite little or no difference in initial genetic endowment.

For the psychoanalyst, this neuroscientific theory also gives us an imaginatively convincing way to think of what we know so well: the stubborn persistence of the effects of early experience. The long struggles we see, in our patients and ourselves, become more comprehensible if we think that we are wrestling with patterns that are inscribed in the actual stuff of the neurons.

Mark Solms (1998) has shown that Freud abandoned his early attempt in the 1890s to describe the neuroanatomical counterpart to psychic events because the theory available in his day was still too crude to encompass them. Freud could work only with a static brain anatomy, in which specific localised 'lesions' had to be invoked to account for 'psychopathology'. Solms and his colleague Oliver Turnbull have also emphasised that Freud was quite aware that future advances in neuroscience might 'blow away' (Freud 1920: 60) the whole complicated structure of psychoanalytic thought (Solms and Turnbull 2002). Edelman's theory does not do that, but it does now give us a dynamic anatomy with a developmental history, far more capable, in principle, of matching the subtlety and complexity of psycho-analytic findings. The notion of 'psychopathology' also becomes more evidently a metaphor: what we are talking about, most often, is more accurately described, not as a 'pathology' of some kind, but as one development rather than another. Whether a given development is functional or dysfunctional depends on many things, including the nature of the society which the child will be called upon to inhabit. Often what presents as 'psychopathology' in the larger society may be a development that was adaptive when the child was growing up, but unfortunately adaptive within a dysfunctional family structure. Or, of course, vice versa: the child may have grown up adapted to a more benign system, only to find himself flung into a situation of collective trauma such as war or revolution.

To come back to the notion of a psychic 'position': there can be no doubt that the depressive and paranoid-schizoid positions do occur, and in the clinical setting it can be extremely dramatic to see a patient go from one to the other, sometimes very abruptly. (The case of Sylvia, in Chapter 4, was an example.) The capacity to think, to see another person's point of view, to be sad and reflective rather than in a state of fury, can disappear and reappear like the flashing lights of a pinball machine. What is happening, presumably, is that changes are occurring in the brain which allow the experience of 'I' to be associated with very different sets of physical events. We may imagine, following Edelman's model, that as a patient comes to have more regular access to depressive position (socially realistic) thinking, new synaptic connections are being reinforced, and previous ones deleted, modified, or brought into association with the new pathways. Psycho-analytic change then takes so long, and requires so much repeated working-through, because of the huge amount of work such physical changes involve after the early phases of brain growth and adaptability in infancy and adolescence.

Changes in psychic 'position' are matched by changes in values, as I showed in my other case example in Chapter 4, that of Sarah. The move to the depressive position is a move towards values that respect the full reality of another person, that respect long-term welfare as well as impulse grati-fication, and that relativise the importance of the peremptory narcissistic 'I' of the paranoid-schizoid position. The word 'position' is well established in psychoanalysis but it is misleading if it is taken to imply a single, static posture. In fact, each so-called position is more like a long road, with recognisable points along it. For example, in the depressive position, I may experience remorse for the damage I have done in reality or phantasy to my 'objects' (to others); but this feeling can occur in profoundly different tonalities, as Donald Winnicott (1963) showed when he distinguished between guilt (which merely feels bad, and fears punishment) and concern (which warmly wants to put right).

We may link these reflections to another famous psychological conundrum, namely: who is the dreamer? Dreaming is so familiar to us that we easily overlook the sheer extraordinariness of it: how can the dream know so much that the dreamer doesn't? For example, in certain sorts of very self-destructive patient, the possibility of progress is often delayed, and is then heralded by a dream in which someone is in the grip of a powerful, seductive, mafia-like organisation. This sort of dream, first described in the psychoanalytic literature by Herbert Rosenfeld (1988), seems at the time frightening or meaningless to the patient, but may be extremely illuminating to the analyst, who can, hopefully, and often over a long period of time, introduce the patient further to its meaning. But how can the dream have happened, in such an uncomprehending patient? Usually, it follows a lot of analytic work, and it will require a great deal more before it offers useful insight to the patient. But the fact that it has been preceded by analytic work allows one to think that the analyst's interventions have already had some preliminary effect in opening up new pathways in the patient's brain; a new 'position' which might be described as the internalisation of some of the analyst's thoughts and attitudes. It is these newly activated pathways which make the dream possible. The further work that is necessary is to do with linking them in with the structures creating the sense of 'I', and easing the 'I', so to speak, out of its habitual pathways.

A fuller account of these processes would require a more detailed discussion of 'internalisation'. It seems intuitively likely that the importance of a degree of positive feeling, liking or trust, towards the therapist is that it allows the more energetic action of sympathy, which makes possible the sort of unconscious or semi-conscious identification which is being described here in terms of its neuronal correlates. Very often with such patients, however, liking or trust is hard to establish, and when it arises, is subject to violent attacks.

To return to the religions: without seeking to answer any questions about the nature of the mind-brain connection, we can nevertheless say that thinking in terms of brain anatomy gives us a way of imagining how different psychic 'positions' are possible, subtly and sometimes radically different from one another. What Symington (1994) would call mature religions aim to give their practitioners access to mental positions which appear to be recognisably similar to the depressive position as it can be arrived at and worked through in psychoanalysis. For example, the qualities of 'justice' and 'mercy' that characterise God in the Abrahamic traditions (qualities, I shall suggest, that await introjection by the believer) are 'depressive position' qualities: they recognise the full reality of human beings and their right to good treatment, equally with the self. The Christian injunction to love one's neighbour as one's self is in the same spirit. The Dalai Lama has commented on the similarity of the basic ethical training of all the main religions: 'when it comes', he writes, 'to cultivating love, compassion, patience, and contentment, or the observance of self-discipline and ethical principles, most spiritual traditions seem to be more or less the same' (Dalai Lama 2007: 5). All these qualities clearly belong in the 'depressive position' series, in which the dominating peremptory 'I' of the narcissistic person is transcended by a recognition of the full reality of at least some others.

The explicit statement of values tells us of the basic axiological orientation of the religion, and it is certainly important, but as far as personal development is concerned it is only part of the story. It operates at the intellectual level, but personal development is too difficult to occur without the energy of powerful emotion. Any religion practised by large numbers of people, such as Buddhism or Christianity, is bound to present a mixture of mature and 'primitive' elements, and the development of the believer, from more infantile forms of belief to more mature, does not necessarily show the sharp discontinuity these terms suggest when they are used in the abstract. If this development is possible within the religion (and there is a great deal of evidence that, at least in the case of most of the major religions, it is), then that is because, as religions, they are able to add to the direct experience of relationship with others, not only an explicit statement of values, but also the emotional experience of relating to religious objects. If we are to distinguish 'primitive' from mature elements, this will be one of the areas in which we need to step carefully.

William James, in *The Varieties of Religious Experience* (1902), examined a great many accounts of conversion, both to and also from religious belief, and considered their place in the longer-term narrative of their subjects' lives. He concluded that, although often the immediate high drama of conversion, with its accompanying emotions of excitement, relief, gratitude and so on, quickly ebbed away, it regularly left a deposit in the form of a lasting change in the subject's life and values, most often described as increased calm, capacity for concern or love for others, and diminished fear of death. If we look at a specific life-story, for example that of George Fox (1694), the seventeenth century founder of the Quakers, we see the process of religious development taking place in a characteristic sequence, moving from intense, emotion-laden interactions with religious objects – despairing petitionary prayers to God or Jesus Christ, or agonising periods of 'spiritual dryness' in which these objects cannot be discovered, alternating with moments of ecstatic delight and adoration – moderating over time to a quieter and more stable security in affirming his own considered values, a capacity to teach and guide others with moral consistency, and steadiness in dealing with criticism and disagreement.

The 'objects' of religion – essentially culturally provided internal mental objects – and the 'objects' of psychoanalysis (above all the analyst as experienced in the transference) are of course extremely different, and I shall end this chapter by considering this contrast and the very different ways in which these objects are used. This difference is, I think, the most striking feature that distinguishes psychoanalysis from the religions.

The use of objects in religion and in psychoanalysis

In a psychoanalysis, what happens is that a patient enters a relationship in which he can have access to some part of his range of feelings and phantasies towards another person – his longing to surrender, his hope for love, his willingness to hate and damage, his fear of catastrophic loss, and so on. Analysis of the 'transference' helps him to see what it is that he brings to the relationship which distorts his perception and response to the actual other person in front of him. If all goes well, he emerges with a better capacity to tolerate his own feelings, and a better recognition of what belongs to him and what belongs to the other. As a result of this experience, he becomes more able to endure and inhabit a world of human relationships, without being overwhelmed and without acting in ways that are damaging to his deepest wishes for his life.

With a religious object, by contrast, no such experience is possible, because the religious object – Jesus, God, Krishna, the Buddha, etc. – has no significant objective existence to be contrasted with its existence in the psychic world of the faith community. What is achieved by worship, contemplation, prayer, meditation and so on, involving these objects, is not a contrast with an actual 'other', but a development, gradual or sometimes sudden, of a 'position' in the mind which conforms to the structure of the founding vision of the religious community. Tradition and the faith community are inescapable, even if individual believers choose to isolate themselves: they are inescapably present in the believer's language and phantasy, because it is they who have shaped, sustained and remembered the religious object (Rizzutto 1979; Black 1993).

The development that psychoanalysis can provide is clearly of great value in the ordinary world of human relationships. A vision involving religious objects opens up the possibility of further sorts of development, which include but also go beyond the world of human relations. We can recognise this, for example, in relation to two issues: mortality and forgiveness. (Perhaps we need a slightly larger term than 'forgiveness', to include something for which there is no adequate single word in English, namely, the giving up of bitterness.) Psychoanalysis can of course talk about both issues, but whether patients become reconciled to their mortality, or are able to forgive those who have injured them, is not something that psychoanalysis can control or even propose as a desirable outcome. It is part of the commitment of the psychoanalyst to stay with the patient in his or her despair, grief, bitterness and so on, and not to give advice or propose solutions unless or until they emerge in the patient's own process and material. Any other reaction would be to encourage splitting or denial. This psychoanalytic posture (correct, in my view, as a guide to clinical practice) leaves unanswered the question of how these things may be thought of in the non-clinical setting.

To consider mortality first: from within the world of human object relating (the psychoanalytic perspective), mortality can only be a cause of loss and sorrow: death can only be seen as a terminus. It is a boundary beyond which no one can go, and the person who dies will make no further contribution to human interaction. Whether one's response to death is to view it as a catastrophe, or to accept it with stoical resignation as Freud did, there is no positive or hopeful light in which it can be seen. At best, its finality can serve to make it a stimulus, to encourage one to make the most of one's life before it is too late – but that is not to find death positive, but to find life positive by contrast.

Similarly, in the world of human object relating, there may be a boundary within the totality of damage done to one, beyond which the victim cannot forgive the perpetrator. If, like the abused child, my capacity for human object relating has been irreparably damaged, that is a wrong that is absolute: how can I ever cease to be bitter? The question has a particular resonance in the early years of the twenty-first century. In the past hundred years, more than ever before, entire populations have suffered terrible psychic damage: can they (and should they) ever let go of their past (which would mean forgetting terrible grievance and injustice to loved ones and relatives), or must they forever nurse their bitter memories and remember their victimhood?

Santayana (1905) famously said: those who cannot remember the past are condemned to repeat it. We may equally say, however: those who cannot let go of bitterness are doomed never to live in the present. W.B. Yeats, reflecting on the Irish situation in his poem, 'Easter 1916', spoke of the memory of 'too great a sacrifice' as making 'a stone of the heart': a stone 'to trouble the living stream' (Yeats 1951: 202–205). Any psycho-analyst who has worked with a patient suffering from traumatic memories, perhaps of torture or of severe childhood abuse, knows how such bitterness can become a lifelong jail sentence. In this perspective, the discussion of human beings in terms of genetics and neuroscience can seem to miss the point. This is because it cannot take into account the peculiar predicament of a creature that carries detailed memories of the past, and also anticipation of the future, including an awareness of its own coming death and the deaths of those around it. Freud's early drive theory, derived from a Darwinian picture of the organism, also failed to fully recognise these factors. In much of his later work, and particularly after he had developed his theory of mourning and the 'death drive', he made a vigorous attempt to take them into account.

From inside the web of human object relating, death and irreparable injury can be seen only as negatives. What religions attempt to offer is a viewpoint from outside the web, a viewpoint from which we can see our life-histories, and those of other people, in a different perspective altogether: not one which renders them unimportant, but one in which their importance is redefined, and past injury and future death can lose their irremediable bitterness. The notion of eternity, which should be distinguished from the notion of everlastingness, is to do with this other dimension from which experience can be viewed.

Without fully registering the fact, in the tremendous push forward that resulted from Freud's late theories, and led on in the work of Melanie Klein and Donald Winnicott to the development of a much more detailed object-relations theory, psychoanalysis took a big step in this religious direction. In a famous paper, the psychoanalyst Elliott Jaques (1988) spoke of the need in mid-life to come to terms with approaching death by reworking the depressive position. He wrote:

> Working through again the infantile experience of loss and grief gives an increase in confidence in one's capacity to love and mourn what has been lost and what is past, rather than to hate and feel persecuted by it. We can begin to mourn our own eventual death. Creativeness takes on new depths and shades of feeling. There is the possibility, however, of furthering the resolution of the depressive position at a much deeper level. Such a working through is possible if the primal object is sufficiently well established in its own right and neither excessively idealised nor devalued.
>
> (Jaques 1988: 245)

Jaques continues, a little surprisingly in view of his generally disparaging attitude towards religion, to speak with great feeling of the possible serenity and confidence of old age. He does so by quoting the supreme imagery of Dante's *Paradiso*: 'my desire and my will, like a wheel that spins with even motion, were revolved by the Love that moves the sun and other stars'.

One of the difficulties with the language of the 'depressive position' is that very different psychic achievements get described in the same words. No doubt by 'primal object' Jaques meant to speak of something deriving from the breast and the baby's earliest encounters with the mother, but in quoting Dante he moved on to a religious vision, in which the love between mother and child, between Mary and Jesus, between Dante and Beatrice, is also the divine Love which is the ultimate truth of the universe. Perhaps he did not quite realise he had done so; or perhaps there is a secret ecstasy latent in the sober Kleinian vocabulary which is rarely allowed to show its face, but does so for a moment here. But what has happened is that Jaques, perhaps because he was reluctant to acknowledge his own religious vision, has elided two levels of reality. Loss, grief, mourning and the depressive position all exist on the level of human object relating, and as such are squarely within the domain of psychoanalysis. Dante's vision, however, whether or not you agree with it, is cosmological: it is an attempt to state a supreme truth about the universe. He is saying – and more than saying, envisioning – that the moral and emotional laws that prevail in the realm of human feeling are also the laws that govern the universe. This is a fundamental teaching in religions: for example, the Jewish understanding of *halakhah* (the Judaic Law) is that it is not only a code for human conduct, but also the law by which God created the cosmos. A similar idea is implicit in the Christian understanding of Creation. It finds a surprising parallel in Freud's thought, in two of his last papers (1937, 1940) in which he unexpectedly suggests that the two great 'drives', Eros and Thanatos, may not just operate within the biological realm: they may, he says, like the cosmic forces of Love and Strife described by the pre-Socratic philosopher, Empedocles of Acragas, be at work throughout the universe. Jaques too has slipped, though apparently without quite noticing it, from psychology to ontology, from psychological theory to mystical or cosmological vision.

Perhaps he had no alternative. Our thoughts about death are not merely the infantile fears, in which death is equated with 'depressive chaos, confusion, and persecution' (Jaques 1988: 242); we also have to cope with ageing and death as empirical realities, which frame and limit our lives. Mature religions, as the myth of the Buddha's Three Heavenly Messengers emphasises, are to do with realities. They face us with entirely non-neurotic questions, and above all the question: how are human beings to see and tolerate their incomplete, damaged and finite lives, in this vast spatio-temporal universe in which they are for a while, briefly in time, locally in space, conscious? How are we to endure these limits?

What Elliott Jaques overlooked, in the transition from a world of merely human object relating to a universal vision, was that such a vision alters the basis on which values are held. Values cease (if the universal vision is correct) to be simply the product of human needs and a human developmental story, and become in some sense 'objective'. This quality of being 'in some sense objective' is, I think, the distinctive note of religious values; it gives rise to philosophical problems which I shall discuss further in Chapter 10. For the moment, however, we need to note that it is this transition that marks the threshold between a psychological and a religious realm. It is a threshold that any serious psychological theory cannot avoid arriving at. When, in psychoanalytic language, we press on the nerve of the relationship to the 'good internal object', we find ourselves on a journey back through countless generations, not one of which could have come into being without sexual desire and maternal care (the presence of a 'good object'), in however harsh or primitive a form. It is this continuity, inseparable from its physical expressions, that roots us in the material cosmos. There is a similar continuity, which may be called cultural, which also plants us ineradicably in the vast psychic world of humans and the higher animals. Language is

the most obvious manifestation of this second continuity: a social construct, without which individual psychic development is derailed. These
material and cultural continuities are non-controversial, I think, and we
may infer from them the impossibility of viewing the individual in isolation
from his or her context; the more surprising step taken by Freud in later
life, and by Jaques (1988) in his paper, is to go beyond biology altogether
and to find precursors of biological drives in the inorganic realm. (There is
a certain echo here of the openness of some modern students of consciousness to 'panpsychism', which I referred to in Chapter 2 and shall
discuss further in Chapter 6.)

Because the ethical principles of the major religions are consistently
based on feelings and attitudes towards others that are within the depressive position series that psychoanalysis recognises, and because of the
unexpected swerve by Freud and some later analysts towards a cosmological vision as they attempt to think about the irreducible, non-neurotic
limits on human life, it seems reasonable to think that the central 'good
objects' of the mature religions are not entirely unlike the 'internal good
object' of modern psychoanalysis. If in places they seem to contradict one
another, that is, I think, because one of the parties, either the psychoanalyst
or the believer, is holding onto convictions as a matter of introjected belief
rather than genuine understanding and experience. Fundamentalisms are
necessarily at war with one another. But the achievement of the familiar
depressive position of psychoanalysis, the capacity to perceive others and
oneself as whole and separate objects, to mourn loss and to be grateful for
good treatment, must be the gateway to all psychological maturity, regardless of cultural and other factors.

It would be a mistake, however, to equate psychoanalysis with the
religions or to say that they operate in the same way or on the same level.
The use of religious objects is quite specific. It is not to discover the contrast
between their reality and our own, which is one of the crucial functions of
psychoanalysis. It more resembles the functioning of the analyst, at an
earlier stage of the analysis, which is seen in the development of the capacity to dream more revealingly: by contemplating, worshipping, paying
homage to, *thinking about* the figure of Jesus, the Virgin Mary, the Buddha
and others, the values and vision they represent become active in the
devotee. The healthy development, then, is to move on from contemplating
the religious figure to introjecting the psychic position he represents into
the believer's own unique circumstances and personality. 'If you meet the
Buddha on the road, kill him!' is an attempt to state the dangers of getting
stuck in the initial stage. Christianity has all too often infantilised its
adherents by turning the contemplation of Jesus into a self-depleting idealisation (he all good, the devotee a 'miserable sinner'), but in Christianity as
in Buddhism there have always remained elements, and often more than
elements, of more mature understanding.

Conclusion and summary

The goal of psychoanalytic therapy is very specific. It is to work through a process, the transference, in which we enact some or many of our characteristic ways of treating another person with whom we have a close relationship, both in actuality and in the inner world of our phantasy. The goal of the process, never completely achieved, is to come to distinguish between reality and phantasy in such a relationship, and in this way to allow the ego to achieve its best possibility of functioning in the social and intimate worlds in which we actually find ourselves. Another way of putting this is to say that we become more integrated, more self-aware, and therefore more able to distinguish ourselves clearly from others.

The goal of religion is to achieve a true view of the universe and our relation to it. Religions take into account that we exist, not only in the social world, but also in the vast realm of the non-human, within which the human world has come to be. Like the transference object in therapy, the objects of religion have a transitional character, but this is not because they have a reality that is to be distinguished from phantasy, but because their function is to be way-stations in understanding. Contemplating, praying to, meditating on them is a means of opening the mind up to the areas of experience, and the values, they represent.

These goals are the sort of thing that is called in modern psychoanalysis a 'position', characterised by a specific disposition towards the world, the self, and other people. The different religions have come into being to cope with different aspects of our existential dilemmas, and consequently have arrived at somewhat different 'positions' in their pursuit of solutions. In the modern globalised world, with giant flows of influence in all directions, the different traditions are all now, whether they know it or not, learning massively from one another. Typically, however, the disposition aimed for in a mature religion is one characterised by love, generosity, tolerance, and the embodiment of certain values (in broad terms very similar across the major traditions, as the Dalai Lama says; the theologian Hans Küng (1974: 92) has made a similar point). As with the psychoanalytic depressive position, we need not assume that the attainment of a religious position is a stable and permanent achievement. On the contrary, psychologically speaking, religious practices represent the continual struggle to re-establish it.

Chapter 6

The ownership of consciousness and the uniqueness of subjects

In Chapter 3 I outlined some of the enormous consequences that flowed from the distinction made by Galileo and John Locke in the seventeenth century between the primary and secondary qualities of matter. The primary qualities were those that appeared to exist independently of the observer and that could be measured; typically, they were expressed in numbers, and they included such things as mass, dimension and velocity. The secondary qualities were those whose character depended on the nature of the human senses; they included such things as colour, taste, heat, beauty and so on. These are qualities which exist in the observer's subjective experience, and we can never be quite certain that one observer's experience of them is the same as another's. Locke (1689) described the primary qualities as 'real', with the implication that the secondary qualities were in some way unreal, or less real.

In the present chapter, I want to rehearse some of the arguments I have used so far, in the light of the general concern of this book for values, and see what preliminary conclusions can be based on them.

The hypothesis of primary qualities has had consequences so epoch-making that it is hard to overstate them. The reason is that, by choosing as the primary qualities of the universe those that are measurable, it became possible to *grasp* the resulting model of the world with extreme accuracy by counting (statistics) and by mathematics. For the first time in history, it became possible to formulate accurately the laws that govern natural events, initially large events like the movements of planets, eventually minute events like the behaviour of quantum particles. The grasp of this method on the physical world was unprecedented, and has proved capable of ever-increasing precision; no end to its consequences can be foreseen. So prodigiously successful has it been in improving the quality of human life, and so dangerous has it become, in creating possibilities of both deliberate and inadvertent destruction, that it dominates our horizon: it is often given authority, in matters such as religion and values, to which it has no title.

We get a nice picture of how the world looks, when we take the primary qualities 'model' for the reality, from the mathematician and physicist Alfred North Whitehead:

> The poets are entirely mistaken. They should address their lyrics to themselves, and should turn them into odes of self-congratulation on the excellency of the human mind. Nature is a dull affair, soundless, scentless, colorless, merely the hurrying of material, endlessly, meaninglessly.
>
> (quoted in Velmans 2000: 112)

The notion that the physical world is meaningless is now virtually an axiom in modern science. The physicist Steven Weinberg (1993) famously said: 'The more we understand the world, the more it seems pointless'.

It can come as a surprise, therefore, to realise that Galileo and Locke, when they formulated their fertile hypothesis, were perfectly aware of its limitations: they did not think they were describing the final truth about the world. In 1615, Galileo – a devout Catholic – wrote a long letter to explain his position. In it, he speaks of two 'books' which God has written: the Book of Nature, which is the lesser book, and which we may read if we are curious about unimportant matters like the orbits of the planets, whether the earth moves or stands still and so on, and the Holy Scriptures, which are supremely important and necessary for our salvation (Galileo 1615). There is no reason to think that Galileo was insincere in saying this, and in fact in some version this was the belief of most of the great rational thinkers of the seventeenth century, including Descartes and Newton. The model of 'primary qualities' was just that: a useful heuristic tool to simplify the world in order that specific facts could be established and certain specific problems could be addressed – for Galileo, in particular, certain astronomical problems.

Once started on its way, however, the astonishing success of the scientific method, and the formulation of natural laws that accounted for more and more of what went on in the world without the need for any input from a supernatural realm, opened an increasingly broad path to sceptics who would regard 'materialism' as a metaphysical stance in its own right. Even so, it took something like two hundred years for this possibility to become clear. The question whether order could proceed from disorder without the intervention of an intelligent designer (Descartes thought it could; Newton denied it) continued to give some plausibility to deistic 'arguments from design' until the middle of the nineteenth century, when Comte and Darwin, among others, convincingly demonstrated a plausible mechanism for such processes (Brooke 1991). To many, belief and piety came to seem embarrassing and childish. 'What is the Enlightenment?' asked Immanuel

Kant (1784), and he answered: 'It is the liberation of man from his self-imposed minority'. The human race was at last emerging from its childishness in the face of nature. Kant is a crucial figure in this fascinating period, post-Newton but pre-Darwin, when it was still plausible to think like Descartes that at the heart of the mind there was a 'soul', an ultimate kernel, so to speak, that was free of time and space and governed by non-natural, perhaps 'supernatural' laws. In Kant's case, this became the sovereign I of 'pure reason', which could be properly autonomous if it was governed by rationality alone. Kant's critical philosophy, both an ontology and an account of values, which he worked out with unrelenting rigour and seriousness, still provides a philosophical landmark for modern thinkers. His attempt to conceptualise the nature and limits of our capacity for experience gives him a fair claim to be called the founder of what later on in the nineteenth century would become the science of psychology.

Kant remained a Protestant Christian. But as the nineteenth century proceeded, and Charles Lyell demonstrated the enormous age of the earth, Hermann Helmholtz formulated the laws of conservation of energy, and Darwin described at last a convincing theory of the evolution of all species, including humankind, it seemed to many as if science and its certainties had swept the board. It seemed there was no longer any place for divine intervention, or for any sort of non-material agency that had real efficacy in the world. 'The more important fundamental laws and facts of physical science have all been discovered', said Albert Michelson in 1899, 'and these are now so firmly established that the possibility of their ever being supplanted in consequence of new discoveries is exceedingly remote' (quoted in Kumar 2008: xv). In 1900 Lord Kelvin, President of Britain's Royal Society, announced that science was on the brink of being able to explain 'every phenomenon in the universe' (Peat 2002: x).

I am telling this familiar story with a purpose. The stunning self-confidence of the Enlightenment was based, as Kant said, on the conviction that rationality and evidence-based, scientific thinking were grown-up and responsible; anything else was childish or 'primitive'. And yet, if we look at the origin of this thinking, it depends not only on rationality and careful observation – characteristics of 'adulthood', perhaps – but also on the abstract model of the world that follows from Galileo's useful hypothesis: the model of the mathematically graspable 'primary qualities of matter' abstracted from the actual world of experience. The world science was so successfully learning to describe was increasingly an abstraction; it was not in a complete sense 'the real world' as we encounter it. (Whitehead's ironic description, quoted above, captures the picture perfectly: the human mind receives a mention, but it seems it has nothing to do with the dull meaningless 'hurrying of matter' that is all Nature is.) For anyone, like myself, educated in the Enlightenment traditions of science and philosophy, this fact, that the world of the physicists is an abstraction, is very hard to grasp:

it is obvious, yet it is hard to take in. This is partly because sheer power is itself daunting, and the power of our modern technology is potentially annihilating: we had better respect it. And perhaps there is something less rational as well, a particular sort of attraction that this picture has for us. The philosopher Mary Midgley speaks of 'physics-envy', with a playful nod to Freud's 'penis-envy', and the psychoanalyst is bound to be intrigued by the insistent imagery of the scientist as dominant male, conquering or mastering female Nature, which is present from the start in the history I am describing. Midgley (2001: 56) quotes Francis Bacon's ferocious injunction to the scientist, to subdue 'Nature with all her children, to bind her to your service and make her your slave'. My quotation from Descartes in Chapter 3 (p. 34) expresses a similarly ruthless and imperial ambition. The irrational appeal of the world of primary qualities, which so skilfully subdues what William James called the 'blooming buzzing confusion' of our actual experience to the clear, apparently affect-free mathematical intelligence, may partly be to do with the wish we all have to be on the side of the big boys, the winners, the ones who do not cry and do not have to experience humiliation: it includes clear elements of what Freud at the end of his life would call the 'repudiation of the feminine' in both sexes. Let Nature, let *her*, be the one to suffer!

The overthrow of Albert Michelson and Lord Kelvin's confident assertions, which was to follow with almost biblical swiftness with Max Planck's first formulation of quanta in 1900 and Einstein's special theory of relativity in 1905, did not however require them to alter their fundamental confidence in their position: the new world of relativity and quantum mechanics continued to be susceptible to mathematical treatment and understanding, even if it had now taken a further step beyond Galileo and ceased to be imaginable.

The exclusion of subjectivity

What did Galileo's theory eliminate from the world? One simple answer might be: the subjectively experienced elements of it. Another might be: consciousness. I want to spend a moment picking up again the subject-matter of Chapter 2 and discuss the words *subject* and *consciousness*, and also another word, *sentience*, which I think will help us to see more of what a modern understanding requires us to reintegrate.

The word *consciousness* is often used, in neuroscience, cognitive science and elsewhere, as if it described the elementary form of the phenomenon they are wanting to discuss. This is misleading. The etymology implies complexity: the *sci-* root – *sci* as in science – means knowing, and the *con* implies together with. Originally, therefore, *consciousness* had to do with knowing of a sort that could be shared with others, and it still carries an implication of a knowing that can at least be shared with oneself –

'conscious knowledge' (Zeman 2002). This is a far from elementary notion. Elementary subjective awareness is better described as *sentience*, the bare capacity for experiencing. In ordinary usage, a frog or a worm may be described as sentient; if someone described them as 'conscious', we would wonder if he was anthropomorphising. The sort of consciousness humans are familiar with is vastly more sophisticated than the sentience of a frog, but both can be called *subjective* because both are experienced by a subjectivity: both frog and human experience pain, which they try to avoid, and pleasure, which they go towards. To a large extent, our ordinary language is bound to be anthropomorphic (i.e. adapted to human experience) but if a poet or a child imagines a frog as having an 'I', my assumption is that that corresponds to some sort of reality. If, as in some children's stories, a clock or a coin is imagined as having an 'I', that, I assume, does not correspond to a reality.

I am assuming in saying this that it can be correct to use the word 'I' of any subject of feeling and not only of a subject of reflexive cognition; in any sentient subject there is, by definition, the capacity for feeling pleasure or pain. (This does not of course imply that the subject will be capable of using the word 'I', which is a sophisticated achievement that arrives relatively late even in human development.) It is likely that feeling and cognition are in origin two aspects of a single function, that of 'experiencing', so the feeling of a frog must be presumed to include some rudimentary form of cognition as well. In saying this I am disagreeing with, for example, Lancaster (2004: 70), who makes the interesting but, I think, unintelligible suggestion that 'to be conscious implies a subject; consciousness does not'. As I understand it, awareness requires and is inseparable from a subject of awareness. This would be true, in contradiction of Hume, for example, even if the awareness were momentary and the 'subject' lasted no longer than the awareness. (Once again, language lets us down: to be aware *is* to be a subject.)

What Galileo's hypothesis excluded from the world, therefore, is best described as *subjectivity*, which occurs at many different levels of sophistication, of which the most elementary we can imagine is *sentience*. *Consciousness* is best kept for more complex levels, such as those ordinarily experienced by waking humans. It is important to remember, however, that this is not how these words are regularly used. Much confusion results from the use of *consciousness* as the general term. For example, when the philosopher John Searle says 'the brain is a biological organ, like any other, and consciousness is as much a biological process as digestion' (Searle 1997: 50), it may sound initially plausible; if we substitute the word 'subjectivity' for 'consciousness', however, the parallel ceases to be persuasive.

Many thinkers, including Sherrington (1940), Teilhard de Chardin (1959), David Chalmers (1996), Thomas Nagel (1979b), Max Velmans (2000) and Galen Strawson (2006), have suggested that there is no logical reason to decide a stopping point for sentience: it may go 'all the way down' into inorganic matter and even into subatomic particles ('panpsy-chism'). Panpsychism is an intriguing speculation which remains beyond the reach of testing (we cannot even imagine an experiment that would enable it to be tested), so in my view we can only suspend judgement. Relevant to our present theme, it also gives rise to the question, previously mentioned, of what could be the subject (who could be the 'owner'?) of a panpsychic consciousness: into what units might it divide itself?

The nature of subjectivity

The nature of subjectivity is that it involves a sense of 'I'. In philosophy, there is the position known as solipsism, which Descartes perhaps flirted with but which no functioning human being can actually believe. The solipsist says: 'I alone exist. The whole world is my imaginative construc-tion, my dream, if you like: none of *you* or *they* have any independent reality, I alone have reality.' Of course, if we met a solipsist, we would say he was mad, but nevertheless his madness – and this is why solipsism is so haunting – would be built on a true perception: his knowledge of his own experience does indeed have a quality that none of his other knowledge has. He knows his 'I' in a way that he does not know the external world, or the 'I' of his parents, or you, or Shakespeare. The jolting realisation of the uniqueness of one's 'I', and the mystery that my 'I' inhabits *this* body and *this* set of characteristics and relationships, and not your body or any other body, and is not disembodied either but is in this particular space, at this particular moment; this mystery is so shocking that, for the most part, we blank it out of awareness altogether. Nevertheless, many people remember occasions when they were struck by it, often in childhood or adolescence.

There is a moving evocation of it in a poem by Elizabeth Bishop, entitled 'In the Waiting Room' (Bishop 1991). The poem is too long to quote in full, but in it she describes her experience, as a little girl of 6, waiting for her aunt in the dentist's waiting room. She passes the time by reading the *National Geographic*, with its vivid pictures of exotic and remote people and places. Suddenly she hears her aunt speak, and she is brought back to the present, but not immediately back to herself. She suffers a moment of complete dislocation:

> I said to myself: three days
> and you'll be seven years old.
> I said it to stop
> the sensation of falling off
> the round, turning world
> into cold, blue-black space.
> But I felt: you are an *I*,
> you are an *Elizabeth*,

you are one of *them*.
Why should you be one, too?
I scarcely dared to look
to see what it was I was.

And then she looks at all the strange people in the waiting room. 'Why should I be my aunt/ or me, or anyone?' It's a wonderful poem, and I regret that here I can only gut it ruthlessly to get at the central point, the mystery of a subjectivity that is nevertheless planted in an objective world, a mystery so familiar and so baffling that in ordinary life we quickly come to overlook it altogether.

This phenomenon brings us to the sharp point of the issue of subjectivity, and I do not think anything we can learn about the functioning or integration of different parts of the brain can help us to understand it. Neuroscience shows us, for example, that anger correlates with the activation of areas of thalamus and cerebral cortex, and that is true both for your anger and for my anger, in our different but similar brains; but what we cannot see is the 'yourness' or 'myness' of the anger. This difference, which from the subjective point of view is absolute, from the objective point of view is undiscoverable. Subjectivity cannot be described by describing neurons, though neurons obviously have a great deal to do with what sort of experience a given subjectivity will have. Subjectivity is about the 'ownership' of sentience or consciousness, the fact that events in *this* brain show up as 'my' experience, and descriptively identical events in *that* brain do not show up as my experience at all – but they do show up, very vividly, as your experience. (This fact is equally true at the level of sentience, though it is only organisms at a high level of reflexive consciousness that can be clearly aware of it.)

Consciousness and subjectivity

Many discussions of 'consciousness' fail to recognise this issue of subjectivity, and contrive to discuss consciousness as if it were merely another objective phenomenon awaiting scientific explanation. The prevailing physicalist theories (including 'functionalism') are of this sort (Churchland 1986; Dennett 1991; Edelman 1992; Crick 1994, and many others). The failure of such theories to recognise the nature of subjectivity has been pointed out by, among others, Nagel (1979a, 1979c), McGinn (1989), Varela (1996), and Velmans (2000). Some thinkers (Nagel and McGinn, in particular) suggest that we are constitutionally unable to resolve these issues, not because they are necessarily 'difficult' but because of where we are sited in relation to our knowledge (as McGinn (1989) puts it, we are either introspecting or doing neuroscience, and we cannot do both at once).

A more radical theory was put forward by William James (1898), who described a transmission theory of consciousness. He suggested that consciousness exists apart from the physical world, and that brains act as receivers of it, much as radio sets act as receivers of radio-waves broadcast everywhere in space. Each brain has its own characteristics, and modifies the transmission it receives, and therefore despite the ultimate unity of consciousness, there is a diversity of unique individual consciousnesses. This theory has the great merit that it allows for the uniqueness of each subjectivity while also offering an account of the fact that brain-states crucially affect the content of experience, and when the brain is dead, that subjectivity has no further experiences (so far as we know).

When the philosopher Colin McGinn (2004) tried to think of an alternative to his own 'mysterian' account of consciousness, the most plausible theory he could think of was very similar to William James's. To McGinn, this was so bizarre that he joked he encountered it only when he was abducted by aliens and carried off to a distant galaxy. He was clearly intrigued by it, but did not want anyone to think he believed it himself. The difficulty with any notion of a disembodied consciousness is that it solves one problem by creating further problems, for example what is this consciousness? How does it relate to the known history of the cosmos? McGinn's alien suggested that God initially created two entirely unrelated universes, and then had to work very hard to invent a clever thing called a human brain to connect them up.

Starting from a quite different standpoint, the pioneering quantum physicist Erwin Schrödinger (1958) also proposed that individual consciousnesses are diverse expressions of something unitary. He approached the issue by saying that we encounter consciousness in two different 'registrations': if I think about *your* consciousness, I can intelligibly conceive it as something produced by your brain – because in fact I do not ever experience your consciousness as it is in itself (as you experience it): I only see what I presume to be your conscious behaviour, interpret as best I can your conversational signals, and so on. I also see that your behaviour and your signalling can be interfered with by brain-damage, drink, drugs and so forth. In John Searle's (1997) fashion, therefore, I can conceive your consciousness as 'like digestion', taking place over there in you, an ordinary product of physical processes (though only because my encounter with it is so limited).

But, says Schrödinger (1958), I also meet consciousness in a second, quite different registration. That is, as my own consciousness, which I know from within and which owns all my thoughts and experiences. (I would prefer to put this slightly differently, to avoid the apparent diversity of 'I' and 'my consciousness': to say, the second registration is my 'subjectivity', the I that 'owns' or is the subject of all my thoughts and experiences.) Schrödinger finds a striking image for this double registration:

> Sometimes a painter introduces into his large picture, or a poet into his long poem, an unpretending subordinate character who is himself. . . . In Dürer's *All-Saints* picture two circles of believers are gathered in prayer around the Trinity . . . a circle of the blessed above, and a circle of humans on the earth. Among the latter are kings and emperors and popes, but also . . . the portrait of the artist himself, as a humble side-figure that might as well be missing.
> 'To me this seems to be the best possible simile of the bewildering double role of mind. On the one hand is the artist who has produced the whole; in the accomplished work, however, it is but an insignificant accessory which might be absent without detracting from the total effect.
>
> (Schrödinger 1958: 136–137)

That is a very clear statement of the conundrum of subjectivity, and the inadequacy of the ordinary account by neuroscience or cognitive science which looks only, so to speak, at the figure in the picture, and not at the artist.

How can there be so many individual consciousnesses, all somehow 'producing' one world? To avoid what he felt to be the intolerable picture of Leibnizian windowless monads, united by 'pre-established harmony', Schrödinger (1958), like William James, suggested that ultimately all our apparently diverse consciousnesses are one consciousness (a thought he links with the mysticism of the Upanishads). It is remarkable that a physicist should arrive at a philosophical position which gives consciousness priority over against physics – but this of course reflects the extraordinary new development of quantum physics, to which Schrödinger had centrally contributed. His solution, however, comes up against a parallel problem to that of panpsychism: what could be the subject of this unitary consciousness?

I want to return to Schrödinger's second registration of consciousness, the one that perceives the whole. In principle, this registration could be the unique subject of a solipsistic universe – one might infer that subjectivity not only perceives the whole, but also creates it. Here psychoanalysis and developmental psychology have a contribution to make. We know now – to use Wilfred Bion's language, but there are many others – that human psychic development requires interaction with other people who also have thinking minds, and who with their thinking minds 'contain' in some sense our mental experience (Bion 1962). 'Contain' is Bion's metaphor and no doubt it splits active and passive roles excessively. It implies a process of 'taking an interest' in the other's mental state – lovingly, angrily, excitedly, playfully, reprovingly, thoughtfully and so on. My rudimentary subjectivity develops into adult consciousness as a result of repeated such encounters which, as I increasingly internalise them, and build up a world of phantasised 'internal objects' (unconsciously imagined internal figures), also become resources for containment and affect regulation that I can now do for myself. More recently, increasingly minute observation of mother–baby interaction by psychoanalysts and developmental psychologists (Stern 1985; Trevarthen and Aitken 2001), and neuroscientific work on the development of affect regulation (Schore 2003a, 2003b; Green 2003), confirm the crucial developmental importance of these early sympathetic emotional interactions.

It follows that when we speak of human subjectivity, we are not speaking of an isolated conscious mind, enclosed like a Leibnizian monad and having a solitary history. Nor are we speaking of the disengaged 'I' of the Cartesian *cogito* (which has no existence except as the subject of the verb to think) or the 'pure reason' of Immanuel Kant. We are speaking of a consciousness that exists in a structure, built up through repeated transformative encounters in human and other sorts of relationship, and which now looks out on a world – a real world, as real as itself – by way of, so to speak, an ever-adapting repertoire of lenses. The internal figures, which play such an important part in this structure, and whose origins are inseparable from actual experiences of encounter, are for the most part unconscious, but their representatives, their avatars, so to say, are to be met with in dreams and imaginative phantasies.

This idea, that the external world is as real as the subjectivity that perceives it (and, of course, vice versa) is a contradiction of solipsism and some forms of mysticism. It is also very different from the picture of positivistic science, because it takes sentience to be every bit as 'primary' as the measurable qualities. In doing so, it allows sentience to be something that can be selected by evolution. I want to spend a moment enlarging on the implications of this.

Three ways in which consciousness plays causal roles

The first implication is that, contrary to the conclusions often drawn from the work of neurophysiologists such as Benjamin Libet (1996), who have shown that neuronal innervations precede conscious decision-making, consciousness plays a significant causal role in the world. (It is not just an 'epiphenomenon'.) In sympathetic interactions, it is your subjectivity, as distinct from the neurons that sustain it, that affects me. Psychosomatic medicine shows that states of consciousness (affective states such as mourning and depression) influence somatic and immune system functioning; and psychoanalysis shows that bringing obscure or half-perceived mental states into the light of consciousness alters them, often making them more accessible to management. Ronald Britton (1998) has suggested that one can securely relinquish a belief one holds, for example a belief that it is ominous to meet a single magpie, only by first making it conscious and then comparing it with the rest of one's beliefs about the world. Similarly, the difference between being 'uncommitted' and becoming committed is dependent on conscious attention and decision. There are many sorts of psychological development which depend on the presence of consciousness. They require the particular focused function of consciousness which is called *attention*.

William James made attention central in his understanding of psychology. My potential experience, he said, is vast and chaotic: it is only my attention that brings it into order and gives it shape. He ridiculed the empiricist's idea that experience is simply received passively 'by the senses'; on the contrary, 'my experience is what I agree to attend to' and I attend to what interests me (James 1890: 402). Charles Sherrington (1940) too, asking our present question about the role of consciousness in evolution, singled out the function of attention, emphasising its practical importance. 'The biological advantage which mind seems to confer on the concrete individual is,' he says, 'improvement and control of the motor act. It seems to attach only to such doings as can be modified' (Sherrington 1940: 201). Learning new skills, for example, which plays such an important role in the lives of human beings and other primates, cannot occur without conscious attention; once the skill has been learned, it can be practised with less consciousness or even with none. As we would now say, an acquired skill goes into procedural memory. Presumably, at the neuronal level, the application of conscious attention causes the brain to be restrained from activating its familiar pathways, and enabled to open up and hold open new ones. The changes that psychoanalytic interpretation brings about can be regarded as a special instance of this more general truth about the causal role of attention.

These thinkers were considering consciousness as a sophisticated cognitive function, in the form in which it appears relatively late in evolutionary history. If we think, however, that cognition was originally inseparable from affect, and is still almost always accompanied by affect, we will notice a more general and elementary way in which sentience/consciousness may have been advantageous in evolutionary terms to the various lineages in which it has been enhanced (some birds, probably, as well as several species of mammals). I think we can see in the fact that consciousness is always 'owned' by a subject – that we cannot imagine experience without imagining a subject of experience – something that has enormous consequence. It causes things to *matter*. Where there is no subject, nothing is of any importance. Whether a rock is at the top of a cliff, or falls to the bottom, whether water is present as gas or liquid, is neither here nor there. But as soon as a subject comes on the scene, things acquire importance: the subject can flourish or fail to thrive. If the rock blocks my path, it matters to me: I want to get home. If water is liquid, I can drink it; if it is in the form of vapour, I may die of thirst.

An organism to whom its survival matters (any sentient organism) will tend to act in its own interest. It goes towards what gives pleasure (food, sex, a comfortable temperature); it avoids what causes pain (any sort of damage). An increase in the intensity of this mattering, therefore, will give the organism an advantage. Similarly, an organism that develops a concern for the welfare of some other organism – for example its young – will tend to improve the chances for that other organism of surviving and flourishing. In a stable environment, blind 'instinct' may be as effective in protecting the young as conscious sympathy; in an environment where threats and opportunities are unpredictable, consciousness gives the advantage. It may also give an increased savagery towards those experienced as dangerous to the cherished other. This is not of course to argue that consciousness – subjectivity – is the only way to achieve these effects; there may be other ways that are as good, or better.

Enhanced competence in unpredictable conditions, and enhanced energy in caring about the subject's own welfare and the welfare of kin, give a convincing base for thinking of the possible evolutionary value of sentience/consciousness. I will mention a third, more speculative factor. There is also a distinctive *joy* that seems to characterise conscious encounter with another conscious being not perceived as an enemy – the wish to play or to enter into relationship. Young squirrels, or fox cubs, unmistakably play together, and it is hard to doubt their pleasure in doing so; in the process they develop quickness and many skills and responses that will help them in their adult lives. But the energising force of conscious interaction, a matter of everyday experience to humans, deserves to be considered at much greater length. It may come at a price. We glimpse more of the human evolutionary background in the work I have already referred to by Stephen Malloch and Colwyn Trevarthen and their colleagues in which they emphasise the solidarity created in human groupings, prior to verbal language, by 'shared musicality' (Malloch and Trevarthen 2009). The need for such musicality may point to one of the dysfunctional features of evolving reflexive consciousness, namely an increased awareness of separation and anxiety.

Emergence

To say that something new comes on the scene when a world, which was, presumably, in the beginning entirely composed of inorganic matter, comes to include living organisms however primitive, is to speak of new properties that emerge at different levels of increasing complexity. As a simplifying hypothesis, I shall assume that one property of emergent life is what I am calling *sentience*. (It is equally possible that life and sentience represent different levels of emergence.) 'Emergence' has recently been much discussed by philosophers. I shall speak in the traditional way, as if emergence can produce wholly new properties (see for example the entry under 'Reductionism' in Medawar and Medawar 1984), but this has been widely challenged (Nagel 1979b; Velmans 2000; Strawson 2006).

It follows from the notion of emergence that new laws, and new values, come into play at the higher level, which had no meaning at the lower. With sentience come new values to do with survival and flourishing. The point at which values emerge is significant. Biologists have spoken above all of the importance of survival and reproduction, and clearly without these things a species becomes extinct; it is bound to be true, indeed tautological, to say of any existing species that it has managed to transmit its genes over a vast number of generations. This is sometimes spoken of as the gene's reproductive success (Dawkins 1976). This is confusing, however, because a 'gene', a stretch of DNA, is not the sort of thing that can be concerned for success. If a gene is regarded as successful when it reproduces itself, that is a value projected by an onlooking subject who has the notion of a purpose; it is the onlooker, not the gene, to whom the value is meaningful.

With the emergence of sentience and subjectivity, however, certain foundational values such as pain and pleasure, desire and aversion, appear in the universe. Hitherto there have been blind processes, just-so stories of quarks and stars, rocks and water. Now there are also subjective experiences such as shocks, perceptions, pains, pleasures, desires and fears. This story cannot be told in the language of physics. It can be told only in the form of narratives involving unique subjects. We have left behind the world that could be fully described in the language of Lockean primary qualities and have entered a world that includes unique subjective experience. Anything we may say about subjective experience at levels other than the human can only be speculation (Nagel 1979a) but the attempt to understand the laws that govern human subjective flourishing has in the past (prior to the existence of psychology) been the concern of religion, and it is worth considering what we may learn from there.

The role of religion

Reflection on unique subjective experience has traditionally been the province of 'religion', a vast realm which has gradually slimmed down as it gave birth to more specific cultural forms such as dance, drama, secular literature and philosophy. Any serious discussion of religious understanding requires acute awareness of the scope and limitations of language (N. Smart 1958; Macquarrie 1966; Panikkar 1989). 'Mystical' truth, often described as unsayable, requires the use of metaphor if it is to be spoken at all. The relation between mystical and mythological language is an issue for all religions, and the confusion of mythology with history in Christianity (and no doubt in the popular forms of all religions) has been one of the most successful grounds of rational attack. I shall not attempt here to discuss these complex issues in detail, but I have argued in Chapter 5 that the emphasis in modern psychoanalysis on the role of 'phantasy' in structuring a meaningful world opens up an important path to understanding the role of mythological and religious objects (Black 2000; K. Wright 2006) – we no longer need to dismiss them, as Freud did, as a mere wish for regressive illusion.

What religious specialists have done is to try to integrate their experience and perceptions with a tradition of thought descending from a poetic and pre-rational past. For all their great differences, religions tend to say certain things in common (differently from non-religious, materialistic ideologies). They tend, specifically, to affirm that the subjective aspect of life has its own laws, which are sometimes construed as comparable to human laws, that is, imposed with threats of punishment if they are broken, but are better understood as analogous to natural laws, that is, attempts to describe the way things are. Thought of like this, the psychological function of religions may be described as an attempt to formulate rules of human flourishing, given the way things are in the subjective realm.

I want to enlarge on this point, which is crucial to understanding what is lost by those who are over-impressed by the achievements of Galilean science. It is that there *is* 'a way things are' in the subjective realm, and not only in the material world. This is a claim that has always been made by religion. What will be the intellectual future of the traditional religions remains uncertain; their present tendencies to fundamentalism and weirdly inward-looking preoccupations with matters of sex and gender can seem a disastrous triumph of their most fearful and ignorant elements. However, setting aside current confusions, several themes stand out that deserve consideration. I shall indicate three.

First, all meditative and contemplative traditions recognise the tendency of the mind to scatter, to evade experience rather than to live with clarity in the present. Psychoanalysis deals with pathological, unconscious aspects of defence, which block the subject from psychic contents he/she needs to be in touch with; meditation enhances functioning in a reasonably integrated personality (Engler 2003). As a result of these practices, possibilities open up of identifying with different 'levels' of the self, less with reactive, peremptory responses to experience, and more with more stable and widely responsible attitudes. Existential themes of death, transience and solitude may be confronted. Freud's claim that religions merely offer consoling fantasy is squarely contradicted by the seriousness of many meditative traditions, for example those of Buddhism, in looking directly into one's deepest fears in relation to death and transience (Buddhaghosa 1964).

Developed meditative traditions go further, and speak of definite sequences of experience that mark different levels of internal attainment. Controlled research is needed (d'Aquili and Newberg 1999; B.A. Wallace 2000, 2007) but if these accounts are correct they provide the clearest evidence we have for a unique structure of the subjective realm. The sort of structures psychoanalysis speaks of (ego, superego, id; or an indefinite number of internal objects organised by changing phantasies) are essentially conceptions relating to the patient's capacity to live as a coherent subject in the present as a new time in his life; meditational concepts of structure describe predictable sorts of experience when present consciousness is entered with profound concentration. They suggest that desirable attitudes of mind, and in particular sound values, can be cultivated without any loss of reality.

Second, psychologically speaking, in religions that speak of a God, he serves the purpose of an internal object onto whom 'perfections' can be projected. This may have a certain beneficial consequence, in that the believer can keep in touch with his highest values, but no longer needs to aspire to perfection, which belongs to God alone. Often the downside, however, is that such a belief keeps him in an infantile state, seeking the approval of a feared/admired parental figure, unfree to own his own adult capacity for judgement (Freud 1927b; Britton 2006). In the Christian world, and in a long-term, transgenerational perspective, God's attributes served to mark out a path of moral development. For instance, in the extremely hierarchical world of the Roman Empire, God was described as 'no respecter of persons' (i.e. impartial in relation to rank). In a society where death and violence were commonplace, God was declared to be concerned for the fate of every sparrow. A religious ideal was set up, sharply contrasting with contemporary social reality, which over the following two thousand years gradually altered the moral climate in Christian countries in the direction of equality, the abolition of slavery, assertion of human rights and so forth. It is possible to say this without in any way being starry-eyed about the extremely imperfect way in which these developments are often implemented; the point is that what used to be conceived of as attributes of 'God' are now widely seen as the commitment of responsible human beings. No doubt we have a great deal further to go in recognising human responsibility for other species and the environment, but it will need to be along the lines of God's concern for the sparrows. Using psychoanalytic language, these developments can be described as a gradual withdrawal of projections, and one function of God in traditional religion has been to be an object onto which the projection of such unattainable values can be made in the first place – not unlike the 'ego-ideal' in psychoanalysis but available down the generations for a society.

This function is obscured by the concretisation of mythology in many schools (particularly where there has been an idealisation of 'sacred Scriptures'), which makes immature attitudes, such as misogyny and homophobia, very difficult to discard. It is more clearly recognised in Buddhism, where a mythological object, such as the bodhisattva Avalokitesvara, who represents compassion, is explicitly stated to be a mental construct.

The supreme values projected onto God in the Abrahamic traditions are justice and mercy. Someone who carries an internal object embodying such values may be greatly benefited, both in times of personal hardship, when he can turn to his God for consolation and strength, and at times of major responsibility, when he can discover non-partisan motives to guide his conduct. In Ignatius Loyola, the founder of the Jesuit order, we can see an example of the great positive value of such internal figures (Meissner 1992). Loyola's knee was smashed by a cannonball in 1520 at the siege of Pamplona. A professional soldier, his career in ruins, he rebuilt his life through passionate internal dialogues with Jesus Christ and the Virgin Mary. These internal 'objects' could serve as resources for consciousness – imagined figures whose characteristics and viewpoint could be related to, and to some extent inhabited by, Ignatius's 'I' at a time when his more ordinary experience was unbearably painful or despair-creating. To think of religious objects as resources for consciousness in this way allows us to make psychological sense of a great deal of religion which can otherwise seem bizarre in its lofty or terrifying imagery.

However, these objective sorts of internal divine figure carry psychological danger because the worshipper is necessarily subordinate to them. As the history of religion all too abundantly shows, the resulting diminishment of the ego is frequently projected outward into the humiliation and persecution of others, condemned as heretics, blasphemers, witches and so on. Ferocious cruelty, paradoxical in religionists who claim to esteem love, justice and mercy, may then be justified as 'doing God's will', meaning identified with an omnipotent righteousness which it would be sinful to question.

A third way in which religions maintain and develop the potentials of the subjective world is by acting on the believer's capacity for emotion. Typically, a developed religion offers a wide variety of emotional experiences – to take examples from Christianity: different sorts of joy at Christmas, Mardi Gras and Easter, restraint and penitence in Lent, profound grief on Good Friday, solemnity and gratitude at the Holy Communion – all these shared and validated by a church community and elaborated, often with great psychological acuity, by theologians and preachers. These emotional opportunities are vastly expanded by different artistic treatments, particularly musical, in which sublime or heart-rending aspects of feeling are developed beyond anything that ordinary distracted social life would allow (Pugmire 2006). This could be a whole topic in itself; here, all that need be said is that without religion and its narratives, many of these capacities for profound feeling might never be actuated.

The implication of all this is that the realm of ethics and subjectivity exists as a rich resource for the human being, but if it is to be fully entered, work has to be done. It is perhaps a bit like the body for the athlete: it can be worked on in many different ways, and different skills and attitudes will result, but because subjectivity has a structure, only specific disciplines will be effective, and without specific disciplines certain capacities will not develop, and some may never even be known to exist.

A multi-level monism?

To speak of religions in terms of this function, of being custodian of the structure and resources of consciousness-owned-by-a-subject, may seem to make a deep divide from the concerns of biological and physical science. Many thinkers would affirm such a divide. We may recall Stephen Jay Gould (2001), who claimed that religion and science are non-overlapping magisteria, two domains of authority, both necessary, but entirely independent of each other. Galileo, saying that God wrote the truth in two books, the Book of Nature and the Holy Scriptures, was pointing in the same direction, though he asserted that scripture always had the primacy. Dualists, such as Descartes, transmission theorists, such as William James, and the alien who abducted Colin McGinn – and many religionists also – would all to some extent agree.

Materialists and 'monists' would not agree. Neither would Freud. In his paper on 'Negation' (1925a) we see his pleasure at finding at last a secure link between the highest faculty of the mind, the capacity for judgement, and the 'drives' which he believed crossed the frontier between soma and psyche. Yet he too was baffled by the nature of consciousness, 'a fact without parallel', he declared at the end of his life, 'which defies all explanation or description' (Freud 1940).

I agree that it is without parallel, but I am not sure that it entirely defies explanation. I have already indicated some significant advantages of consciousness, and of the fact that consciousness has an 'owner', which may have caused evolution to select for it from a basis of primary sentience. In the light of this evolutionary picture, how can we understand the 'structured' nature of our subjectivity, as it appears in the light of developed religions and contemplative traditions? Such traditions seem to go far beyond sympathy with the young, hatred for what threatens them, and delight in meeting safe conscious others like oneself; indeed, in many cases, they include attitudes of contempt for bodily pleasures.

In talking about religions we have to be willing to make major allowance for perverse developments and 'spandrels' (Gould's term for evolutionary developments which occur, not because they confer any advantage, but because they are incidental to other developments which *are* positively selected for). This is in part precisely because the apparently independent laws of the subjective realm – independent, that is, of the material realm – have encouraged religionists to build verbal structures of increasing complexity without having to observe the discipline of a science, the repeated comparison of theory with observable fact. Many 'spandrels', for example, can be generated simply by an adroit use of the negative: if 'all men are mortal', it is rather easy to create the impressive concept of someone who is 'immortal'; if all our experience is imperfect, we can create the notion of perfection. These verbal creations, which correspond to nothing in our experience, can then go on to generate huge and intriguing intellectual structures. Much of the attack on religion by professed atheists such as Dawkins (2006) and Dennett (2006) is made plausible by these purely verbal constructions.

I call the laws of the subjective realm 'apparently independent' because I think the predictive quality of the attributes of God – which so to speak stored-up certain values and preceded or made possible their development in human beings – indicate that such structures are not in fact as independent of the ordinary world as they seem. When we attend centrally to subjectivity, we become aware, perhaps initially in a disorganised way, of many things we know, many things that 'matter' to us, which we ordinarily overlook in the rush of daily doing and social life. Jonathan Lear (2006) has discussed the function of the visionary dream in Native American religion, with reference in particular to the Crow chief, Plenty Coups, who in 1856, aged 9, had a vision predicting the loss of the traditional Crow way of life, and hinting at a way to cope with this devastating development. To have this vision, it was necessary for the young boy to go off alone into the wilderness; when he at first failed to have a suitable vision, he compelled himself to take what he was doing with complete seriousness by cutting off part of one of his fingers. This was not a way of going away from the concerns of his society but, on the contrary, coming closer to them.

Psychoanalysis too is very aware of this need for isolation from the rush of everyday busy-ness, and of the difficulty of focusing and making oneself serious. Hence the strict boundaries around the analytic session, the exclusion of all intrusions, and so on. Meditators and creative artists, specialists in subjectivity, have a similar need for segregation from distracting influences. In the resulting solitude, there is not only a risk of distortion and madness, but also the possibility of access to 'depth' of feeling and phantasy, which will then have its part to play later, when one returns to one's ordinary social context.

One element that I suggest structures subjectivity is the range of application of the different levels of values that it relates to. Thus at one level we are concerned for values to do with our own comfort and pleasures, at another with the welfare of those close to us. Plenty Coups was felt to have had his vision 'for the Crow'. Because human beings have such abundant sympathy and imagination, and because we so readily form 'transferences' which transfer feelings from biological kin to friends, colleagues, clans and sometimes remarkably tenuous, verbally defined groups of 'people like us', our values and concerns tend to fluctuate wildly. The attempt of the meditator is to organise these fluctuations into 'levels', and to downplay the shallower levels in favour of something deeper and more stable. Plenty Coups's vision stayed with him throughout his long life, and for many decades it helped to guide his gifted leadership of the Crow as they underwent the transformation he had obscurely foreseen. The values discovered by earnest reflection on narratives involving God have similarly guided much of the moral development of the Christian West.

The larger ideals projected onto God – those that unite mercy with justice, or love and concern with truth – give rise to a ladder of expanding identifications: not only the self, or even the Crow nation, but also a concern for the totality of life. From this standpoint, the judgements implicit in, for example, biologists' language when they speak of the reproductive 'success' of a particular species, or historians' language when they speak of the 'success' of scientific and rational thinking, may call for modification when they are confronted with a viewpoint concerned for the welfare of the entire ecosystem, 'Gaia', or perhaps even something larger.

In principle no doubt, such a ladder of concerns might be climbed on an intellectual basis, without the addition of faith or religious devotion. Empirically, however, there is reason to doubt whether intellectual recognition alone generates the energy to alter psychic structure and therefore to effect radical changes in the individual's value-system. Hence, in psychoanalysis, the importance of the emotions of the transference and the prolonged process of 'working through'. What religious faith and devotion represent is emotional engagement with other levels of values.

Profound attention to subjective experience ends by returning us to the ordinary world of values and human concerns. Subjectivity causes things to matter, and can be selected by evolution because it promotes the welfare of self and others; but this development has a downside, because in seeing, say, the young as precious, it creates an 'us' who are precious over against a 'them' who are of no concern, whom 'we' are entitled or encouraged to treat ruthlessly. With the emergence of an all-conquering instrumental approach to the world – 'science' as Bacon and Descartes conceived it – the danger in this aspect of our values has become overwhelming. The short-term concern for human welfare has put at risk the long-term and more profound human dependence on the survival of the ecosystem as a whole. There is a challenge to mount another rung on the ladder of values, and to reconceive the meaning of the 'we' with whom we need to identify.

Conclusion

Let me try to summarise where all this has got us, in the light of Galileo and John Locke's hypothesis of primary qualities. I think, first, that we can no longer speak of primacy between subjectivity and the world of physics. You can give the priority to subjectivity, to consciousness, and you will have some very impressive thinkers on your side. Above all, you will have

Buddhism and Advaita Vedanta, two vast and profound systems of thought, which in some ways anticipate the 'introspective science' that William James envisioned; you also have James himself, Schrödinger, and Colin McGinn's alien. But you come up against three problems. First, evolution tells a story in which consciousness must necessarily have an instrumental function (why else would it have been selected?). Second, developmental psychology and psychoanalysis show that the human self cannot emerge in isolation, but requires an affectively rich, sympathetic, intersubjective environment. It acquires its necessary capacities, including its capacity for self-regulation, from a history of many encounters with other subjectivities like its own. And third, the knowledge you have of any consciousness other than your own is because of physical experiences. There is no access to any other subjectivity except by physical signals of various sorts. And new subjectivities originate in the physical act of sexual intercourse.

So we cannot simply give priority to consciousness. But can we give priority to the material world? Perhaps in a purely temporal sense we can. But now that sentience and consciousness have 'emerged' and evolved, they too have become fountains of causation; the 'reasons' of human action, incomprehensible at the level of the quark or the atom, are the causes of vast events in the physical world. We can no longer believe ourselves to inhabit a world just of primary qualities, nor can we believe consciousness to be present but inefficacious, like Benjamin Libet, Max Velmans and many recent neuroscientists. It seems likely that consciousness, having evolved for biologically understandable reasons, has a structure and laws of its own which have to some extent been intuited by traditional religions, but have often been obscured by pre-scientific, mythological stories, presented as objectively true, which we can no longer believe. Philosophically, there is a need for a new scientific vision which, as best I can phrase it, is of a 'multi-level monism' in which both physical and subjective realities have their distinctive laws and properties, and mutually influence one another.

'Vision' alone, however – were such a thing possible – may give rise to understanding, but cannot give rise to 'values', which necessarily require an affective – emotional – engagement. If we are to approach the issue of values, we will have to follow the clue of 'uniqueness' which we discovered when we reflected on the ownership of consciousness. The recognition – or, better, the experience – of values, does not, like the positivist scientific vision, lead to generalisation, and an attempt to understand the laws by which causes produce effects in a world of intrinsically unimportant objects. Instead, it sees everywhere subjects, irreplaceable individuals, and feels the poignancy of their vulnerability and transience. It inhabits the same world as positivistic science, but it perceives it quite differently. It is just as valid, but recently it has often been intimidated by all-dominating attitudes of 'materialism', which can conceive flourishing only in material terms. It is only when we recognise the irreducible uniqueness of subjects that we see why, to give an account of the world, such terms are necessarily inadequate.

As I have said previously, the word 'materialism' needs nowadays to be used with care. The 'matter' of pre-Darwinian dualisms was very different from the matter of the present-day monist. One might say facetiously that the matter of traditional dualism was free to be a slob: it could be 'inert', 'mechanical', 'base' and so on, because its only function was to be a 'tenement' and the soul would shortly be along to tenant it, and to supply it with higher functions. The matter of the new monism has to meet much heavier demands, and meet them single-handedly. Prince Hal has become King Henry; the new 'matter' has to be something that can blossom as time goes on into subjectivity, initiative, uniqueness, and 'values'; it brings us the physicist as well as the physics. To speak of this as 'the triumph of materialism' is confusing because that is to still speak the language of dualism. The 'stuff' of the new monism is not the matter of the old dualism, though Darwin and Helmholtz probably thought it was. It is far richer, far stranger, and far more interesting than that.

Chapter 7

Mapping a detour

Why did Freud speak of a death drive?

Is there any cause in Nature which makes these hard hearts?

King Lear

you are right in inferring that I have often been compelled to make detours in following my own path.

Freud, letter to Fritz Wittels (1924b)

Introduction

Banquo in *Macbeth*, startled by the vanishing of the witches who have just foretold his greatness, exclaimed: 'The earth hath bubbles, as the water has'. It should probably now be accepted that Freud's (1920) account of the death drive,[3] which appeared in his thought for the first time when he was 64, was such a bubble. Nevertheless, just as Macbeth's witches, despite their bubble-like unreality, served mightily to advance the plot, so too that first account of the death drive has exerted remarkable traction in the subsequent development of psychoanalysis. It makes up a fascinating and instructive episode both in the history of ideas and in the history of psychoanalysis, and I shall attempt in this chapter to spell out in pedestrian fashion, step by step, the central line of it.

The death drive is important because it served to focus psychoanalytic thinking on the topic of destructiveness. Freud's initial focus on sexuality and 'the libido' caused him to overlook other aspects of human motivation, and especially the extraordinary propensity of human beings to act destructively, both towards others and towards themselves. Any psychoanalyst who attempts, as I have done in Chapter 4, to assert the crucial importance of *sympathy*, quickly encounters his colleagues' deeply

---

3 Freud's word *Trieb* is a problem for English-speakers. I shall use *drive* for it throughout, but when quoting from Strachey's *Standard Edition* I have to use his translation, *instinct*. The reader is asked to remember that these two words are the same in the original. The death drive is the death instinct.

ingrained suspicion that too much sympathy will result in a sentimental failure to look objectively at destructiveness and self-destructiveness, and the ways in which people act to create or connive in their own problems. Hence in part the preference I described within the profession for using the less vulnerable-sounding word *empathy*. I have argued that we need to retain both words, *sympathy* and *empathy*, which describe the capacities we have to perceive other people as 'subjects' and as 'objects' respectively. We are not going to be able to understand the true power and importance of moral values unless we hold onto the reality of other people as 'subjects'.

The topic of destructiveness, however, introduces a new element into the mix. Destructiveness is not just about treating other people as 'objects' because one is favouring oneself as the only 'subject', that is, as the only person whose subjectivity need be of concern ('narcissism'). Destructiveness is about the satisfaction we can feel in our power to treat other people badly. Paradoxically, destructiveness brings in sympathy by the back door: we would not enjoy our power so much if we were not at some level imagining the suffering of the other person (or, if we are speaking of self-destructiveness, of some other part of the self). So the psychoanalytic suspicion that to speak positively of sympathy may overlook the fact that sympathy can also collude with destructive motives is not without merit. The word *sympathy* is subject to constant slippage, partly because of its double meaning (the 'capacity' which I called sympathy sense one, and the emotion, compassion, which I called sympathy sense two). For example, if we 'sympathise' too freely with clinically depressed patients, we may fail to see how much anger is concealed behind their meek demeanour, and how destructive they are being towards themselves and the other people who are close to them. Our 'sympathy' may collude with their own belief that they are only the sufferer, in no way the active agent. When I was training as a psychoanalyst, I was taught that, in trying to understand a suicide, it is often useful to ask oneself the question: 'Who is murdering whom?' Depressed people are often furious with someone, perhaps a spouse or a parent, and are unable to acknowledge it or even consciously 'know' it. They may, however, by being constantly depressed, in phantasy and very often in reality keep the actual other in a state of constant guilt and frustration. Similarly, their savage attack on themselves ('I am the worst person in the world') makes their own life a misery. If we sympathise too warmly with the (perfectly real) suffering, we may fail to notice the attack that provides the feedback loop that keeps the whole structure of the depression in place.

Freud remarked that he was surprised he had been so slow to find a place for aggression in psychoanalytic theory. It was not until 1920 that he described his theory of the 'death drive', an alleged drive in the organism taking it towards its own death. Destructiveness then was to be understood, he said, as a deflection of the death drive outwards, from the self to the other. This theory failed from the outset to convince many even of Freud's most loyal followers: although it did seem to capture something about destructiveness, and about the echoes between destructive and self-destructive behaviours that we meet in depression, it also seemed inherently improbable: far simpler and more plausible explanations of destructiveness immediately suggested themselves, particularly in the light of Darwin. In this chapter, I shall look in some detail at the history of this odd but important piece of psychoanalytic theory-making. If we reject it finally (as I think we have to), it nevertheless serves to remind us to keep an eye on the need to balance our 'sympathy' (in the second sense, compassion) with a clear-sighted remembering of the power, often hard to see and, when seen, often profoundly intractable, of human destructiveness.

In general, in this book, I want to avoid technical language, but in this more historical discussion I shall be compelled to use it sometimes in order to explain the neurological background of Freud's thinking. I apologise for that. The non-psychoanalytic reader may prefer to skip this chapter, or certainly the section I have headed 'An alternative derivation of the death drive'.

Freud's overt argument

The part of *Beyond the Pleasure Principle* (1920) in which Freud first proposes the repetition compulsion and the death drive is a very curious piece of writing. One of Freud's skills as a rhetorician is that he often disarms his reader by acknowledging his own doubts about his theories, but in this paper his diffidence goes beyond rhetoric and he seems to be struggling with a strong impulse to abandon his line of thought altogether. He warns us in advance that what we will meet is 'speculation, often far-fetched speculation' (Freud 1920: 24), and after many further hesitations along the way, at the end he says the reader may wonder

> how far I am myself convinced of the truth of the hypotheses that have been set out in these pages. My answer would be that I am not convinced myself and that I do not seek to persuade other people to believe in them.
>
> (Freud 1920: 59)

There need, of course, be nothing to apologise about in speculation as such. As Freud says repeatedly, one is entitled to follow up hypotheses. What is odd here is the sense one has in reading this paper that Freud himself is guided by something that is elusive or not explicit. 'One may have made a lucky hit,' says Freud (1920: 59), 'or one may have gone shamefully astray' – he is not really sure himself what has caused him to generate these thoughts. I shall come back to this, but initially I shall try to follow the relevant portion of his text quite carefully.

As Freud speaks of the compulsion to repeat – also described for the first time in this paper – we become aware that something of a repetitive kind is also happening in the writing itself. Freud is returning repeatedly to his own early writings, and particularly to the *Project for a Scientific Psychology* (1895), the remarkable attempt he made, just as he was leaving his career as a neuroanatomist, to base his psychology on the brain-science of the 1890s. Never published in Freud's lifetime, it was essentially out of this rich compost of neurologically based ideas that the science of psychoanalysis was to grow. Freud in 1920 is revisiting, though with variations, much of his own early speculation on the relation between what he called the 'mental apparatus' and the brain.

He goes on to describe the compulsion to repeat as urgent, drive-driven (*triebhaft*, translated by Strachey as 'instinctual'). He gives examples from post-traumatic dreams, children's play (in particular a game in which Freud had watched his little nephew again and again throw away a cotton-reel on a thread, exclaiming triumphantly *fort!* (gone!), and then haul it back into sight, exclaiming delightedly *da!* (there!)), the 'malign fate' that rules some neurotics' lives and the transference in psychoanalysis. He continues:

> But how is the predicate of being 'instinctual' [drive-driven] related to the compulsion to repeat? At this point we cannot escape a suspicion that we may have come upon the track of a universal attribute of instincts [drives] and perhaps of organic life in general. . . . *It seems, then, that an instinct [drive] is an urge inherent in organic life to restore an earlier state of things* which the living entity has been obliged to abandon under the pressure of external disturbing forces.
>
> (Freud 1920: 36, original emphasis)

This enormous and far-reaching generalisation is made on the basis of a few rather special examples and almost no discussion, only an 'inability to escape a suspicion' which, it must be said, the ordinary reader might well have managed to escape. What Freud has plausibly demonstrated is that some repetitions have a drive-like urgency which overrides the principle of pleasure-seeking. He could undoubtedly have made the larger case with a more powerful argument, but, again, it is as if he is enacting something of what he is writing about: he is carried along by an urgency, a *Triebhaftich-keit* perhaps, which causes him to present his theory as far-fetched specu-lation at one moment, and immediately afterwards ('It seems, then') as if it is the outcome of solid argument.

Freud is clearly aware that he has made a curious move at this point. He says that the conclusion to which he is tending may make an impression of 'mysticism or sham profundity' ('but we can feel quite innocent of having had any such purpose in view'); he speaks of it as an 'extreme line of thought' (Freud 1920: 37, 37n). In fact, however, he has not really followed a line of thought: he has made a speculative leap, and, in view of the odd echoes between style and subject-matter, the reader may wonder if Freud is not writing at this point in a manner more like a poet than a scientist.

He now pulls himself together and says, with an air of propriety: 'We seek only for the sober results of research or of reflection based upon it; and we have no wish to find in those results any quality other than certainty' (Freud 1920: 37). In the following paragraph he introduces the death drive.

> It is possible to specify this final goal of all organic striving. It would be in contradiction to the conservative nature of the instincts [drives] if the goal of life were a state of things which had never yet been attained. On the contrary, it must be an *old* state of things.
>
> (Freud 1920: 38)

Since everything living returns for internal reasons to the inorganic state, we are 'compelled to say that "the aim of all life is death"', and, looking backwards, that "inanimate things existed before living ones"' (Freud 1920: 38). There is, in short, a death drive. (The quotations, which he leaves unattributed and which may not be recognised by an English-speaking reader, are from Schopenhauer.)

I spoil the vivacity of Freud's argument by excerpting it, but that in essence is the route by which he arrives at the notion of the death drive. The argument is gossamer-thin, not to say non-existent in patches, and it is only the agreeable urbanity of Freud's prose (we are 'tempted', 'compelled', 'unable to escape the suspicion') which carries us over the voids.

The death drive at which Freud has arrived is one in which, in the course of evolution, primitive life-forms, which die quickly and without complication, are gradually compelled by 'decisive external influences' to make 'ever more complicated detours' before reaching their aim, which is death. These detours are preserved by the always-conservative drives, and come to make up our picture of 'life'. However, somewhat inconsistently, there are parts of these life-forms which do not tread the path to death (despite originating also, presumably, in inorganic matter). These are the germ-cells, which separate themselves from the dying organism and as a result of sexual intercourse pursue a path of 'potential immortality'.

The drives which determine the fate of the germ-cells, therefore – the sexual drives – are true 'life drives', and work in opposition to the death drive. It is these to which Freud soon after gave the encompassing name, Eros. He havered for some time over the ordinary life-preserving motives (desires for food, warmth, sleep, self-protection and so on), initially putting them under the heading of the death drive (on the grounds that they simply create some of the 'detours' on the path to death); later, this became too paradoxical, and the self-preservative drives were also subsumed under Eros.

We should stop for a moment to see what Freud has 'proved' in this energetic and tenuous argument. It is simply that all life has a 'drive' to return to the inorganic state.

What is a drive, exactly? It was not until 1905, with the *Three Essays on the Theory of Sexuality*, that the word *Trieb* began to appear freely in Freud's writings (Strachey 1957). He was always aware that with the notion of a drive we touch on supremely important and deeply puzzling matters: he defined it once as 'a measure of the demand made upon the mind for work in consequence of its connexion with the body' (Freud 1915: 122). Drives are precisely an expression of the link between mind and body, 'the psychical representatives of organic forces' (Freud 1911: 74), and Freud saw clearly that to use a word like 'drive' might be convenient but failed to answer any of the necessary questions about this link. In particular, to use this language failed to resolve body/mind dualism, and was in conflict with Freud's deeper commitment to a materialistic monism.

In 'Instincts [drives] and their vicissitudes' (1915), we see him struggling to define them further. He suggested there that we shall not understand the drives, or know properly how to classify them, if we look at them only from the psychological side: we also need a contribution from 'biology'. (We would now say neuroscience, which at that time was still at too primitive a stage to provide that contribution.) Perhaps the combination of diffidence and emphasis with which Freud argues his case, five years later, in *Beyond the Pleasure Principle* reflects his frustration at having to remain on the psychological side of things: the 'biology' he dreamed of came into existence only with the invention of PET and fMRI scans forty or fifty years later, and even now it is unable to answer Freud's questions with any degree of fullness.

So far, however, so reasonably clear. The drive, making its demand on the mind for work, is something that appears at the psychosomatic frontier (Freud 1915: 121–122); it is mysterious, no doubt, because it represents the body–mind link, but we are clear what mystery it is we are dealing with. However, in *Beyond the Pleasure Principle*, Freud stretches the concept into new realms. I am not sure he entirely realises he is doing so. His examples initially come from the familiar repertoire of psychoanalysis – dreams, children's play, neurotic symptoms – but suddenly the drive he is talking about, the death drive, is something that operates in every cell of the body (Freud 1920: 44ff). Cells can of course be seen as individual living beings, each having its own life, way of functioning, and death, but they are not usually thought of as having a mental life. Freud has moved from the 'psychosomatic frontier' to biochemistry.

Because Freud never quite clarified this confusion – neither argued for an extended use of the word *drive* nor thought up a different vocabulary to describe the biochemical precursors of drives as defined in 1915 – drives came to seem more and more mysterious to him. Towards the end of his life, he wrote: drives 'are mythical entities, magnificent in their indefiniteness. In our work we cannot for a moment disregard them, yet we are never sure that we are seeing them clearly' (Freud 1933a: 95).

But to return to the line of the argument. Freud's death drive in *Beyond the Pleasure Principle* is reached essentially by two steps. First, he says, all drives aim to restore a previous state of the organism, and second, *repetition of a previous state of the organism* includes *reversion to a previous state of the matter of which the organism is composed*. The first of these steps Freud argues for, but his argument, as I have said, is little more than rhetorical assertion.

The second step Freud does not argue for, and perhaps he does not even notice he is making it. Yet it is even more in need of support than the first. It is at least conceivable that the aim of a drive could be to restore a state which the organism has experienced and therefore may in some sense remember; it is much harder to conceive that a drive could aim to restore a state which, being inorganic, could by definition not be experienced, nor could it lay down any memory trace. (This is not even the same as Freud's saying, above, that the death drive operates at a cellular level. The logic of his argument now would require it to operate at the molecular level.) Freud gives us no argument for this move, and it is hard to imagine how it could be supported.

Moreover, as many thinkers have pointed out, repetition of an earlier event is by no means the same thing as reversion to an earlier state. Repetition implies that an event, similar in some ways to an earlier event, is enacted and then emerged from; otherwise it cannot be done repeatedly. We may want to say, using a more modern psychoanalytic language, that the repeated events are 'the same in unconscious phantasy', but even so repetition requires that each of them has a shape in time which returns the person to a condition in which the repetition can happen afresh. Reversion is very different: it implies the literal return to the earlier material condition.

Finally, even if we ignore these various objections, and grant both these steps, there would still remain the question of what they carry us to. Certainly not to a drive that corresponds to Freud's earlier definitions. The return of organic matter to the inorganic state does not make a demand on the mind for work; it happens reliably with or without the mind's participation.

An alternative derivation of the death drive

What I have sketched above is, so to speak, the overt route to the death drive. But, as I have said, there are also indications in *Beyond the Pleasure Principle* that Freud was remembering much of his neurological thinking of the 1890s, and in particular the *Project for a Scientific Psychology* (1895), that fascinating seed-bed of ideas, never published in Freud's lifetime, in which the links between early psychoanalytic ideas and Freud's previous career as a neurologist were clearly visible.

Freud makes use in the *Project* of a notion he calls Q. Q stands for 'Quantity', and Freud uses it without ever making quite clear what it is a quantity of. The nearest he gets to a definition is to say it is 'what distinguishes activity from rest' (Freud 1895: 295). He wanted Q to point to something which had two aspects. One was a sort of 'excitation' or energy, which distinguished activity from rest, and which was also capable of exact measurement and thus conformed to the requirements of his materialistic conception of science. One is reminded that Freud, through his mentor Martin Brücke, was a follower of Hermann Helmholtz's scientific circle, committed philosophical materialists who sought ultimately to account for everything in terms of the basic laws of physics and chemistry (Sulloway 1979).

The second aspect of Q is not so obvious. In a paper written in the previous year, 1894, Freud had described a mental version of Q. 'In mental functions,' he wrote,

> something is to be distinguished – a quota of affect or a sum of excitation – which possesses all the characteristics of a quantity (but we have no way of measuring it), which is capable of increase, diminution, displacement and discharge, and which is spread out over the memory traces of ideas somewhat as an electric charge is spread over the surface of the body.
>
> (Freud 1894: 60)

There can be little doubt that this mental quantity and Q when it occupied the psychological (psi) neuron system were to be regarded as two aspects of a single entity.

Freud at this point was already wrestling with the question that he would address, twenty-five years later, in *Beyond the Pleasure Principle*. How are we to imagine the link across from the body and its needs to the mind and its 'drives' or representations of those needs? What is the relation between excitation (physical) and affect (mental)? It is a variant on the question this present book repeatedly addresses using the language of *objects* and *subjects*. In 1895, Freud seems to be envisaging something like a 'dual-aspect monism', which he lost again when he developed his theory of drives.

The use Freud made of the notion of Q would turn out to be crucial in the evolution of his psychoanalytic thinking. When a neuron fills with Q, it becomes 'cathected', in the language of Freud's English translator, James Strachey. The German for 'cathexis' is simply *Besetzung*, the quite ordinary word meaning *occupation*. A neuron becomes occupied, filled, with Q, and its response is to try to empty itself. It 'divests itself of Q', or 'discharges its cathexis'. The affective accompaniment of the sensation of discharge is *pleasure*.

Here we arrive at one of the fundamental *a priori* assumptions of the *Project*, its First Principal Theorem. 'Neurons tend to divest themselves of Q' (Freud 1895: 296). This is the 'principle of neuronal inertia'. It will persist as a hidden basis to much of Freud's thought in later life, governing his conviction, so often puzzling to readers coming to his work for the first time, that pleasure is always linked with a reduction of tension. As we shall see, it may also have influenced his account of the death drive.

But why should Freud think this? Why should neurons tend to divest themselves of Q?

The answer lies again in one of Freud's invisible *a prioris*, derived from the group of physical scientists, including Helmholtz and Freud's early boss, Brücke, who gave him the essential materialist philosophical under-pinnings of his approach to science. They were less gung-ho, and less of a coherent group, than they are often painted (Sulloway 1979: 65–66), and one of their number was Gustav Fechner (1801–1887), the remarkable pioneer of 'psychophysics' and a man of wide-ranging culture and intrigu-ingly idiosyncratic views. (He believed the earth to be a living being, and wrote what was 'probably the first monograph devoted to the psychology of plants' (Ellenberger 1970: 217).) Freud greatly admired him, and in his Autobiography he writes: 'I have followed [Fechner] upon many important points' (Freud 1925b: 59). He refers to Fechner by name in both the *Project* and *Beyond the Pleasure Principle*.

What Freud had taken from Fechner, in thinking about the behaviour of Q, was Fechner's 'principle of stability', which says that systems tend towards either inertia or regularity of movement, and having achieved such states they will remain in them until acted on by new forces, either internal or external. Fechner distinguishes, however, between organic and inorganic systems, and says that organic systems tend towards movements which are only approximately regular (heart-beat, peristalsis, and so on). Freud appears to have misunderstood Fechner's principle and, perhaps by some confusion with entropy, assumed it to imply that organic systems tend towards inertia (Sulloway 1979: 404–406).

Freud's principle of constancy, therefore, is slightly different from Fechner's, and it takes the form of asserting that the neuron tends to divest itself of Q, and become inert (meaning: at rest). Twenty-five years later, the alternative derivation of the death drive will argue that the entire organism takes a similar path: it tends to divest itself of life and become inert (now meaning: dead).

The modern neuroscientist, Allan Schore (1994), has identified in this pervasive 'principle' one of the fundamental failings in Freud's attempts to picture the mind. He writes that every model of the mind conceived of by Freud is based on a mechanism that maintains a state of non-stimulation by disposing of excitation . . . [Freud] overlooked the essential role of the *energy-conserving* parasympathetic branch of the autonomous nervous system and its reciprocal relationship to the energy-expending sympathetic component in the overall maintenance of organismic energy balance.

(Schore 1994: 536, my emphasis)

The philosopher Jim Hopkins (2000), writing specifically about the death drive, has also made a rather similar point. 'Instead of seeing the brain as creating order . . . Freud made [the disordering principle of entropy] the essence of neural functioning' (Hopkins 2000: 16). Freud therefore (through no fault of his own, given the state of contemporary neuroscience) made at this point a fundamental mistake.

Hopkins (2000) considers that this argument, which I am calling the alternative derivation of the death drive, was in fact the essential one in Freud's mind. In my view, the evidence is inconclusive. In a certain way, Freud presents the death drive as in opposition to Fechner's principle of constancy, which he refers to explicitly (Freud 1920: 8–10) as underlying the notion of the pleasure principle. It is this principle which he is now going 'beyond', as his title says, to establish the new concepts of repetition compulsion and death drive.

Nevertheless, when he returns to the death drive in later papers (e.g. Freud 1923, 1924a), he does clearly link it with Fechner's 'tendency towards stability' (which he may be confusing with entropy). Either at the time or shortly afterwards, therefore, it is certain that this alternative derivation did establish itself in Freud's mind.

Modern neuroscience compels us to reject this line of argument. We know now that, as Hopkins (2000: 15) puts it, 'far from working to divest itself of energy, the brain works to accumulate and concentrate it'. No more, therefore, than the evolutionary argument – the 'overt route' – does the alternative derivation from the principle of neuronal inertia give us a base for believing in Freud's death drive.

Affective roads to the death drive

The unsatisfactory nature of Freud's arguments for the death drive has been apparent from the outset. His follower Ernest Jones, embarrassed and struggling to be respectful, wrote that Freud had never written anything so speculative before, 'and this in itself is a matter of the highest interest to any student of [Freud's] personality' (Jones 1964: 504–505). Freud too was conscious that his arguments were unlikely to carry conviction, and feared that his critics would look for their true origin in the events of his personal life. When in January 1920 his daughter Sophie, pregnant with her third child, died in the flu epidemic that followed the First World War, Freud got Max Eitingon to testify that he had already seen a draft of *Beyond the Pleasure Principle* before her death.[4]

This precaution did not prevent many of Freud's commentators from going down that road (cf. Freud 1924b: 287 fn), and other similar ones. Freud was 64; he had sometimes predicted in a rather superstitious way that he would die at younger ages; perhaps the death drive was an expression of his weariness with life. He had just lived through the First World War, which had appalled him like many others with its vast and mindless carnage; two of his sons, Ernst and Martin, had fought in it and he had been deeply worried for their safety; perhaps the death drive was an attempt to make sense of this apparent madness that had overtaken Europe. He was incubating the cancer which finally killed him; it was not formally diagnosed until 1922, but already in 1917 he had detected a 'painful swelling in the palate', associated with his excessive smoking (Jones 1964: 440), and wondered if it might be cancer; perhaps the death drive expressed his intuitive knowledge of his condition.

And so on. Such speculations are intriguing, but they are by their nature unprovable. There is a sense in which, ever since 1913 and his break-up with Jung, something had changed in Freud's conquistador-like temperament; he was the triumphant father who has killed his favourite son and, although he was too militant not to relish his triumph, the surgent high spirits of those earlier years never really returned to him. If I were to add my own two-cents worth of speculation, I would suggest that the affect which lay behind the creation of the death drive may derive from the events of 1913.

The subsequent history of the death drive

Given such unpromising beginnings, one might have predicted that the death drive would quietly disappear from psychoanalytic history, one of those odd quirks of Freud's thought like his Lamarckism or his weakness for Thomas Looney's theory that Shakespeare's plays were really written by the Earl of Oxford (Gay 1988: 643). If the death drive, even to its formulator, seemed so doubtful, why would it survive?

---

4 According to the respected Freud scholar, Ilse Grubrich-Simitis, who has examined the manuscript of *Beyond the Pleasure Principle* in the Library of Congress, the correct story is this: Freud indeed wrote a draft of *Beyond the Pleasure Principle* prior to Sophie's death – but it was one that included no reference to a death drive. The chapter introducing the death drive was inserted into the manuscript in May or June 1920, a few months after Sophie's death in January (Grubrich-Simitis 1996: 189). Freud's embarrassment about letting this be known does not, of course, necessarily imply that her death was the true source of his hypothesis, merely that he feared it would seem so.

The answer is that, almost from the start, the death drive was used in two derivative ways. One was that it was combined with Eros to account for the 'fused' or 'bound' nature of the drives that we actually encounter in ordinary experience. The notion of 'boundness', with its corollary that our motives are necessarily always mixed, had always been present in psychoanalysis (again going back to the *Project*) as the way in which the random directness of primary process functioning becomes adapted to secondary process. However, it was unclear how such binding occurred. We see it too, for example, in Freud's early idea that perverse sexual impulses were 'component drives' of full genitality which could, so to speak, get loose and operate in isolation. Sadism, in the first edition of the *Three Essays on the Theory of Sexuality* (1905), was the aggressive component of ordinary sexual activity; it became a perversion when it was no longer constrained by other components.

However, on closer scrutiny, this argument was not quite satisfactory. Sadism is not just energetic violence, but a specific pleasure in the suffering of the loved object. How could this be understood? And what, in an evolutionary sense, could be its origin? (Sadism is a nice example of a familiar human motive which is a profound puzzle to the Darwinian. What could be the evolutionary advantage of enjoying the suffering of one's mate?)

Writing in 1920, Freud realised that his death drive, 'under the influence of the narcissistic libido' (Freud 1920: 54), could be forced away from acting on the self and could then be directed against another. Such an account might then begin to make sense of sadism as no previous theory had done (and because the death drive, at least in Freud's mind, was satisfactory from a Darwinian point of view, sadism could cease to be an evolutionary puzzle). At the time, in the hesitant mood characteristic of this paper – 'limping', as he puts it – he takes the matter no further, but if we wonder more deeply what was his underlying motive in pursuing speculations which he found so doubtful, perhaps the most plausible suggestion would be that already at the back of his mind he glimpsed the enormous potential of both these ideas: the new version of 'boundness', and the huge explanatory range of a death drive that could be projected outward.

So great is Freud's diffidence in 1920, that the unwary reader may be taken by surprise to re-encounter these ideas in 1923, in *The Ego and the Id*, stated with definition and firmness as the basis of Freud's thinking. 'I have lately developed a view of the instincts [drives] which I shall here hold to and take as the basis of my further discussions' (Freud 1923: 40). But while holding to the death drive, he now says it is almost totally silent; it finds its normal expression through being 'directed onto the external world' by means of the muscular apparatus. It expresses itself, he says, 'though probably only in part', 'as an instinct of destruction directed against the external world and other organisms' (Freud 1923: 41).

With that mild parenthesis, 'though probably only in part', what is correctly called the death drive recedes into metapsychology. Freud is acknowledging that what we in fact meet is a destructive drive, pervasively in the form of ambivalence, less frequently though still very often in more unbound forms. Apart from a small guest appearance in 1924, 'tamed' by Eros into 'primary masochism' (Freud 1924a), the future of the death drive will be as a destructive drive.

There is something very surprising about this development. It is not that human destructiveness in itself is surprising: we see it about us, and within us, every day. And whereas, in spite of Freud, the idea of a death drive has never persuaded most Darwinians, a drive to violence is eminently explicable in evolutionary terms. We have been very powerfully selected for a capacity for violence, both to protect ourselves and our young, and to slaughter our prey – see for example Pinker (1997: 509–517). What is surprising is that it took Freud so long to arrive at an account of destructiveness, and when he did so, it was by such an unconvincing and convoluted route.

A few years later, in *Civilization and its Discontents* (1930), Freud virtually says this himself. 'I can no longer understand', he writes, 'how we can have overlooked the ubiquity of non-erotic aggressivity and destructiveness and can have failed to give it its due place in our interpretation of life' (Freud 1930: 120). He goes on: 'I remember my own defensive attitude' when the idea was first mooted in analytic circles – presumably a reference to the much earlier ideas of Wilhelm Stekel and Sabine Spielrein. Three years later, in the *New Introductory Lectures* (1933a), Freud writes in the same vein. He initially skates over 'the origin of this novelty' and simply speaks of two classes of drive, the sexual and the aggressive. He blames the resistance to the idea on the human wish to perceive man as naturally good. Later, when he outlines the death drive proper, he fears it will be set aside as merely echoing Schopenhauer.

Freud's biographer Peter Gay (1988: 397) plausibly suggests that this resistance was Freud's own: Freud was reluctant to recognise his own capacity for violence and aggression. If that is correct, it would make sense of many things, not least the extraordinary combination of diffidence and compulsion that characterises *Beyond the Pleasure Principle*, which perhaps can now be read as a key text in Freud's lifelong self-analysis. Surely this is what Freud was sensing when he concluded his paper with the words of Rückert: 'what we cannot reach flying we must reach limping'.[5]

---

5 Ilse Grubrich-Simitis considers that Freud's self-analysis retained its 'pre-eminent function' throughout his life, 'although its intensity varied according to the pressure of his suffering'. She was speaking in particular of his 1939 work *Moses and Monotheism* (Grubrich-Simitis 1997: 89).

Concluding remarks

To sum up: probably the death drive, as such, merits no future in psycho-analytic thinking. Even Freud could find no plausible argument to support it, and there are far more convincing hypotheses to explain the evolution of the human capacity for violence. However, it makes an interesting episode in the history of ideas, and a number of lessons can be drawn from it. Let me conclude this chapter by spelling out a few points of interest.

First, it shows that an idea does not have to be true to be fruitful. Just as the square root of minus one, an intrinsically impossible number, is used in some mathematical operations to arrive at a correct solution, the death drive allowed Freud's thought to move on from its initial sexual one-sidedness to a much wider and more stable conception of the human psyche, with huge implications for the whole future of psychoanalysis.

Second, the notion of the mutual 'binding' of drives has gone on to have a great future, not always recognised as such because different names have been used. Melanie Klein's account of the development of the depressive position (discussed in Chapter 5) is a much elaborated, more carefully psychological expansion of Freud's relatively elementary thoughts about ambivalence. Klein's account in turn provoked a protest by the Scottish psychoanalyst and psychiatrist Ronald Fairbairn that schizoid ('unbound') psychological factors were being under-recognised, to which Klein responded by formulating the paranoid-schizoid position (Klein 1946). Out of this crucial exchange, all the main schools of psychoanalytic object-relations theory have developed and branched. It is likely that the image of 'binding' in various forms will prove to be one of the inescapable metaphors of psychoanalytic thinking. As our history reconnects with neuroscience, it is already becoming more possible to understand the physical events that stand behind this pervasive metaphor.

Third, to recognise a pleasure in violence as one of the fundamental modalities of human motives, with a force comparable to that of sexuality, is indeed a corrective to any amiable wish to perceive humans as 'naturally good'. Freud's winding path to this perception, however, created two enduring confusions. On the one hand, Klein and her school rightly followed him in insisting on the fundamental nature of violence, but by continuing to use Freud's early designation for it – death drive – she failed to free herself from an unnecessary theoretical thicket. It is simpler to say that self-destruction is a variant of externally directed violence than that all destruc-tiveness is a variant of a death drive. It is simpler still to say that we can find pleasure in violence and vehemence regardless of their object, and precisely because they disregard their object.

On the other hand, some non-Kleinian analysts, rightly rejecting the death drive as such, have underestimated the fundamental nature of violence in human behaviour and motivation. There is a natural tendency among civilised and decent people to overlook the ubiquity of our cruelty, malice, envy, hatred and violence, our capacity to revel in destructiveness or be terrified by fears of annihilation. The clinical value of the death drive has been that it gives a simple banner under which to rally all these forces: it has helped us to keep them in mind and think about them. We shall miss it, if we give it up, and perhaps it will not be easy to agree another single term to replace it that unites this wide spectrum of motives.

Finally, when I first studied psychoanalysis, I was very puzzled by Freud's resolute dualism with regard to the drives. Initially, there were the sexual and the self-preservative drives; these then were replaced by another pairing, the narcissistic and object libido; and when he moved on from that picture, he replaced it with Eros and the death drive. He insisted on gathering the self-preservative drives under one or other of these flags – first one, then the other – ignoring the obvious solution of saying that there were three or more categories of drive. Modern neuroscience suggests that there are many different fundamental motives, which cannot be reduced to one another in this way (Hopkins 2000).

Probably, in this matter too, Freud was in a literal sense wrong, but in his stubbornness he was holding on to something real that his language could not quite bring into focus. Working with patients, one becomes aware that there is a broad Yes or No in human attitudes, however entangled it may be in the masses of autobiographical detail. Perhaps the fundamental twofold conflict that Freud glimpsed and held onto so resolutely lies there, not in the 'drives' as such (another term which probably does not have a future). As I conceive it, this Yes/No conflict is primarily psychological but cannot be properly understood in terms of a one-person psychology. It depends on the nature of the love the person has received in his or her unique experience: it requires a psychology of real relationships if it is to be made sense of. As we now know that 'real relationships' modify brain-structure, to call it 'primarily psychological' does not take us away from neurons: it is a comment on how causation flows. This issue has been discussed by many psychoanalysts since Freud's day (for example Bion 1962; Rosenfeld 1988; Symington 1993).

In terms of Freud's own development, the struggle to formulate his 'mythology' of Eros and the death drive proved profoundly fertile: it opened his thought to the issues of religion and civilisation, the public and social themes that preoccupied him in his final years. When he began to write about them, he was so relieved that he described it as the triumph of his life (Freud 1927a: 253); his medical career, he declared, had been a detour. Later still, reflecting on the drives led him to a cosmological picture. In 1937, he proudly compared himself to the pre-Socratic thinker, Empedocles of Acragas, who described the whole universe as the battleground of Love and Strife. Perhaps, he thought, the drives operated throughout the cosmos.

Acknowledgement

I am grateful to Dr Jim Hopkins for permission to quote from his unpublished paper on 'The Death Drive' (2000).

Chapter 8

An outline of a 'contemplative position'

> Two birds, companions always united, perch in the same tree. One eats the ripe fruit, the other looks on without eating.
>
> Svetasvatara Upanishad

Introduction

I suggested in Chapter 5 that the psychoanalytic notion of a psychic 'position' may give us a key to understanding what religions do, psychologically. The word *position* allows us to have the idea that what we regard as 'I' is not always, so to speak, in the same posture in relation to its world: in particular, there are times when we are very aware of the reality of other people as subjects like ourselves, we can be concerned for them, sympathetically imagine their motives, and so on, and there are other times when we are dominated by our own concerns, perhaps our fear, excitement or ambition, and the reality of other people as subjects seems to be lost to us. Neither of these ego-states or 'positions' need be seen as pathological in themselves: it seems to be part of normal experience to have access to both and to move between them.

These two positions are called in Kleinian psychoanalysis the depressive position and the paranoid-schizoid position, two rather clunking titles which disguise the fact that both are part of ordinary experience. Each position conceals within it a multitude of micro-positions: I might, exuberantly telling you of my prowess on the sports field, forget that you have just had the bad news of your mother's cancer; suddenly I recall it, and am stricken at my crassness in being so self-centred. In ordinary experience, a switch of 'position' of this sort happens easily and requires no psychopathological commentary. If, on the other hand, star-struck by my own success, I remember your mother's cancer and am impatient with it, and still expect you to have no feelings but adoring admiration for me, then, we might think, something is wrong and I have failed to find a necessary psychic flexibility. The essence of the paranoid-schizoid position is intolerance of the fact that other people have full mental and emotional lives, separate from one's own. The person suffering from pathological jealousy, for example, is unable to allow that his partner has ordinary sexual feelings and will, therefore, inevitably sometimes notice that other people are also attractive. Freud (1914) tells a story of going for a walk with a young poet (sometimes thought to have been Rilke) who was unable to enjoy the beauty of nature because he was so aware that it was all transient: he was unable to suffer the sadness of this awareness, and unable therefore to soften and allow nature to be beautiful in spite of it, or perhaps even to experience nature's beauty more vividly because of its transience. Freud's poet was, so to speak, rigidly stuck in one position.

Religious language offers many clues that what religion is about, psychologically, is a change of position. The language of 'conversion', or repentance (in Greek *metanoia*, change of mind (Parsons 2006)), of being blind and now seeing, of awakening from sleep or of 'turning around in the deepest seat of consciousness' (a Tibetan Buddhist formula (Govinda 1966)), is all redolent of the sort of thing psychoanalysts mean by a change of position. When these changes occur in the psychoanalytic consulting room, they are often accompanied by a similar feeling of relief, and a similar imagery (coming home, 'finding oneself', feeling 'forgiven'), to what we find in the religious literature (James 1902). George Fox, the founder of the Quakers, writing in the seventeenth century, described the painful and chaotic period of depression he suffered in early adulthood before he had formulated the main principles of his beliefs. He used the metaphor of 'openings' to describe the glimpses he had during that time of an alternative and more stable psychic position which eventually he became able to occupy more reliably. He wrote in his *Journal*:

> Now though I had great openings, yet great trouble and temptation came many times upon me, so that when it was day I wished for night, and when it was night I wished for day; and by reason of the openings I had in my troubles, I could say as David did, 'Day unto day uttereth speech, and night unto night showeth knowledge'. And when I had openings, they answered one another and answered the Scriptures, for I had great openings of the Scriptures; and when I was in troubles, one trouble also answered to another.
>
> (Fox 1694: 9)

With this notion of 'answering one another', Fox captures well the sense that each position has its own coherence, despite the incursions of the other. As his 'openings' stabilised into settled insights, in the sort of process familiar to psychoanalysis as 'working through', he acquired the moral steadiness that allowed him to found and give leadership to his new Society.

Positions and levels

When Melanie Klein first used the word *position* as a psychoanalytic technical term, she used it rather freely: there was for example a manic position as well as a depressive one. As her thought became more structured, she realised that manic defences were a typical way of avoiding depressive pain, and therefore the manic position was better thought of as one characteristic aspect of the depressive position as a whole: each of the two major positions had its typical defences, as well as its typical sorts of painfulness, anxiety, and modes of treating other people.

Psychoanalysts usually say that the depressive position is more socially realistic than the paranoid-schizoid one. This is because in the depressive position other people are seen as 'whole objects', as having mental lives which are different from ours, and we can allow them to have relationships from which we are excluded, and to make mistakes; we recognise that we will need to explain ourselves if they are to understand us, and that we may need to do some thinking if we are to 'see where they're coming from'. In short, to live successfully in a social world, we need to be able to inhabit the depressive position. On the other hand, more recent psychoanalysis has emphasised that we also need the paranoid-schizoid position, in which our own wishes are at the centre of the world; it may be narcissistic and less 'realistic', but it is in touch with the intensity of our feeling and our imagination, and with what makes us unique, vivid individuals. In an earlier psychoanalytic vocabulary, Freud valued the 'reality principle' above the 'pleasure principle', but more recent psychoanalysts have emphasised that both are essential if we are to live fulfilling lives and be adequate, fully contributing members of society. We seem to have arrived at a recognition that the two positions exist in a hierarchical relationship, but neither must eclipse the other and both are necessary.

I want in this chapter to consider whether the notion of a 'position' gives us a way to understand the notion of 'transcendence'. Transcendence is a word often used in talking about religion (and perhaps, if it has no meaning, 'mature' religion also becomes unintelligible), and it is necessary too if we are to think about different levels of values. We saw in Chapter 6 how the young Plenty Coups, the future Crow Indian chief, isolated himself and even chopped off one of his fingers in his determination to have a meaningful dream 'for the Crow'. There is an implicit picture here of, so to speak, a deeper level of seriousness, which could be reached only with difficulty, but which was worth reaching because it opened up greater scope for understanding and even, as it turned out, allowed Plenty Coups to glimpse a creative way of coping with a potentially catastrophic situation, the destruction of the whole way of life of his people. Similarly, when a Buddhist monk goes into 'retreat' to meditate in solitude on a mountain for three years, we can make sense of what he is doing only if we think that it relates to contacting a 'level' in his experience which is not available to him if he lives an ordinary life surrounded by the distractions and stimuli of a city. What are we to make of this idea of levels, which is pervasive in accounts of religious experience, and hard to avoid when one thinks of psychological development? At first glance, it seems to be at odds with the modern neuroscientific picture, in which mental states correlate with neuronal states: how could one neuronal state be superior to (or 'transcend') another? A neuronal state might, no doubt, be more complex, or involve more parts of the brain, than another, but the idea of meditative levels implies another sort of difference than mere complexity or even logical level: it implies a 'vertical' dimension involving superiority in value. (Neuroscience is of course well able to speak in its own terms of a vertical hierarchy of functioning, but that hierarchy is logical and without the affective element that is present when one speaks of value.)

What I shall do in this chapter is to explore one possible way in which, without departing from the broad consensus of current psychoanalytic and neuroscientific understanding, and making use of the Kleinian notion of 'positions', the idea of 'transcendence' may find a meaning – not quite the meaning of traditional religious thought, but not a meaning, either, that is wholly subordinate to our current psychological understanding. Scientific argument by its nature is never going to settle the questions about value, and in the two final chapters I shall try to look further into the philosophical issues which ultimately underlie them, but the scientific argument can at least clarify the possibility that there are different 'levels' of apprehension of the world, and that these different levels may have different degrees of validity or comprehensiveness, and therefore make different levels of claim on us to influence our motives. If we want to go further than this (and we are bound to do so if we are serious about trying to understand more of the basis of value), we need to enter the philosophical territory. In saying this, I am again differing from those who might wish to claim that science and values are simply two independent domains of human thought, both authoritative and both necessary, which exist in different dimensions and in no way impact on one another. To my understanding, by contrast, there must be some overarching picture which will enable us to see the two things as part of a single coherent universe.

I shall begin by proposing an experiment in how we think about consciousness.

The impact on consciousness of 'conversation'

The first question I want to ask is this: what are the consequences of the fact that our conscious experience comes to be structured so strongly by language that it is hard, perhaps impossible, to imagine living in a world which is not differentiated and structured by formulas of a linguistic and grammatical kind; and yet, initially, in infancy, our conscious experience was not verbally structured? There is a persistent strand in our thinking, in philosophy, art, and also in religious mysticism, which suggests that language imposes a distortion on experience, but that it is difficult, perhaps impossible, to escape from the many-layered webs that language lays over the world. (The psychoanalyst Jacques Lacan was one of those who believed that such escape was impossible.) But we continue to be intrigued by stories such as those of Kaspar Hauser, or the wild boy of Aveyron, in which a human being has developed without language, as if somehow they might give us access to some truth that language hides from us. In fact, of course, in these cases, what we encounter are human beings who are sadly impaired in their social and cognitive capacities. The fascination for children of stories in which animals speak – like the Dr Dolittle books – is perhaps a variant of the same theme, capturing a sense of loss the child feels about entering the human social world.

The philosopher Thomas Nagel, in a famous paper entitled 'What is it like to be a bat?' (1979a), came to the conclusion that we have no idea what it is like to be a bat. We can only, he says, imagine conscious states that we might in principle experience ourselves, and since we do not have a bat's nervous system and sensorium, its experience is quite simply beyond our ken.

If so, perhaps we have to give the same answer to the question, what is it like to be a baby? After all, a baby's brain, with no verbal language, no capacity for episodic memory, and minimal communication between the two hemispheres, is extremely unlike our own; and the internal stream of verbal consciousness which is so familiar to us can be no part of a baby's awareness; yet we have all been babies, and our interaction with babies is compelling and feels intelligible, at any rate sometimes – it would seem strange to think we have no imaginative access at all to a baby's states of mind.[6]

As an experiment, I shall approach this question by provisionally setting aside the familiar psychoanalytic account of two mental states, conscious and unconscious, with their various subdivisions of preconscious, repressed unconscious, system unconscious, and so on. This picture, known in psychoanalysis as Freud's First Topography, is extremely useful from the point of view of therapeutic practice, but it nicely demonstrates precisely the problem that using words inflicts on us: they focus the light of consciousness from a particular angle, and what they illuminate they reveal

6 Recent research has emphasised that 'musicality' is the key to what transcends the threshold of verbal communication and episodic memory; more profound than our semantic meanings are our shared musical capacities, and babies live in a social world because they participate from birth in exchanges characterised by qualities of timing, rhythm, pitch and synchronisation (Malloch and Trevarthen 2009).

very clearly, but what they put in shadow they hide from us. For the sake of this thought experiment, I shall propose, therefore, a different model: that we have several grades of consciousness. These grades of consciousness can each be inhabited by ego or the sense of 'I', though ordinarily at any given moment one of them is particularly the location of ego. How many of these grades are there? Well, perhaps indefinitely many, but certainly more than one.

On this model, what happens in psychoanalytic work is that the analyst's understanding and interpretations allow the patient to inhabit a different grade of consciousness. Suppose, for example, a patient in individual therapy who is also in a group, whose conscious motives are entirely benign – she 'only wants to help the group reach a deeper level' – recurrently describes episodes in the group in which she has spoken in ways that create resentment and anger, and leave her feeling misunderstood and unaccountably isolated. The analyst is initially puzzled: the patient's account of her contribution sounds anodyne, or perhaps genuinely insightful. But then it occurs to him to wonder about the non-verbal signals which may have accompanied the contribution – its timing, tone of voice, underlying motivation and so on. He suggests to the patient that, when she made these contributions, perhaps she was in fact angry herself, was feeling outside the net of communication in the group, and her 'desire to help' concealed another set of motivations, to attack angrily, to be noticed, and so on. One patient (let's call her A) might respond to such an interpretation by refusing to 'go there'; she denies that anything of the sort was going on, and she stays with her own account. Another patient, B, might agree, on reflection, that something like that was happening, and might agree that it played a part in the disappointing response she received.

Interpretation of this sort is continually going on in any analytic session, and in much ordinary social interaction. It is essentially to do with change of focus. Patient B, who accepted the interpretation (unless she was merely being compliant) was changing her focus from one part of the remembered episode to another, and also consenting to *really attend* to something that was not unconscious but from which attention had been withheld. (It was preconscious, in Freud's language.) With an extra-transference interpretation, this can often take place at a mainly cognitive level; the same thing done in the immediacy of the transference relationship is likely to bring in the more disturbing, affective elements.

We now know (Gabbard and Westen 2003) that cognitive and psychoanalytic interpretations – and I am assuming that every psychoanalytic interpretation inevitably includes cognitive elements – affect different parts of the brain, the cognitive component affecting mainly cortical layers, long-term psychoanalytic work also affecting subcortical structures. If in the course of therapy patient B becomes able to be more consistently in touch with her own motives for her actions, and able to take them seriously, she comes to use her brain in a somewhat new way, regularly drawing on a larger range of the energising factors it makes available to her.

An important point here is that such changes are initiated by verbal interaction. I shall use the word 'conversation' as a general term for verbal interaction, stretching its ordinary meaning to include all sorts of verbal interactions, including social chat, analytic sessions, lectures, listening to the radio and reading. All such verbal interactions result in continual modification and stimulus to mental structure, and presumably – following the ideas of Gerald Edelman (1992) and others – to actual brain-structure as well.

Conversation is a necessity, and is intensely desired. The psychoanalyst Edwin Wallace (1991: 269) writes: 'language does not merely express the psyche, but is constitutive of it; it is the very vehicle by which one presents oneself to the world and by which one receives and responds to it'. Deaf children without deaf peers invent their own sign-language (Economist 2004). Babies blind from birth, who have never seen hands, either their own or anyone else's, spontaneously make expressive gestures using their hands (Trevarthen and Aitken 2001: 6).

What happens when a psychoanalytic interpretation 'works' is that the area of consciousness of the patient is enlarged and to some extent relocated by the interaction with the analyst. What we speak of as the goals of psychoanalysis, the greater capacity for intimacy, the increased tolerance of ambivalent feelings, the withdrawal of projections and recognition of introjections, the more accurate drawing of the boundaries between self and other – all these things are testimony to the power of 'conversation' in shaping awareness and thereby modifying the world the patient invests with affect-and-cognition (two words, like psyche and soma, which cry out for a unifying term). A patient's use of language is reshaped to some extent in the course of an analysis, hopefully in a way that creates a more accurate 'fit' with his experience, and encompasses a larger range of it.

What happens in psychoanalysis is a variant of what happens at 15–42 months

The child's entry into the web of human conversation begins overtly at the age of 12 months or so, when he or she begins to use recognisable words. The take-up of new language then occurs at prodigious speed until about age 5, after which it slows up, but it continues throughout childhood and adolescence and, more slowly, throughout the rest of active life. To learn a new language is, at least temporarily, to adopt a somewhat changed personality, as well described by Eva Hoffman (1991) in her autobiography.

Prior to the age of 12 or 15 months is the stage often described in psychoanalytic writings as pre-verbal. This term is not really satisfactory, as there is no stage of babies' lives in which they are not interacting with adults and older children who use words to them, and they respond, if not to the precise semantic meaning of the words, to the musical and gestural components of the communication. Already by the age of 2 weeks babies show clear signs of recognising specific words used by their mothers (Share 1994). Babies in general are highly responsive to communications couched in words, particularly in 'motherese', that is, words spoken with dramatic variations of pitch and emphasis, and accompanied by highly expressive facial and gestural signals. Malloch and Trevarthen (2009) use the word 'protoconversation' to describe the musical social interactions that precede the infant's use of language. It includes of course a lot of ordinary language on the adult side, and mimicry of language by the child. Analogously, the term 'proto-verbal' is preferable to the term 'pre-verbal' when describing the developmental stages prior to active language use.

What is changing, as the infant moves through the proto-verbal stages and enters the overtly verbal phase? We could, of course, describe it in many different dimensions. Freud initially, constructing a one-person model of the psyche, spoke of the changing bodily locations of desire. Later, as he became more aware of the huge role played by aggression, mourning, guilt, among others, the fundamental importance of object-relations forced itself upon his attention (Freud 1917, 1923). Melanie Klein accommodated these insights more systematically by giving a central place to anxiety and phantasy, and projected back into proto-verbal babyhood a picture of phantasy activity based on what could be learned from children who had reached the stage of verbal functioning.

Nowadays, with ever more precise observation of babies, it has become clear that classical psychoanalysis underestimated the extent of the infant's capacity both for self-organisation and for intersubjective awareness. There is now abundant evidence that babies are born anticipating a sympathetic interpersonal environment in which they will be proactive as well as respon-sive, and without this they are traumatised. Filmed studies of mother–baby interaction reveal orderly age-related transformations in the baby's inter-action throughout the first year, intricately coordinated with the mother's reciprocally changing patterns of play and communication (Stern 1985; Trevarthen and Aitken 2001). As Trevarthen and Aitken emphasise, attach-ment alone is not enough; the baby also requires companionship; com-panionship in the first weeks and months of life is mediated above all by communications with musical features of rhythm and pitch (Malloch and Trevarthen 2009).

The outcome for the infant of these intense interactions with one or more companions is a set of 'implicit relational expectations' (Daniel Stern's (1985) phrase) which will influence him throughout life. The expectations derived from the first year are 'implicit', that is to say, unconscious and non-verbal, and are very difficult if not impossible to change in later life, no doubt because they are imprinted in complexly embedded patterns of synaptic connections in the brain. For this reason, the tendency of much recent research is to emphasise the continuity between proto-verbal and verbal functioning. In this chapter, however, I want to foreground some of the *differences* created by the shift from proto-verbal to verbal mental functioning. It involves a profound change in the *sort* of consciousness with which the child apprehends his or her external and internal world. I shall ask two questions of this transition. First, what is gained by it? And second, what is lost by it? I also want to keep in mind the view that many religious practitioners express, of language as a potential obstacle to some sorts of awareness.

What is gained by the transition to verbal consciousness?

Essentially, one crucial gain results from this transition: the child joins as an active participant in the ever-changing web of 'conversation' which unites human beings into society. There are, in any society, certain agreements about what constitutes meaningful behaviour, what it makes sense to be interested in or to attend to, and the child who is to be a successful member of the society needs to enter comfortably into these agreements. In psychoanalytic language, the child internalises and identifies with objects which affirm these skills and goals and approve the child pursuing them. Neuroscience tells the same story in terms of neuronal pathways which are enriched and strengthened, or alternatively deleted, in response to social interaction (Edelman 1992). 'The ball' in so many childhood games – football, baseball, cricket, tennis and so on – is a symbol of the social consensus. Children have to learn to 'keep their eye on the ball', and also to catch, throw, kick, use a bat or racquet, and the majority of children learn to do so adequately without too much difficulty. Autistic children, however, do not see the point: they may attend no more to the ball than to any other point in their visual field. They fail to enter the social consensus, and are not set to succeed at society's goals. At a less pathological level, children from migrant families often suffer a related confusion: goals that are 'obvious' to their school-mates are not obvious to them.

Language, the instrument that grasps and gives clarity to conscious experience (Freud 1923), is the medium in which these goals are set up and communicated, and the charm of verbal communication is a very large part of the bonding that holds together friendship, work and family groups, which together generate, designate and pursue these socially understood goals. Reciprocally, shared exercise of social skills and shared pursuit of social goals reinforce in turn the bonding of these groups. It is hard to overstate the importance, therefore, of the transition to verbal consciousness. When a child learns language, people are only half-joking when they say he or she is joining the human race.

Precisely because of its power, however, the transition carries a great danger. It is that society's goals distort or supplant the child's own biological goals. The child comes to have essentially a double definition: he or she is both a member of society and a biological unit, and while the child has to succeed as the one, he or she must also succeed as the other. If the society the child joins – which in the first instance is the couple of baby and primary care-giver, but then rapidly widens out to the family as a whole and then in a range of further directions – if this initial society exerts influences which take the child away from his or her biological goals (which means primarily finding a sexual partner or partners and achieving some degree of social status), then psychological damage is likely to result. This 'double definition', like so many of the terms we have to use in psychology (mind and body, nature and nurture, etc.), involves invoking two entities which cannot in reality be fully differentiated. As I once heard Raimon Panikkar put it, they can be a 'creative tension', so long as we do not allow them to become a 'lethal dichotomy'.

If we tell this story in neuroscientific terms, we are speaking here of the development of the neural networks of the two hemispheres of the brain. Until about the age of 18 months, the largely non-verbal right hemisphere is dominant; from 18 months, prefrontal callosal axons begin to grow across from the left hemisphere, and dominance begins to shift from the right hemisphere to the left, which is primarily associated with verbal activity. From the age of about 3½ years, the left, verbal hemisphere becomes dominant, and it will remain so for the rest of life (Solms and Turnbull 2002; Schore 2003a). (Functions are not of course sharply demarcated, as between left and right hemispheres, so this account is inevitably somewhat simplified.)

The age of around 3½ years figures in a number of developmental schemas. It was the age at which Freud, though not Melanie Klein, reckoned the Oedipal phase to begin, and it is also the age identified by Peter Fonagy and Mary Target (Fonagy and Target 1996, 2000; Target and Fonagy 1996) as marking the start of the capacity to 'mentalise', that is to imagine others as having minds which can have different content from one's own. According to the neuroscientist Allan Schore (2003a), it is also the age at which psychic conflict, between the verbal self-representations of the left hemisphere and the non-verbal self-representations of the right hemisphere, becomes a possibility. Part of what psychoanalysis has described under the heading of the Oedipus complex can also be viewed in terms of struggling towards a reconciliation of left and right hemispheric functioning.

The picture is, then, that in the first eighteen months of the child's life, brain development is occurring at prodigious speed and above all in the non-verbal right hemisphere. Just as the chemical composition of breast-milk changes according to the developing baby's needs, so too the emotional and gestural responses of the mother adapt unconsciously and with great subtlety to the changing capacities of the growing infant. The word 'attachment' is used to describe the product of this process. Attachment to the primary care-giver is the medium in which the development of the right hemisphere takes place and it strongly influences the patterning of the synapses which become established or deleted. Donald Winnicott's famous remark, that 'there is no such thing as a baby', is a vivid way of emphasising the absolute dependence of babies on their early attachments for their psychological development (Winnicott 1964: 88).

To pick out one suggestive point. Allan Schore (2003a) emphasises in particular that the internalisation of a capacity for affect regulation is one of the fruits of the mental structure that results from the protoconversation. Affect regulation, he says, 'is not just the dampening of negative emotion. It also involves an amplification of positive emotion, a condition necessary for more complex self-organisation' (Schore 2003a: 34). This will be worth recalling when we come to think more deeply about the functioning of a moral ontology.

All subsequent emotional development takes place on the basis of this profound unspoken inwardness of right-hemispheric consciousness. Learning to keep an eye on the social ball makes huge demands on the developing child, which require so much attention that they can become serious causes of distortion or derailment. For example, psychoanalysis describes patients who use what we call intellectual or manic defences. These are people who have learned to speak with some coercive quality of intelligence or exuberance, which tends to put both themselves and others out of touch with crucial aspects of the emotional reality of their situation. Winnicott (1960) wrote of the 'false self' which develops when a child is not free to express its own needs, and learns instead to comply with the apparently greater needs or demands of the mother. Distortions of this sort may be introduced whenever internal conflict becomes unbearable, often because of quite ordinary requirements. The need to fit in to the psychic structure of a sibling set is an example of one such ordinary but hugely influential requirement. Frank Sulloway (1996) made a comparison of scientists at times of scientific revolution, who either rapidly came to support the new theory, or who adamantly opposed it, that is, those who were adaptable and those who remained conservative. His very consistent finding was that conservative scientists were predominantly firstborn siblings, more flexible ones laterborns. A fact of this sort is highly suggestive of the pressures within sibling sets that lead in the long run to profound, unshiftable differences of character-structure.

The gain of the transition to a verbal consciousness, if things go reasonably well, is a capacity to unite social and biological aims and to live satisfyingly in the social world without forfeiting or frustrating the fundamental biological motivations that are the bedrock of long-term personal fulfilment. The painful adjustments that these often contradictory requirements entail are one way of describing the content of what Melanie Klein called the depressive position. It is significant that the depressive position is conventionally described in terms of the capacity to unite parts into wholes, parts of the self as well as parts of the object.

What are the losses of the transition?

The losses of the transition to verbal consciousness are above all to do with the immediacy and vividness of experience. What Freud described as the 'primary process', characteristic, he said, of mental functioning in the system unconscious, includes many elements of Klein's paranoid-schizoid position, in which intense desire or hostility is directed to parts of bodies (nipple, breast, penis and so on) rather than to whole persons, and there is the chaotic instability of 'deep unconscious phantasy'. Freud I think had in mind the blind unconscious 'will' or 'striving' of Schopenhauer, which was the ultimate reality of the 'inwardness' of a world given to us in two modes, from the inside (first-person) as 'will' and from the outside (third-person) as 'representation' (Schopenhauer 1819). The unconscious can do nothing but wish, as Freud put it.

This (relatively speaking) immediate contact with 'wishing' or willing is the joy and misery of the proto-verbal stages of development. This is where we meet what Freud called 'the initial pleasure-ego', with its peremptory judgements on reality, 'It shall be inside me' or 'It shall be outside me'. In Freud's (1925a) language, the ego-alien, the external and the bad are initially synonymous, and they are matched by the ego-syntonic, the internal and the good. These abrupt and peremptory infantile judgements in turn constitute the mechanism that establishes what Klein (1946) would later describe as the primary (and actually necessary) splitting of the world and the self into good and bad.

The uninhibited vividness of this present-tense experience is lost with the transition to a verbal consciousness. The attraction of hallucinogenic drugs such as LSD and mescalin is perhaps that they reinstate some of the babyhood intensity of physical sensation – both in its clarity and in its 'timeless' (and intensely interesting) quality. No doubt the power of music in adult life also links with the sensual features of the protoconversation. It seems that part of the compelling power of music is that it relieves us of the burden of feeling ourselves to be solitary individuals: it creates a feeling of solidarity with others, which can be delightful, as in dance and group-singing, or can give the individual a sense of enhanced power, as when soldiers march in step to a regular drum-beat or Nazis on a torch-lit parade. The ubiquity of 'ceremonies' in tribal societies, usually involving music and dance as well as colour, ritual and extravagant costume, points to the relief of a return to a world of pre-verbal sensual experience (Dissanayake 2009). More pathologically, the absolute certainty which is so startling when we meet it in paranoid people probably has its roots too in the same mechanisms as some of these very early responses.

However, whether *states* of consciousness are reversions to earlier *stages* of conscious development has been a vexed question in psychoanalysis. It has led some thinkers to believe that primary-process thinking, with its 'symmetrical' or reversible grammar, is characteristic of infancy, and that ego-states such as the paranoid-schizoid position are representative of proto-verbal stages of development. Increasing evidence shows that this is to underestimate the 'normality' of much proto-verbal functioning. There are several senses in which the proto-verbal consciousness is in out-standingly accurate contact with its experience and these are obscured if it is judged by the standards of later consciousness.

One of these senses is the vividness of its physical sensations. Perhaps another is the quality of its contact with certain sorts of emotional experi-ence. Freud in *Moses and Monotheism* (1939) returned to the philogenetic argument he had first put forward in *Totem and Taboo* (1912–1913), and claimed that 'an experience in the primaeval ages of the human family' had left 'permanent traces' in the human mind (Freud 1939: 129). This argu-ment reads oddly nowadays and is generally rejected by modern biologists, who believe that changes in DNA can occur only at random and uninflu-enced by the experience of the organism. If that is correct, it leaves homeless Freud's idea that such 'permanent traces' might become the basis of religious conviction. However, it is possible to reinstate his thought if we think that, instead of relating to the past experience of the species, the conviction carried by religions, for example, may depend on vividly experi-enced episodes in the proto-verbal stages of the individual's life – not remembered in verbalisable form (episodic memory depends on a brain development, the maturation of the hippocampus, which does not occur before the age of 18 months), but which are nevertheless stored in implicit memory in the structures of the right brain.

Clinical evidence suggests that even very early experiences may be carried through in some way into verbal consciousness, though not in the form of episodic memories.

Mr S, a competent 50-year-old man, whose treatment I supervised, would become extremely angry with his female therapist. He would be first very withdrawn, and then contemptuous and despairing. What he said repeatedly was: 'You don't pick me up!' Both she and he were at a loss to know how to understand this statement, and the passionate hatred into which it carried him. It was only after the therapist had quietly stayed for many sessions with the fact that this was his experience, that he happened to mention that he had been born prematurely and had been in an incubator for the first week of his life. His mother had been allowed to watch him through the glass screen, but not to touch him. (As the therapist subsequently commented: 'the preverbal communication went both ways . . . he was also able to put me in touch with being an angry inadequate mother who was completely helpless, as she must have been'.) Whether his enormous despair, hatred and contempt were directly connected with this early situation we had, of course, no means of knowing, but the therapist's careful interpretation of his passionate feeling of 'not being picked up' in terms of that early experience proved remarkably successful in resolving what had threatened to become an impasse.[7]

What I am suggesting is that the baby's experiences in emotional inter-action may be particularly clear, and not gainsayable. The rapture of the 2-month-old baby during interactions to do with feeding and changing with a loving, lively and sympathetic mother may be conceived as laying down in the right brain a 'knowledge' – a certainty – which if it were verbal we might summarise as a knowledge that to be loved and to love are wonderful and life-giving. Subsequent experiences with loved and loving others serve to confirm that primal certainty, and in adult life the compelling delight and liberation of falling in love, and the conviction of the goodness of self and other that is part of it, re-contact that early irrefutable, non-ambivalent emotion. On the other hand, if the mother is ambiguous, fearful of the intensity of her own passions, or doubtful of her own worthiness to receive love, the baby may be given a confusing signal, which causes him too to become in later life ambivalent or avoidant in the presence of ardour and the possibility of love.

Similarly, there can be moments of great peace in mother–baby inter-action, moments when there is nothing to be done, when the baby experi-ences the maternal reverie without excitement or apparent content. At such times, perhaps the breathing of the two parties is the chief object of conscious awareness. Such moments are probably not infrequent, and like experiences of more excited loving they may carry with them an unques-tionable quality of 'goodness' and safety.

The psychoanalyst Rachel Blass (2003) has suggested that in his late work, *Moses and Monotheism* (1939), Freud allowed himself to wonder about the origin of his own (non-religious) convictions, such as his belief in the pursuit of truth, which he held powerfully but without regard to observable 'evidence'. Perhaps some of the characteristics of the mother's early communication with the baby are relevant here too. We may speculate that the open face and uncomplicated emotional expression in 'motherese' are a source of great joy to the baby (and by contrast emotionally complex or shaded expressions may be a source of pain or sadness), and the origin of the love of truth may lie in these responses. We are speaking here of qualities of feeling which may be experienced with great clarity and accur-acy by the baby, for which language, when it develops, may be too distant and imprecise an instrument.

7 I am grateful to Mrs Dot Phillips for permission to use this material.

This account of the origin of later-life 'convictions' depends on the assumption that certain sorts of experience can make a bridge between proto-verbal and verbal consciousness. To establish a unity between these two sorts of consciousness has perhaps a very special power, felt to be 'significant'. The psychoanalyst Hans Loewald (1978) has suggested that experiences of 'eternity' reported by mystics – eternity not in the sense of everlastingness but in the sense of a 'timeless moment', a *nunc stans* – may derive from an enlarged construction of consciousness when 'primary and secondary modes of mentation may be known together'. Perhaps the power of art also has to do with this bridging across between verbal and proto-verbal consciousness – a successful work of art being one that communicates in some way similar or harmonious messages both to the verbal, thinking brain and to the non-verbal, sensuous, emotional right brain. This would help us to understand the reciprocal importance of 'form' and 'content' in a successful work of art, and its peculiarly satisfying, stabilising quality that can be present even when the subject-matter is tragic or harrowing.

I think such an account gives a reasonably persuasive picture of why certain convictions, or certain subjectively experienced moments of aesthetic satisfaction, occur and have a compelling power for us. However, it fails to give an adequate basis for responsibly held, enduring convictions. Experiences, however impressive, are always open to interrogation as to their meaning, their relation to our existing values, our larger world-view, and so on. Exciting moments of insight often prove, on reflection, disappointingly trivial or even dangerously misleading. We need to be able to distinguish between exciting but unreliable moments of 'certainty' – some conversion experiences are of this kind – and enduring, responsible, principled convictions, such as the concern for truth of a John Locke or a Darwin, or the religiously based concern for justice of a Martin Luther King or a Dietrich Bonhoeffer.

This question of the basis of principled conviction takes us into new realms, because to answer it would bring in the importance of validation by a like-minded group. Despite the myths of solitary seekers, the reality is likely to be that great principled achievements take place in dialogue, internal or external, with others who share one's concerns. ('Conversation', once again, is essential.) However, I want to focus here on the inward template that influences such conversation, and we may glimpse its origin when we think of early experience in the proto-verbal, protoconversational stages of development, influencing the structure of the right hemisphere of the brain. Such experiences can support later 'convictions' of many kinds, including not only no doubt negative ones such as settled murderous hatred or pathological jealousy, but also positive ones such as convictions of the importance of love and sincerity. Where connection can be made to moments of peace between mother and baby, moments when nothing needed to be done, then perhaps the way lies open to a conviction of 'goodness' of an ontological rather than a passionate kind. Such a conviction might resemble those described by religious people as deriving sometimes from informal, spontaneous events, and sometimes from more formalised experiences attained through prayer and meditation. It is perhaps also this unconscious contact with protoconversational early experience which later on allows the individual a degree of independence from the glamour of group membership. Wilfred Bion in one of his *Cogitations* (1992: 152) suggested that Plato's famous image of humankind as a group, seated in a cave with their backs to the light, essentially expresses a recognition that the enticements of group solidarity may be so compelling that they prevent us from turning to look at what, if we looked, we could 'see' to be true.

What is at stake in this argument, and how does it relate to our starting-point?

What have we achieved by this discussion? We set out in this chapter to conceptualise some sorts of what Freud called 'unconscious', and Melanie Klein called 'positions', as different sorts of consciousness. Doing so brings into view the possibility that consciousness exists in a layered series, of which the paranoid-schizoid and depressive positions are two members (or two large classes of members). What characterises each member of the series is that it includes the data of its predecessor in a more economical synthesis, allowing a larger overview of the subject's total situation and a wider extension of sympathy to the denizens of the subject's world (usually in psychoanalytic language called his 'objects'. As I have said in Chapter 4, this is odd in relation to sympathy because sympathy is with the other perceived as a subject).

If, in addition to our various theoretical models, designed to cope with different aspects of psychic development, we include this layered, hierarchical picture, it becomes possible to conceive of a further layer, a contemplative layer or 'contemplative position', which can be accommodated without prejudice to the existing developmental and structural models. This 'contemplative position' is one from which the experience of being alive in the world can be perceived and thought about without the need for immediate action. A developmental and neurological origin for this contemplative position can be glimpsed in times of tranquillity between mother and baby, which are then inscribed in implicit form in the non-verbal structures of the right hemisphere.

What happens in some sorts of meditation, such as Buddhist *shamatha* or attention-training, is that the compulsive action and response that characterise our ordinary relationship with the world are stilled and seen increasingly by way of non-verbal, more steady experiences of consciousness which are hard to access (and harder still to maintain). These more steady experiences reach deeper than the conscious verbal levels to contact implicit emotional memories of a stable 'contentless' togetherness with the mother during the proto-verbal phases at times when there was nothing that needed to be done. There has been much discussion in recent years of the possible relations between psychoanalysis and meditational experiences. It is well recognised now that meditation causes significant and measurable effects, for example in improving recovery times from physical trauma, in enhancing the working of the circulatory and immune systems and in creating stable and repeatable patterns of neural activity measurable by fMRI scans (Benson 1976; d'Aquili and Newberg 1999; Goleman 2003; Meikle 2004). It has been hard to find a place for these findings in the psychological picture given by psychoanalysis. However, the fact that meditation has benign consequences for body and emotional functioning suggests that it should be taken seriously as creating an identifiable structure that contributes to 'health' in the widest sense. Some psychoanalysts have claimed that this state also gives access to a more accurate or far-reaching recognition of reality, as in a discussion between Jack Engler and Stephen Mitchell of the Buddhist no-self doctrine (Engler 2003; Mitchell 2003).

The 'contemplative position' is a position comparable to the familiar depressive and paranoid-schizoid positions, that is to say, an ego-state or series of ego-states with definable characteristics. These include above all tolerance of frustration, anxiety and excitement and a willingness to contemplate rather than act on motives that happen to arise. Remembering Allan Schore's (2003a) emphasis that successful affect-regulation involves an amplification of positive emotions, we may note that positive emotion is often deliberately enhanced in Buddhism, for example, by meditations that set out to create a 'compassionate' state of mind. The emphasis on affirming devotion and love in other religions performs a similar function.

Like other states of mind, the contemplative position can be idealised. It is not uncommon to meet meditators and religious people who are dismissive of ordinary relationships and responsibilities. For such people, meditation has become a psychic retreat (Steiner 1993). Unidealised, however, experience of the contemplative position may enable meditators to become more reliable and give them more consistent access to their deeper feelings.

Finally, to come back to the starting-point, the contemplative position allows us to find a possible meaning for the word 'transcendent'. The contemplative position 'transcends' the ordinary motives of pleasure-seeking and pain-avoidance, not by abolishing them, but by establishing a further layer of recognition and understanding. Coupled with an acceptance of the central importance of sympathy, it makes comprehensible that there can be a compelling desire for motives of justice and compassion, rather than seeing justice, for example, along Freud's lines, as desirable solely as a consolation for unfulfilled narcissistic longings (Freud 1921). We may understand the contemplative position too in relation to the different functioning of the two hemispheres of the brain – a position in which verbal and 'protoconversational' awareness may be maintained in relation to each other.

The contemplative position is *not* transcendent, however, in the sense of giving access to some 'higher reality' or ultimate truth, and in this respect it may be disappointing to some religionists. We cannot escape from what the neuroscientist Francisco Varela (1996) called 'the intrinsic circularity in cognitive science wherein the study of mental phenomena is always that of [i.e. a study done by] an experiencing person'. We remain in the phenomenal world, and the world of 'noumena' remains closed to us. Nothing a scientific thinker can say, therefore, can dispense with the need for conscious 'faith', an act of subjective commitment beyond what can be guaranteed by evidence, if convictions are to be maintained or values securely under-pinned. This is seen vividly with the large-scale values, such as justice and compassion, which clearly compete with our ordinary drive-based motives, but in fact it is true even in the more intimate sphere of values which psychoanalysis has perceived so accurately in its account of the depressive position and the role of envy, love, cruelty, remorse and so on in our treatment of our objects. 'Faith' is the product of an act of commitment by individual 'subjects' prepared to entrust themselves to their own subjective conviction; it cannot be guaranteed by objective evidence because, in the last analysis, subjectivity cannot be discovered in objective evidence objectively considered (Nagel 1979b; Velmans 2000). The capacity for faith must itself depend on some of these earliest experiences, from which Erikson (1968) derived his category of 'basic trust'. I shall attempt in Chapter 10 to discuss the nature of faith, and the conditions in which, though it can never be the product wholly of the intellect, it may deserve intellectual respect.

This picture of a contemplative position also makes room for the reser-vation that many psychoanalysts feel towards religious ways of thinking, that they can serve as an escape from the real conflicts of the patient's social and biological life. It does so by emphasising that a 'higher' level of consciousness can indeed be used defensively to bypass conflict at a lower level, and if so the result is weakness and incompleteness, sometimes of catastrophic dimensions, in the patient's life as a whole. We see this for example in the not uncommon case when a patient has tried to bypass the struggles of adolescence and adopted attitudes of precocious 'adult' matur-ity, which often lead to breakdown in his or her middle or late twenties. I remember that when I started to work as a psychoanalyst, I was surprised by the number of my patients who had been unusually high-achieving at school or university. I came to realise that this was no coincidence. Too one-sided a spiritual aspiration can often carry similar psychological dangers.

Chapter 9

Selves and no-selves

Introduction: initial questions

Reflection on the contemplative and other positions makes one aware of how many different 'selves' or aspects of the self can be inhabited, some involuntarily and even against one's conscious wishes, others more voluntarily. Some of the most important of one's 'selves' accrue slowly, perhaps over a lifetime, as a result of important moments of active, 'self-defining' decision which are looked back on, later, as landmarks in one's personal history. Sooner or later, in any life, the issue comes up of such decision: choices, for example, of career and sexual partnership – including the avoidance or postponement of such choices – which are inescapable to anyone living an ordinary life in Western society. In other societies where, for example, marriages may be more or less forcefully 'arranged' by the person's family, the element of choice remains present but is partially shifted to the decision whether one will participate whole-heartedly in the arrangement, or subvert it in one of a number of ways that are socially recognised if not necessarily approved (for example, brothels, gambling, drink, quarrelling, extravagant piety).

Many other choices are also self-defining: to choose one's religion or one's politics can be momentous; even to choose the football team one will support, the hobbies one will pursue, the musical instrument one will commit oneself to learning to play – all these decisions unfold down unforeseeable paths into the future, and have the effect of shaping the life that keeps faith with them. 'Commitment', that threshold at which so many of our psycho-analytic patients balk, is a moment of decision, of accepting to *be* in the future continuous with the self one is or can envisage now. These moments are bound to be of interest from the point of view of values: choices, as we have seen, are necessarily made from within a horizon of values; they are bound also to be made from within a perspective of historical time and an assumption of the continuity in it of the self and/or the self's objects. (We have to add: in reality or phantasy.) In the absence of a moralised landscape, a landscape including values, the notion of meaningful choice would be unintelligible.

What we mean by a 'self' is in some respects rather like a psychoanalytic 'position': a certain structure of the 'I', but viewed not in terms of 'characteristic anxieties, defences, object-relations and impulses' (Hinshelwood 1991: 393) but as a centre of action and reaction in an enduring world. A self is an 'I' with a degree, even if a very limited degree, of structure and duration; it is not just a 'subject', in the minimal sense in which I used this word in Chapter 6, as the necessarily implied 'owner' of any experience. It is meaningful to ask of a 'self': 'What are his or her (or my) values?' And in important ways one assesses other selves by the values they are discovered to hold. An external social description, 'Male, age 45, lawyer, married, three children', tells us little about the self. 'But what is he *like*?' we ask, and the answers we are crucially looking out for relate to other questions: Will I like him? What precautions will I need to take with him? Will he exploit me if he gets the chance? Will he be sympathetic to the fact that I am a subject like him, with vulnerabilities, failings and idiosyncrasies, and will he treat me with respect? Or will we basically be in a fight, jockeying for advantage, keeping weakness out of sight, exploiting before the other exploits, and so on?

The answers of course will not be simple. And one's own self is not a given. We embark on 'voyages of self-discovery' and come back 'changed', or we come back saying ruefully that, wherever you go, you cannot get away from your self; or we say we were not ourself when we assaulted the police officer. Trust and mistrust are key notions in relation to selves: we trust someone if she appears to be the same self each time we encounter her (even if we don't like her, we know where we are with her), but we mistrust her if she seems evasive or unpredictable, or if we hear she has said something to someone else not compatible with what she told us. We mistrust ourself when we discover how dishonest we can be – towards ourself as well as towards others. We thought we meant it when we made that generous offer – but now, when it comes to the crunch, we find ourself backing away, making excuses. Goya depicted infidelity with two faces, looking in opposite directions. Infidelity to another is infidelity to oneself, or at any rate to one version of one's self.

The difficulty of saying all this is because the self is not a unity. Cardinal Wolsey in Shakespeare's *Henry VIII* poignantly laments: 'Had I but served my God/ As faithfully as I have served my King', he would not in old age have been left naked to his enemies. Fidelity comes at a price, and part of the price is other fidelities, which we may later judge were more important. We owe to Donald Winnicott (1960) the idea of a true self and a number of false selves, and one way of approaching the topic is to ask whether that distinction is meaningful. Can I make a choice which is somehow 'not true to myself', and if so, who was it then who made the choice? More generally, psychoanalysts speak of people who are 'split', or who make choices in a state of dissociation or denial, or with some part of their motivational repertory inaccessible or unconscious. Such people are unable to make choices by reference to the whole of themselves, and so their choices are unsafe and may be at risk of bewildering reversals or sudden incursions of doubt. Other people may make seemingly contradictory choices: to choose to marry, but retain one's lover, to become a Muslim, and yet continue to get drunk several nights of the week. Such confusing behaviours are often called hypocritical, but sometimes it seems more accurate to say that both activities are engaged in sincerely: a contradiction is perceived by the onlooker, but does not trouble the person acting, who appears to be fully involved in both settings. There is a vivid account of such a person in Naguib Mahfouz's novel *The Cairo Trilogy* (1991) in which at the beginning Al-Sayyid Ahmad is both a devout and severe Muslim paterfamilias, and a much-loved and colourful boon companion in Cairo's night-world of drinking and sexually available singers and entertainers. When a divided life, lived by values which are incompatible, is socially supported, it may be sustained indefinitely: we might ask if 'integration' is necessarily desirable. Perhaps (as Al-Sayyid Ahmad would no doubt claim) the divided person lives the richer life?

The latent issue behind these two questions is: Do we need to aspire to a coherent 'self'? Might not a human being just be a Darwinian animal getting by, getting through life in such a way as, hopefully, to survive and reproduce, and all the rest is window-dressing? This of course is a position widely believed, or at any rate asserted, in our times.

A third question is prompted by Buddhism, which is generally held to claim that there is 'no self'. Buddhism is so wary of intellectualising that some thinkers say that what is dangerous is to become 'attached' to any concept – to become attached to the idea that there is 'no self' might be just as damaging as to believe that there is a self. The Dalai Lama, however, quotes as authoritative a Tibetan teaching that the no-self teaching is definitive of Buddhism: 'The assertion or refutation of the basis for the view of self is what separates followers of the Buddha from others' (Dalai Lama 2007: 120). The crucial Buddhist doctrine of *pratitya samutpada* (translated as 'conditioned co-production' or 'dependent origination') states that no individual thing has independent existence: everything is a transient manifestation arising in a vast interrelated network of causal sequences. It follows that there are ultimately no individual selves just as there are no individual 'things'. At a lesser pitch of ultimacy, Buddhism allows things and selves to be spoken of as 'conventional designations' (Dalai Lama 2007: 29–40).

These arguments of Buddhism are impressively similar to those developed in the eighteenth century quite independently by David Hume (1739), who also said that when he looked into himself he found only this or that particular idea or impression, but never a 'self', and therefore he concluded that the self must be a fiction. Nowadays all these arguments seem to invite us to take a deeper look into the nature of language, but nevertheless they focus our third question: how can we understand the persistence and importance of the notion of the self, when it is so hard to identify it with clarity?

Self in psychoanalysis

Psychoanalysts, confronted with the word *self*, almost reflexively catch themselves murmuring: *and other*. Selves, we are continually reminded, and as I have discussed here in Chapter 6, owe their existence to a continual exchange and dialogue, real or imagined, with 'others'. We are accustomed to the idea that who 'I' am is continually fluctuating in relation to 'you', the you I experience you as being, who may or may not resemble the person *you* experience yourself as being, your 'I'. The notion of projective identification is relevant here. If I am angry with Jane, and I meet you who are also angry with Jane, I may start to speak about Jane in a very moderate and reasonable way, because I have projected my anger into your anger and I am now free to occupy a different part of my reaction to her – to be, to this extent, a different self because of who you are.

A similar mechanism may be employed when I am very hurt by what you have said to me, but don't want to experience myself as vulnerable. I may then behave towards you 'in all innocence' in a way that finally makes you very angry with me, and we then have a quarrel in which I feel entirely in the right. In this case I have been unconscious, or only very obscurely conscious, of my anger towards you for hurting me, but by my behaviour I have now 'projected my anger into you', and you are the one who is angry. When we quarrel, our quarrel is about something else, and I have now regained the ascendancy: I am morally in the superior position, and I continue to protect myself from knowing how hurt I was by the initial event. A great deal of marital conflict has this kind of shape, and is so difficult to resolve because the overt quarrel has been carefully separated from the initial grievance, of which neither party may ever have let themselves be quite aware.

The 'self' in an intimate relationship is continually fluctuating, and our best hope of wholeness is if we can over the course of time inhabit most of the different bits of ourself, and not get trapped in any one of them. Eric Berne (1964), in the simplified version of psychoanalysis he called Transactional Analysis, created a schema of three typical roles we can all play, which he called Parent, Adult and Child. If I speak to you in Parent mode, I am apt to evoke a response from you in Child mode; or you may respond by becoming even more parental than I, in an attempt to force me to carry the childish, humiliating end of the stick. On the other hand, in sexual activity for example, it may be fun if we can both be in Child mode for a while. In reality, roles are far more complex and detailed than this schema suggests, and sometimes they involve quite lengthy sequences of role-taking and role-imposition, played out over time and very hard to discern without prolonged attention and reflection. (Berne noticed this too, and gave amusing names to some of these repetitive dramas: 'Look What You Made Me Do', in which your role is to be helplessly guilty, or 'Gee, You're Wonderful, Professor Finkelbaum', in which unless you are alert you are likely to end up looking embarrassingly stupid.)

But to speak of roles is misleading if it suggests that there is a consistent actor behind them, taking off one mask and putting on another. Jung's technical term, 'persona', which is often compared to Winnicott's 'false self', was derived from the idea of an actor's mask (*persona* in Latin), but if it has any validity it is only in the case of exceptionally accomplished social performers, diplomats or habitual seducers, perhaps, who are quite consciously 'acting' in their social relations. Far more often, there is an actual change of 'self', and the person is not playing but has become the new role. In health, the transition between selves can often be managed quickly and without forgetting or undue embarrassment (between being a parent fooling about with one's children and being a responsible professional, for example); in other situations, embarrassment is often the marker of clashing selves.

The question of selves is crucial to the question of values because different selves hold, or are governed by, different values. You cannot have a value unless there is a 'subject' to which the value is precious, and in human life that subject is bound to be a self. Many people nowadays who come to a psychotherapist have wanted to 'keep their options open' with regard to some important area of life – marriage, career, gender orientation – and are now suffering from a sense of 'not knowing who they are'. They feel uncomfortable and trapped when they find themselves in any settled situation, as if it isn't 'the right one'. One patient said in each of a succession of work situations that he came to feel 'his face didn't fit' – he had to move on.

What is typically happening when there is such a complaint is that the adaptive self which has initially 'fitted in', is now being encroached on by other motives or other 'selves' which were excluded by the initial adaptation. If we use Winnicott's (1960) language, we would say that a false self is being encroached on by the true self, but to put it in this way underestimates the 'truth' of the fears, desires and defences which set up the adaptation in the first place. It is preferable to say that the different selves are all equally real, and the question is more to do with the freedom the person feels to adopt, abandon or move on from them. The person who is unable to commit himself fails to provide himself with a context in which the evolution of his self and his values can proceed; he is often, paradoxically, confining his experience to a rather narrow and repetitive band within his wider spectrum of possible selves, and hence, over time, the frustration he comes to feel.

An opposite difficulty in understanding confronts us when we meet the ideal presented by many religions and philosophies that speak of 'wisdom'. They describe a stability we cannot believe in: the saint, the Enlightened being, the sage who has achieved an unalterable single self, a coherent stable personality that he (rather rarely she) can always be relied on to be. This self is usually characterised by calm and benevolence, unfazed by passion or misfortune. The Bible tells us for example of 'the righteous': 'I have been young and now am old, yet saw I never the righteous forsaken, and his seed begging their bread' (Psalm 37: 25, AV). Or, with the rather different verbal manners of the English eighteenth century, the Earl of Shaftesbury tells us of 'the good man', who 'becomes the architect of his life and fortune, by laying within himself the lasting and sure foundations of order, peace, concord' (quoted in Taylor 1989: 259). Living in the twenty-first century, we can hardly read this sort of thing without inwardly satirising it. We know only too well how many good people have died terrible deaths, and how often the unrighteous have flourished.

I want therefore to address several questions in this discussion of selves. Can I (not being under duress) make a choice which is somehow not 'true to myself'? Is integration – the pursuit of a single, coherent self – necessarily desirable? Why is the notion of a self so important, given that it is so hard to identify it? And lastly, is there still any value in the widespread picture of the religious person who has 'made it', the avatar, bodhisattva, saint or sage who presents a stable self reliably expressive of the values of his religion or his philosophy: what is the use of such a picture?

Can I make a choice which is not true to myself?

The question of true and false selves is bound to arise, because the terms are in common use and also because, in psychoanalysis, Donald Winnicott has given them a further currency. We all know what it is to be compliant with someone and afterwards regret it (or the only slightly different variant of this, to be defiant towards someone and then regret it), and in such cases it is natural to say: I wasn't being true to myself. But all we mean is that the (perfectly real) motives which at the time caused my compliance have proved to be less lasting, less serious and less embedded in the continuing texture of my feeling-life (Pugmire 2005), than the feelings I am experiencing now. To call them false is to make a claim from the perspective of the present, but at the time they were not false and it is not illuminating – indeed it trivialises them and makes them harder to think about – if we speak in this way.

There are many special instances which it would be interesting to spend time on – the person who 'acts', the compulsive liar, the person who breaks up her mind and prefers not to know and so on – but for our present purposes I shall treat all selves as equally 'real' in the moment of their manifestation.

Is integration necessarily desirable?

Psychoanalysis is based on the assumption that integration is desirable, that is to say, that the different parts of the personality, including its impulses, desires, emotions, moral attitudes, knowledge of the world, and so forth should all be so to speak in dialogue with one another: that decision and action should be the outcome of a sort of internal self-consultation. Put like that, it sounds excessively complicated, but of course in the healthy person this consultation, or contact with different parts of the personality, is not at the expense of spontaneity. Indeed, inhibition and lack of spontaneity are often the indicators that the inner connections are not operating smoothly, and one of the aims of psychoanalytic interpretations is to bring more of these inner elements 'into consciousness' and into the joined-up process.

It is never easy to know what language to use to describe these internal realities. Freud's early oppositions, consciousness/unconsciousness, with the later addition of the preconscious, are useful but now seem over-simple. Much that psychoanalysis brings to consciousness was never really that unconscious: it was more that the patient had never really reflected centrally on it, or had never felt able to entertain it with proper seriousness. What is brought 'into consciousness' by interpretation or as part of the analytic process often disappears from consciousness again very shortly afterwards, but may still exert a changing influence on the patient's relationships and behaviour.

A patient who had a strong dislike of using the seat-belt in his car suddenly, one day, had an image of himself as a small child protesting bitterly at being strapped into a push-chair. His aversion to car seat-belts disappeared from that moment and didn't trouble him again. Presumably the conscious remembering of the push-chair enabled him to separate the current experience of the seat-belt from it, and therefore from the painful and rebellious emotion associated with it.

Unfortunately, significant change is rarely achieved so simply. The embarrassing thing about psychoanalysis, the great length of time it takes, is no doubt because the slow cumulative impact of repeated exposure to a non-judgemental interpretive environment allows patients to feel that it is safe to inhabit more of their mental world – to explore thoughts and feelings without fearing that they will suffer violent rejection or criticism or be overtaken by unmanageable emotions. The metaphors of exploration and inhabiting seem to carry an implication that the terrain will turn out to be a coherent mainland, so to speak, and will not be split up into mutually inaccessible islands.

The development of psychoanalytic theory, proceeding hand-in-hand with increasing understanding of brain development in childhood, and also increasing recognition of the need of babies for a sympathetic interactive 'protoconversation' – huge topics which I touched on briefly in Chapter 8 – has led to a wish to speak of psychoanalysis too in relationship terms: object-relations theory in Britain, relational psychoanalysis in the United States. The personal feelings of the psychoanalyst in response to the patient, initially perceived as slightly shameful distractions from the objective and surgically precise task of 'analysing', are nowadays regarded as inevitable and significant ingredients in the process. To what extent they should be spoken about directly in the work remains controversial; among my British colleagues, the general view is that they should inform analysts in reaching their interpretations, but to speak of them directly to the patient is likely to be more confusing than illuminating and should ordinarily be avoided. (I agree with this.) In terms of our question, the involvement of analyst and patient in a one-to-one relationship also creates an 'integrating' structure, in which the analyst's containing mind, presumably a consistent unit, is there to receive and process whatever the patient brings. In what Freud called the 'fundamental rule' of psychoanalysis, patients are invited to say what comes into their mind and to hold nothing back, so in the ideal picture patients bring 'everything', including their splits, confusions and defences, to the receptive and thoughtful mind of the all-noticing analyst, who by his or her interpretations links it all up and returns it in usable form to the patient. Reality of course is very different but nevertheless the ideal picture shows clearly that the goal of psychoanalysis, contrary to its name, is to help the patient to achieve an integrated mind.

Put in terms of selves, we could say its goal is to help patients experience their different selves, the different 'I's they can at different times be, as tolerable and mutually related. As different selves are not separated from one another by hard boundaries (generally speaking), it is not quite possible to say whether integration of this sort is like a committee, in which so to speak the different views of each self have to be considered, and decisions involve processes like negotiation, compromise, and even a final vote, or whether the final decision is made by a whole self who is discovered only through the debate. Perhaps the greater decisions of life are more like the latter. But the difference between selves is very real, seen most dramatically when there are 'hard boundaries' as in Jekyll and Hyde, or patients with latent psychosis, but present even in ordinary experience in wayward thoughts, dreams, daydreams. As Richard Wilbur says in his poem 'The

Sirens': 'I never knew the road/ From which the whole earth didn't call away' (Wilbur 1989: 301).

But should we assume that integration is desirable? If the divisions in a person's mind cause him to be unable to reach a decision – or, having made the decision, to be promptly unfaithful to it – then we can see that such a person will either become unhappy himself or cause unhappiness in others; in a quite recognisable way, the inability to 'be' a settled 'self' creates a problem. But it is possible to imagine a society, Mahfouz's 1920s Cairo perhaps, where a split life can be led with consistency and significant social support. Al-Sayyid Ahmad's wife maintains decorum in his home: she admires her strict, dominating, worldly-wise husband unquestioningly, is loyal to him and devotes herself to bringing up the children; and in his night-time persona he is a generous, funny, and relaxed, if at times domineering figure in a group of similar husbands, who drink alcohol (contrary to Muslim law) and have sex with charming, seductive, available women whose way of life this is. Al-Sayyid is not a 'split personality' of the Jekyll-and-Hyde type, where one self is criminal and anti-social; both his selves have social support, and have in some respects admirable qualities.

From my own experience in the consulting room, the capacity to live a radically divided life seems to show up more frequently in men than in women. Perhaps this is only because women are still in general more strongly anchored by kitchen and children (if not by church – I am thinking of *Kirche, Kinder, Küche*) than men are. I have several times worked with female patients who have been astounded to discover that their husbands, to whom they have been loyal, have been conducting an entirely separate love-life, sometimes with a succession of casual partners, but on two occasions with a 'serious' alternative partner, virtually in a second marriage. In all cases, the men are described as accomplished liars, able to produce convincing stories to account for their many absences, and apparently unaffected by remorse at deceiving their wives and children. Perhaps in the nature of the case, the male partners of such women less frequently come to analysis.

I have only once worked with a man who was clearly split in this way. He was a successful, middle-aged businessman, somewhat hypomanic, who repeatedly arrived at sessions telling me with enthusiasm about the 'wonderful girl' he had just met on his latest business trip. When in a positive mood he would speak with infectious exhilaration and high spirits which made it easy to understand why he was so successful as a seducer. In analysis, he gradually became more in touch both with his guilt towards his wife and children, and also with his genuine love for one of his girlfriends. Unable to choose between them (to decide 'which self to be'), he became increasingly desperate. He had a dream one night in which he was pursued by a cheetah; he fled in terror up and down a street which proved to be a cul-de-sac closed at both ends. The situation resolved only when he had (it is tempting to write: 'when he unconsciously staged') a severe skiing accident, in which he nearly died. His wife was the one who visited him in hospital, and it was to her he returned when he came out of it.

The importance of integration, in such cases, can seem more obvious when one considers the person's objects – the other people in his life – than when one considers him in isolation. This was true as well for Al-Sayyid Ahmad. When his wife and growing children began to get wind of his alternative life, the children lost respect for him, and his wife was devastated. The strict but moral and well-regulated household could not survive the revelation of the failure of morality on which it was founded; the impact on the contemptuous, angry and disillusioned children launches the narrative on its later volumes. This pattern – that the damage caused by a split way of life makes itself felt first in others – was equally apparent in the female patients I have mentioned. The difference between 'splitting' and 'repression', two psychoanalytic 'mechanisms' by which unwanted contents are kept out of consciousness, may be described by saying that splitting is often quite successful, at least initially, in allowing the person to live a life as two or more different selves, but it damages others; whereas 'repression' – the less extreme process, which allows the self to remain more coherent – leaves the repressed content secretly acting in the patient's life so as to undermine it, by causing symptoms, by depression, ambivalence, lack of motivation, and so on. Of course, as so often with these psychological matters, the distinction is not a hard-and-fast one.

Religious moralists have traditionally been unhappy with the idea that individuals who are 'sinful' – a word that can often, psychoanalytically, be translated as 'split' – will not themselves suffer for their sins. It does not seem good enough to merely point out that they damage others, and 'sufferings in the afterlife' has been a good way to satisfy the sense of injustice people often feel when they hear that some 'monster' – a Stalin, a Mao, a Josef Mengele – has died a natural death without remorse. No longer relying for justice on the afterlife, however, we have to face the fact that split people often die without becoming aware, in any emotionally significant way, of the damage they have caused to others, and certainly without suffering the punishment or remorse that might be deemed 'appropriate'. Gitta Sereny's studies of criminals from the Nazi era (Sereny 1974, 1995) offer detailed evidence of how such split states of mind can be maintained over a lifetime.

Do we have to say, therefore, that the price of 'splitting' may be borne wholly by others, and the person who uses this psychic defence against living fully in his emotional world may 'get away with it' scot-free? In an everyday sense, yes, undoubtedly. Splitting, projective identification, irresponsible acts of cruelty and seduction, are part of everyday life, and it would be quite unreal to imagine that every one of them is subsequently suffered or repented for, even by those who are morally sensitive. Such self-protection seems to invite the criticism of the moralist. But, to take another sort of example, every profession, including politics, the military, and medicine, has its official language, which 'trains' its practitioners to perceive reality from certain angles, and to be blind to others: this too is a form of socially supported splitting, and it is necessary if people are to be willing to perform roles in society in which mistakes will cause true damage to individuals. Recently in the UK a number of news stories in which horrendous child abuse has gone unrecognised by the social services, and children have died as a result, have been reported in the press with a great deal of vilification of the social workers concerned. As a result, there has been a serious decline in the number of people willing to train as social workers. Professionals need their socially supported splitting if they are to endure the guilt of their inevitable mistakes.

Nevertheless, the motive of integration is a powerful one, and is a principal driver of maturity. I shall use the word 'maturity' as a term of art, without making any attempt to define it; it describes a state of mind which can accrue only upon emotional experience, and which may remain unachieved despite a great deal of 'experience' in the external sense of activities, relationships entered into, and so on. The nature of experience, and the ways in which experience may be lived and yet not fully 'experienced', have been discussed with great sensitivity in the psychoanalytic literature, and in particular by Wilfred Bion (1962) and Donald Winnicott (1971). Over a long period, the failure to fully experience one's life gives rise to a curious intangible form of suffering which is frequently met in the consulting-room.

From the point of view of our overarching theme of values, the importance of integration and maturity is pointed to in a word I used two paragraphs ago: 'irresponsible'. Responsibility is the willingness or the determination to be answerable for one's acts, including one's words: to be 'the same person' as the one who did or said them, so as to be a reliable point of reference in the human world for one's partner, children, colleagues, or indeed more generally. The wish to be responsible is often actuated by the discovery that one has not been responsible, that it is very easy to say one thing to one person and something incompatible to another (out of a wish to please), or to gossip 'behind someone's back' (and express a malice one would never express to their face). Up to a point, such things are normal, and it depends on the sensitivity of the individual conscience how much one is shocked by them. But at some point, the person who has the potential to mature becomes uneasy: is this just gossip, or is it betrayal? Is this just my pleasant social manner, or is it degrading sycophancy? If there is an I, it seems there must be such a thing as where I stand.

It is now that integration becomes an ideal. The poet W.B. Yeats wrote in a memoir that when he was in his late twenties:

this sentence seemed to form in my head, without my willing it, much as sentences form when we are half asleep: 'Hammer your thoughts into unity'. For days I could think of nothing else, and for years I tested all I did by that sentence.

(Ellmann 1979: 115)

With his rich imagination, it was very easy for his thoughts to run away with him, and Yeats's history is an impressive study of a struggle over many years to unite his thoughts and embody his values in a lived life. In his fifties he wrote a little poem which expresses the struggle well:

Hands, do what you're bid:
Bring the balloon of the mind
That bellies and drags in the wind
Into its narrow shed.

(Yeats 1951)

The person who remains split may not consciously suffer as a result, but the person pays a price nonetheless, which is that he or she is not able to achieve what I am calling maturity. Maturity includes embodying one's values, and being discoverable as holding them: *representing* them. (Embodying one's values is likely to include the rueful discovery that not all one's values are fully compatible with one another: the values of quality and the values of equality are notoriously of this kind.) 'Maturity' is not necessarily the best word for this development, as many people in our society are called mature who have not achieved it; but perhaps there should be some other word for those who have merely grown old unexceptionably. Whatever name we give it, however, there is a quality of being that accrues upon the struggle for integration that is not attainable in its absence. The psychoanalyst Erik Erikson (1968), in his chart of developmental stages through life, named the final phase 'Integrity', and characterised the failure to reach it as 'Despair'. Erikson's Integrity bears some resemblance to the account I quoted earlier from Elliott Jaques of the 'deeper working through' of the depressive position in relation to the realisation of one's own death, which caused Jaques to reach for the imagery of Dante's *Paradiso*. One marker of Integrity, Erikson (1968: 139) suggested is 'a sense of comradeship with men and women of different times and of different pursuits who have created orders and objects and sayings conveying human dignity and love'. Not all who fail to reach this stage necessarily suffer conscious despair: the despair is often hidden behind attitudes of disgust or 'a chronic contemptuous displeasure', as Erikson (1968: 140) put it. I think by 'mature' I am trying to describe what Erikson called Integrity: the common theme in all these various accounts is integration.

Why is the notion of the self so important, given that it's so hard to identify it?

Our third question follows rather oddly after the second, in which I have spoken in definite terms about the self and such characteristics as splitness and integration. Now is the time, however, to remember the arguments of Buddhism and David Hume, that the 'self' is a sort of intellectual illusion, and when I look carefully I can find no trace of it.

This is a philosophical argument and we shall not lose sight of it. But before coming to it in its own terms, perhaps I could remind the reader of the psychoanalytic picture which is a preliminary step in the same direction. When Melanie Klein first formulated her account of depression as a collapse of the person's internal capacity to hold together the tensions of love and hate, resulting in an inability to suffer and work through the pains peculiar to the 'depressive position' – guilt, remorse, 'pining' (Klein 1940: 348), regret, sadness and so on – she received a powerful challenge from the Scottish psychoanalyst Ronald Fairbairn. Fairbairn (1944) claimed that patients who suffered such collapse almost always showed, if one looked deeper, a more obscure pathology. This pathology he called 'schizoid' and it involved deep splits in the psyche which had never been addressed and which might perhaps never have been visible until the patient's integration was threatened by the need to cope with some major life-event, whatever had caused the 'depression', such as bereavement or the failure (or sometimes, paradoxically, the success) of a cherished project. Klein was impressed by Fairbairn's argument, and in response in 1946 she formulated her theory of a 'paranoid-schizoid' position which underlay the achievement of the depressive position (Klein 1946).

This exchange has been hugely fruitful in terms of the development of psychoanalytic theory. The notion that even in the healthy individual there are underlying 'psychotic mechanisms' – that is to say, tendencies to split off experience rather than to digest it into the larger, coherent self – has been illuminating of many previously baffling or inaccessible mental states. It is likely that such underlying mechanisms are universal; without digressing into a lengthy discussion, one striking piece of evidence is the difficulty that most people have in withstanding prolonged solitude. Solitary confinement is a notoriously painful punishment, because we are intensely dependent on other people to play their part in the projective and introjective processes by which we maintain our ordinary mental equilibrium. In the prolonged absence of others we are increasingly exposed to our own irrational phantasies: some people 'go mad', and others may retreat into depression, meaning an anaesthetised avoidance of their crazy thoughts and feelings. Those who cope best are those who can construct others in their mind, perhaps through religious belief, or through vivid memories of loved ones, or by remembering poetry, music and so on.

If we apply this picture to our discussion of the self, it suggests that the 'I' which psychoanalysis is concerned to identify and affirm is a construct in need of a great deal of maintenance. This does not mean that in ordinary circumstances it is not quite robust, but we all know of bewildering states – perhaps when we awake in the middle of the night, or have a fever – when we struggle to 'remember who we are'. One of the most graphic accounts of such an experience comes from William James, and although it has been much discussed (including by Erikson (1968) in his study of identity), it bears repetition.

On the night of 12 February 1906, James, then aged 64, had what he called 'the most intensely peculiar experience of my whole life'. Fortunately, with his remarkable gift for introspection, he was able to describe it:

> I awoke suddenly from my first sleep, which appeared to have been very heavy, in the middle of a dream, in thinking of which I became suddenly confused by the contents of two other dreams that shuffled themselves abruptly in between the parts of the first dream, and of which I couldn't grasp the origin. Whence come *these* dreams? I asked. They were close to *me*, and fresh, as if I had just dreamed them; and yet they were far away *from the first dream*. The contents of the three had absolutely no connection. One had a Cockney atmosphere, it had happened to someone in London. The other two were American. One involved the trying on of a coat (was this the dream I seemed to wake from?), the other was a sort of nightmare and had to do with soldiers. Each had a wholly distinct emotional atmosphere that made its individuality discontinuous with that of the others. And yet, in a moment, as these three dreams alternately telescoped into and out of each other, and I seemed to myself to have been their common dreamer, they seemed quite as distinctly not to have been dreamed in succession, in that one sleep. *When*, then? Not on a previous night, either. *When*, then? and *which* was the one out of which I had just awakened? *I could no longer tell*; one was as close to me as the others, and yet they entirely repelled each other, and I seemed thus to belong to three different dream-systems at once, no one of which would connect itself either with the others or with my waking life. I began to feel curiously confused and *scared*, and tried to wake myself up wider, but I seemed already wide-awake.
>
> (Richardson 2006: 470–471, original emphases)

As he reflected on his experience, James became more and more frightened:

> Presently cold shivers of dread ran over me: *am I getting into other people's dreams?* Is this a 'telepathic' experience? Or an invasion of double (or treble) personality? . . . Decidedly, I was losing hold of my

'self' and making acquaintance with a quality of mental distress that I had never before known.

(Richardson 2006: 471, original emphasis)

It is this 'losing hold of the "self"' that I wish to comment on now.

James, like Yeats, was someone of enormous intellectual and imaginative energy, though he never developed Yeats's superb (or perhaps superb affectation of) self-confidence. But for him too, to 'bring the balloon of the mind' into the narrow shed of an actual life's work had not been easy. He had been profoundly depressed in his twenties, unable to decide on a direction for his career, and even when he had decided, and was married to a wife whom he loved and was enjoying considerable professional success, he was subject to dramatic excitements and alterations of mood; his life shows recurrent signs of considerable instability, held in check by strong ties of love and friendship, and a huge and overflowing articulacy. (In this too he resembled Yeats, whose wife christened him 'William Tell' because he talked about everything.)

So this disturbing dream experience did not come out of nowhere. What it seems to show is something of the incoherent psychic material out of which the regular daily achievement of 'being William James' was built. I am assuming that this is a general truth, that all human selves are built out of comparably incoherent material and 'subpersonalities', but James is helpful to us because his instability gave him more direct access to these foundations, and his gifts as a self-observer allowed him to report what, by its nature, must have been extremely hard to grasp hold of.

If we attempt to look directly into the mind, or to stay with mental experience as far as possible independent of experience of others or of the external world, we become aware of incoherence; this can be profoundly disorienting, as in James's bewildered attempt to remember his dream, or in the experience of the person in solitary confinement. This potential for breakdown is sometimes thought to imply the insubstantiality of the self, but in fact what it highlights is the significance of the integrated self: the actions of the person in breakdown or disorientation no longer express the values and meanings of the integrated person.

David Hume's self-observation, which discovered no 'self' but only 'ideas and impressions', is practised more systematically by Buddhists, who may meditate in solitude with minimal external distraction for periods of up to three years. Buddhist psychology is highly developed, and it differs from Western because instead of looking at experience in relation to the external world (or in the case of psychoanalysis in relation to others), it seeks to attend to consciousness directly, or as directly as possible.

There are broadly speaking two categories of meditation in Buddhism, one, known as *shamatha*, to achieve stability of attention, and the other, *vipashyanâ*, to investigate and achieve insight into the nature of mental reality (B.A. Wallace 2007). (The Buddhist, I think, would say 'reality', not 'mental reality'.) In the next few paragraphs I shall largely follow the clear summary of basic Buddhist teaching provided by the Dalai Lama (2007) in his 'Key Principles of the Buddhadharma'.

As mentioned in Chapter 8, according to the Dalai Lama (2007: 35), the meditator discovers that there are 'two levels of truth': how things appear, and how they really are. There appears to be a self, but if we look closely, we don't find it; we find only the five *skandhas* or 'mind-body aggregates', which are listed elsewhere as form (or matter), feelings (of liking or disliking), perceptions, impulses and acts of consciousness (Conze 1951: 14; Rahula 1967: 20–27). Rahula (1967) gives the flavour of much Buddhist teaching when he quotes two lines from Buddhaghosa:

> Mere suffering exists, but no sufferer is found;
> The deeds are, but no doer is found.
>
> (Rahula 1967: 26)

All mental reality can be assigned to one of these five 'aggregates'. But if we look deeper into each of these *skandhas* in turn, we discover that they too 'have no true identity'; if we view them 'as permanent, truly existent, a source of pleasure, and pure', we are mistaken: in reality, 'there is nothing to be found'. And 'the more we examine the way things really are, underlying the way they appear, the clearer this fact becomes' (Dalai Lama 2007: 34). The Dalai Lama continues:

> The same applies to the whole spectrum of phenomena, all functioning as causes and conditions, interconnected with one another, for better or for worse. If we are not content with appearances, and we examine their ultimate essence, their absolute way of being, their fundamentally unconditioned nature, it is unfindable. . . . This is how phenomena are said to be *false* and are not found to be truly existent. Their true existence, which is what is being refuted here, has never actually been the case. The very nature of things is such that they are there, but they cannot be established as existing.
>
> (Dalai Lama 2007: 34, original emphasis)

This is also described using the word *empty*. All outer and inner phenomena 'are said to be *empty of inherent existence*' (Dalai Lama 2007: 37, original emphasis). However, 'when we say that a flower is empty of inherent existence, we are not denying the reality of the flower'. The flower is 'self-empty', meaning empty of intrinsic existence, but not 'empty of itself', which would mean that there was nothing there to blossom and produce fruit. 'Rather we should understand that any given thing, since it is produced in dependence on other conditions, is empty in the sense that it has no inherent existence of its own' (Dalai Lama 2007: 38).

I am labouring this point because all Buddhism depends on a profound alteration of one's perception, to which this issue of 'emptiness' is crucial. Something is 'devoid of inherent existence' if it is impermanent and if it depends on causes outside itself. Since this is true of everything in the empirical world, including our 'selves', everything is devoid of inherent existence. There is then the familiar philosophical puzzle of how to describe the difference between things that nevertheless do have empirical reality – like flowers – and others, like unicorns, that do not – but this is a sideshow. The big question that survives is whether anything at all *does* have inherent existence, and if so, what?

The Buddha himself always refused to answer this question, no doubt recognising that any answer would send his followers back into the world of delusory religious entities from which he was trying to liberate them. His goal, as formulated in the Four Noble Truths, which are generally agreed to be one of the foundation statements of Buddhism and may well go back to Gautama Siddhartha himself, was to help people overcome their suffering; he had no wish to propagate more, always dubious, theories (with which India, at the close of the Upanishadic period, was already abundantly supplied). However, such intellectual austerity could not survive when Buddhism spread and became a popular religion. Schools came into existence such as the Madhyamikas (who emphasised the teaching of emptiness) and the Yogacarins (who claimed that ultimately there was only consciousness); these gradually separated out from the earlier views to form, some five centuries after Gautama's life, the huge movement known as the Mahayana or 'Great Vehicle', which increasingly seemed to give an ontological freighting to precisely 'the void' which had been designed to refute it. The notion of 'going for refuge to the Buddha' seemed to give Gautama a certain ongoing survival, despite his own silence about the idea, and in Tibetan Buddhism, which perhaps went furthest of all in this direction, the 'clear light' to be found at the heart of the meditator's experience even came to be given a personal name: it was called the Buddha Samantabhadra. When Buddhism disappeared from India (in about 1000 CE), it was because developments of this sort, an increasing reification and even personification of 'the void', had allowed Vedantic Hinduism to annex it; the Buddha was declared to be yet another of Vishnu's several incarnations.

However, the philosophical fascination of Buddhism remains that in its developments outside India it never wholly succumbed to the pull of ontological positivism. Buddhists never quite forgot that however like other people's gods and demons their bodhisattvas and guardians of the Dharma might look, the basic teaching remained clear: these were no more than mental constructions. They might be used in visualisations, and might even be invoked and prayed to, but this was not because they were 'real' but merely because these methods were helpful in acting on the mind. Whether this would necessarily have dismayed Vedantins I am uncertain, and correctly speaking it should not even have been a shock to the Christian tradition of apophatic mysticism – the tradition that declared God to be beyond the reach of concepts – but nevertheless this linguistically sophisticated teaching has always been quite openly maintained in Buddhism, and it is what makes Buddhism of particular interest to psychological thinkers.

The Dalai Lama, like many others, compares the Buddhist teaching that the self is 'empty of inherent existence' to the findings of quantum physics: what seems solid to ordinary experience seems when you look closely to dissolve into empty space and subatomic particles. And even the subatomic particles prove ungraspable: 'finally there is nothing to be found'. (Thinking about the same issues in dialogue with Stephen Mitchell, Jack Engler, one of the pioneers in the dialogue between Buddhism and Western psychotherapy, came to a slightly different conclusion: quantum physics, he thought, shows that whether reality is finally perceived as continuous or discontinuous, waves or particles, is a function of our constructing minds. But – and here he makes the move made by the Mahayana as a whole – surely our mind itself, consciousness, that which observes the world 'with infinite affection', cannot itself be the product of its own constructive activity (Engler 2003; Mitchell 2003; Safran 2003). Surely consciousness finally is the reality which is not to be found elsewhere. It is as if Descartes had arrived at the *cogito* without a God to guarantee the veridicality of his perceptions.)

There can be no question that the Buddhist vision is a profound one. It embodies an important truth, and its liberating potential in relation to psychological and emotional compulsions has been recognised by the adoption of Buddhist mindfulness techniques into a significant movement in cognitive psychotherapy (Kabat Zinn 2001; Segal et al. 2002). But, from a theoretical point of view, how can we relate its insights to more ordinary notions of the self, which are required by psychology, psychoanalysis and more generally in living daily life?

Lakoff and Johnson (1999) have given us the useful notion of a 'basic-level category': the level in a logical hierarchy of concepts 'at which most of our language is organised' unless we are experts in a field. It is also 'the highest level at which category members have similarly perceived overall shapes' or gestalts, and the level at which the hierarchy is first named and understood by children (Lakoff and Johnson 1999: 26–28). To borrow one of Lakoff and Johnson's own examples: chairs are a basic-level category in a logical hierarchy of furnishings, because we still have a mental image when we conceive a chair, even though we know that any actual chair will be more specific (i.e. lower in the hierarchy: an armchair, a kitchen chair, a rocking chair). And we know too that there are higher levels of the hierarchy, such as 'furniture' – but these are now so general that we no longer have a mental image when we employ them. The word chair is used correctly by children from an early age, and by ordinary people with no special knowledge of furnishings.

Using this notion, we may say that selves are a basic-level category in our perception of subjectivity, even though we know that at other levels of contemplation we would see the self break down into subpersonalities and subsidiary narratives (as in William James's moment of mental chaos) or Buddhist *skandhas* or 'ideas and impressions', or perhaps even disappear altogether. I argued in Chapter 6 that unless one gives an absolute priority to consciousness over the external world (i.e. adopts a radically and exclusively phenomenological standpoint, as William James tried to do from time to time, and as some Buddhist schools do), and the logical terminus of such a priority would be solipsism, it is not possible for a 'subject' to entirely disappear from any level of conscious experience. It always remains possible to ask: 'Who is the subject of this experience?' and to point to another subject who is not. This continues to be true even if the experience is of mental chaos, Buddhist enlightenment, and so on. When we think of issues to do with responsibility and with responsibly held values, the elimination of a subject who is an integrable 'self' becomes unintelligible: responsibility is inconceivable without a self, and it requires a self that endures in relation to other comparably enduring selves.

The analogy from quantum physics has a certain value from the point of view of pure ontology. It allows us to see a hierarchy in which one level is basic and familiar, and other levels are vertiginously different or virtually unimaginable. And it is unhelpful to say, either of quantum physics or of subjectivity, that one level gives us reality and the other illusion – who is in a position to decide this? The fact is that we perceive 'the same thing' in radically different ways – at radically different magnifications, so to speak – but this in no way implies that one magnification gives us access to 'reality itself' or to something 'more real' than the other levels.

In short, the idea of the self remains essential as a basic-level category, indispensable in the living of an ordinary life in society, however much at other levels of examination it becomes questionable or even dissolves altogether. In particular, a self capable of integration is a necessity if the notion of responsibility, fundamental to morality, is to have any meaning: a responsible person is by definition one who remains discoverable to answer for his or her acts and decisions, and does not scatter into a blur of *skandhas* or ideas and impressions. (One way to avoid responsibility is to plead mental incapacity.) There can be values without an integrated 'self' (though there must be a 'subject' who is able to experience the preciousness of the value) but an integrated, persisting self is necessary if there is to be morality and a locus of responsibility. That in turn is necessary if society is to have dependable structures and if children are to develop emotionally, become integrated and achieve psychological competence.

To put the same point in the language of emergence: if responsible commitment is a possibility (responsible commitment will be the subject of the next and final chapter) the self cannot be wholly accounted for by a story told in the language of subpersonalities, Buddhist skandhas, or Humean ideas and impressions (or, for that matter, Freudian drives or selfish genes). The 'emergence' of new qualities has created a new situation, in which events occur because of the existence of the higher-level unit which can be described but not understood from the level of its constitutive entities. The higher unit (in this case the self who enters into responsible commitment) has so to speak acquired interests of its own: in the image I used in Chapter 6, it has become a fountain of causation, causing effects at the lower levels which are not comprehensible from the lower levels.

Coda: on avatars, saints and others

It is unlikely that fundamental human experiences that appear in one major cultural tradition will find no expression in others. What in psychologically minded, non-theistic Buddhism is reached by experiences described as being of 'no-self' or emptiness is, I think, reached by other religions that use the notion of a God who is beyond all description or conception, and it may be of interest to reflect briefly on this more mythological way of conceptualising the matter. There is always the paradox, of course, that what is beyond description cannot be put into words at all, and the attempt to describe the ineffable is clearly doomed to fail; nevertheless there have been many imaginative efforts, including the use of silence, music, dance, and drama, which have been felt to be valuable. Language can be stretched in ways that go beyond meaning, deliberately so in the koans of Zen Buddhism. I have mentioned the apophatic Christian tradition, and the mystical path known as the *via negativa*, and there is the famous 'neti, neti' (not this, not this) of the *Brhadaranyaka Upanishad* (1953); there is the use of paradox ('smaller than the small, greater than the great' of the *Bhagavad Gita*, or the 'felix culpa' of Christianity) or St Augustine's circle unknown to geometry 'whose centre is everywhere and whose circumference is nowhere'. And there are the overwhelming visions, like that of Job, whom God crushes with his transcendent greatness ('Where wast thou when I laid the foundations of the earth?'), or that of Arjuna when Krishna grants him the vision of Vishnu, hundred-headed, devouring the stars. These visions, 'too great for mortal sight', have a vertiginous emotional quality, so traumatic that the visionary begs to be released from them.

The psychoanalyst Ronald Britton (2006) has discussed the story of Job from a psychoanalytic angle, in which God is understood as an overwhelming superego from which the ego, Job, needs to be emancipated. Britton approves Job for maintaining his own judgement despite God's overwhelmingness, and suggests that Job's submission at the end of the story is a pious replacement of an earlier ending in which Job retained a healthy scepticism about God's alleged 'goodness'. That is certainly a congenial reading to psychoanalysts who know how important it is for patients to crawl out from under overwhelming, guilt-inducing parental imagos and make their own choices in life.

But if we think of religious objects as 'resources for consciousness', as I suggested in Chapter 6, it is possible to read the Book of Job differently, and to think that God and Job represent two different standpoints for consciousness. Job needs to be able to make his own judgements in order to be a 'self', successful in society, able to cope with competition, guilt, envy, moral choices and all the requirements of human social life. But 'God' represents an enormously enlarged consciousness, an awareness of the huge mystery of the cosmos, and of the tininess of an individual person's knowledge and power within it. Such an awareness can indeed be paralysing, and a distraction from successful social functioning. But it isn't for that reason invalid. In the eleventh chapter of the *Bhagavad Gita*, Arjuna's vision is not dissimilar to Job's:

> Ablaze with many-coloured flames You touch the sky, your mouths wide open, gaping, your eyes distended, blazing: so do I see You and my inmost self is shaken: I cannot bear it, I find no peace, O Vishnu!
> I see your mouths with jagged, ghastly tusks reminding me of Time's devouring fire: I cannot find my bearings, I cannot find a refuge; have mercy, God of gods, home of the universe!
> (*Bhagavad Gita* [1969] 11: 24–25, trans R.C. Zaehner)

The insignificance of human lives and concerns in the face of this vastness that infallibly destroys them can be terrifying: it can be known, conceptually, but what is described here is an emotional experience of it. I have quoted previously from the American psychoanalyst Hans Loewald, who in 1978, when it still required courage for a psychoanalyst to criticise Freud, suggested that Freud 'by avoiding a further understanding of religion remained . . . on the safe ground of the rational ego' (Loewald 1978); what Loewald was pointing to was the protective function of human social activity: we are protected from the terrifying awareness of Job or Arjuna because we are caught up in our 'love and work', our everyday concerns, and in the many layers of social meanings in which our culture cocoons us.

The musical scholar Ellen Dissanayake, attempting to imagine the lives of early hominids, as they developed for the first time in the history of the universe a capacity for memory of the past and foresight concerning the future, has suggested that the ceremonies that are a universal feature of tribal societies are above all to do with anxiety control. There is a need, she says, for 'emotional reassurance that the group's efforts will prevail'. 'Having "something to do" in times of stress', she writes, 'such as moving and vocalising rhythmically with one or more companions, would be more soothing, and safer, that going one's own isolated, anxious way' (Dissanayake 2009: 26). Imagining early human life, it is likely that we should hold onto this idea of a background of ever-looming existential terrors.

Arjuna, like the Buddha, has seen that everything in the empirical world is transient. His mighty vision of Vishnu comes when he asks Krishna to show him 'what does not pass away' (11: 4): what the Buddha and the apophatic mystics refuse to put into positive words is supplied by the tremendous vision of Vishnu, both creative and destructive, but above all so vast and overwhelming as to be traumatising.

What makes the difference between Job's vision and Arjuna's is the presence of Krishna. Krishna is Arjuna's thoughtful and understanding charioteer, who in Arjuna's moment of crisis, when his nerve fails him before the battle, listens to what he has to say and responds. But Krishna is also an avatar of Vishnu; the vision which overwhelms Arjuna, does not overwhelm Krishna because Vishnu *is* Krishna. And at the end of the vision, 'the great-souled One assuming His gentle form consoled him who was terrified' (*Bhagavad Gita* [1965] 11: 50, trans. Swami Chidbhavananda). Krishna has revealed himself as Vishnu; now Vishnu reveals himself as Krishna.

In other words, by the time of the *Gita* (dates are vague, but it is usually taken to date from two or three centuries after the Buddha, and one or two centuries prior to Jesus), there is now another 'religious object', another resource for consciousness, which is intermediate between the overwhelming God and the hapless human subject, which can hold in a single mind both the vision of existentially terrifying vastness and transience, and the recognition of the need to live a human life and to fulfil one's *dharma* and caste-duties, or as we might say to love and to work in the society in which we happen to be. The avatar is a gearing-system, so to speak, that mediates between scales and, instead of paralysis, allows energy to be exchanged between the systems. It makes possible a third way, between pious surrender of one's own interests before the terrible priority of God, and blasphemous rage and rejection of him: to see ordinary everyday human life as also precious in God's eyes and therefore to believe that one has divine support in pursuing one's own goals in society.

As resources for consciousness, however, avatars, like the Supreme Gods they embody, retain too much divinity to allow the human subject to be entirely comfortable. Too much gratitude, adoration and apology deplete us, and we are apt to deal with our resentment by hating others who are not constrained by the same emotions. In the centuries following the *Gita*, Christianity developed both the most elaborated conception of an avatar in human history, and also showed the ferocious persecution of heretics and outsiders that is always likely to be the backside of a too lofty ego-ideal.

One attempt to solve this problem was the inclusion in the religion of stories of saints and followers who were ordinary human beings, who unlike avatars suffered from the doubts and weaknesses of ordinary human subjects. St Peter is a good example, a man who despite his emphasised failings was paradoxically declared to be the 'rock' on which the church was built. Erich Auerbach (1953) has shown what an extraordinary literary innovation the Christian Gospels were, inviting us to take fully seriously the thoughts and feelings of ordinary people, such as fishermen and tax-collectors, who in classical literature would either have been overlooked entirely, or would have been figures of fun. The attempt to present Jesus as not only an avatar but also an ordinary human being, though never entirely persuasive, was also a step in the same direction.

Looked at with a psychological eye, and seeing these various figures – Supreme Gods, avatars, incarnations, saints – as 'resources for consciousness', it makes sense to think they all represent different magnifications at which the telescope of consciousness can perceive the world. These figures represent other possible subjects which human selves can transiently be, and they persist as 'internal objects' when they are not emotionally related to or identified with. Contact with them, and the experience of relating to them by worship, prayer, contemplation, for example, have the effect of developing the personality in particular directions, and of gradually making it possible to come to terms with or assimilate what is found in the object. Values that the self has glimpsed may be 'worshipped' (affirmed as powerful), and either endorsed or repudiated (demons, devils and so on). If endorsed, they can be further explored, strengthened, and then more resolutely worshipped or identified with. We are, to borrow a phrase from Richard Wilbur, 'enlarged by what estranges'; but what, that estranges, we find to be enlarged by will be a function of our incipient values.

Chapter 10

The basis of responsible commitment

> Any enquiry into our ultimate beliefs can be consistent only if it presupposes its own conclusions. It must be intentionally circular.
>
> Michael Polanyi (1958: 299)

Introduction

This book has looked at a number of crucial topics relating to its core concern with values: neuroscience, religion, sympathy, the uniqueness of the subject, Freud's attempt to understand destructiveness, the nature of selves. But it has left a gaping hole at the centre of the topic. What is the glue that holds the self and its values together? Or, to alter the metaphor, what is the fuel that powers responsible action, assuming it is not mere compliance with external *force majeure* (or internalised *force majeure* such as a super-ego)? In Chapter 9 I used the phrase, to 'keep faith' with a commitment. That seems correct, but what does it mean? What is faith? How does it work? Why 'keep' it? How are we to respond to the cynic, who sniggers at all talk of 'faith' and is often psychologically rather acute?

To answer these questions, we shall have to divest ourselves of our prejudice against circularity. I have introduced this chapter with a quotation from Michael Polanyi, and I am glad to do so, because his brilliant discussion of commitment in his book *Personal Knowledge* (1958) has probably influenced what I shall say here more than I know; but I do so too because he recognised that if we are not merely constructing an argument (we have all been taught that argument should not be circular and thereby 'beg the question'), but if we are also attempting to describe a 'basis' for something, a psychological structure which can carry weight, then a circularity, or a reciprocity of action between the parts, is bound to underlie it. The recognition of a value will always depend to some degree on a preparedness to recognise the value; without that, not only the cynic, but also those who sincerely hold other values, will remain so to speak tone-deaf.

What I say in this chapter, therefore, will be vulnerable to the charge of circularity. The alternative would be to adopt the position of William

James's celebrated old lady, who, asked what the world rested on, answered, 'A rock'; and then, asked what the rock rested on, answered, 'Another rock; it's rocks all the way down' (James 1882: 104). She rightly saw that the alternative to circularity is endless regress.

The problem of responsibility

The basis of commitment has to lie beyond rationality, because it has to trump argument and rational doubt. It would be easy therefore to say it depends on feeling, but if the commitment is to be responsible that implies that certainly ordinary feeling, which is changeable, is not in sole charge: commitment also and precisely stands against the fickleness of changing feelings.

If to get our bearings we look across to religion, the solution has been provided in the past by the notion of something transcendent, not subject to the transience and mutability of 'this world'. I attempted in Chapter 8 to think about 'transcendence' in terms understandable to a scientific world-view, and the notion of a contemplative position can perhaps give us one element of what traditional 'transcendence' provided – the notion of a vertical dimension of consciousness, a ladder of 'positions' in terms of which things can be more profoundly or more shallowly seen – but it cannot free us from transience and mutability, or provide the unshakable stability of the traditional mythological religious picture. It cannot free us, finally, from the need to form our own 'opinion'. Kant gave a philosophical account of transcendence, which perhaps got closer to the traditional meaning, but it was too abstract for ordinary use and depended on a purely rational subject, a rational 'I', which is no longer convincing. But the mythological picture shows well enough how transcendence works. In the words of Samuel Johnson's hymn: 'In vain the surge's angry shock,/ In vain the drifting sands;/ Unharmed upon the eternal rock/ The eternal City stands'. Johnson was envisaging an unchanging God, steady as a rock, outside of space and time, and the faith that could be founded on that rock was proof against Time's shocks and reversals. One question which this book has repeatedly turned around to examine from various angles is: on what can commitment (fidelity, faith) be founded if we stay within the scientific vision and no longer have such a picture of 'the supernatural', a realm outside of and superior to 'nature', the world of what is born and dies (the word *nature* is cognate with *nascent*)? In this final chapter I want to address this question directly, and at least attempt to give a clear response to it.

One immediate consequence of living in a unitary universe, in which the great dualities of body and mind, matter and spirit, Creator and Creation, cease to be stark dichotomies and come to be perceived as different aspects of something unitary, is that the 'eternal City' ceases to be altogether proof against the sea and the shifting sand. In other words, the world of the fundamentalist becomes no longer a possibility for us: commitments cannot be wholly independent of circumstances. This is because 'I' and 'my circumstances' also cease to be a stark dichotomy: in the last analysis, I am continuous with my environment. In this sense, the loss of the supernatural takes us a step nearer to the Buddha's vision. As in Buddhism, there is no longer a place for the heroic moralities: lifelong vows that cannot be broken, honour feuds that must be bloodily pursued generation after generation, blind obedience to ancient texts declared to be 'the word of God' – and for those whose mind-set is fundamentalist or literalist, that loss is catastrophic: it causes first despair (or a ferocious reaction to refuse despair), and later shallowness. It is as if, for such a person, the loss of an absolute morality is the loss of all morality, 'responsibility' can find nothing to 'respond' to, and the place of morality will be usurped only by various sorts of greed, for food, money, power, status, sex and so on, or by the pleasures of hatred: racism, class resentments, the persecution of particular categories of offender – all of which at best make up a foreground, against a deeper background of futility and anomie.

Such a change in values has appeared to be supported in recent decades by the willingness to speak of human beings as 'consumers'. A 'consumer society' presumably is one in which things can be valued only in so far as they conduce to consumption, which in itself is amoral. A consumer society, therefore (supposing it were possible), would confirm the worst fears of fundamentalists.

Psychoanalysts on responsibility

If the notion of responsible commitment is to survive the loss of the supernatural realm, it can only be grounded in ordinary 'nature' and natural motives compatible with our evolutionary history and psychological and cultural development. What then can it be 'to'? And – a second but related question – how can it be 'responsible'?

The psychoanalyst Donald Meltzer has given a central place to the notion of responsibility, in his account of the Kleinian notion of the depressive position. He writes:

> the very heart of the depressive position is the realisation that security can only be achieved through responsibility. . . . Responsibility entails integration, that is, accepting responsibility for psychical reality, for the impulsivity and affects and attitudes, for all the different parts of the self *vis-à-vis* internal and external objects. Inherent in the concept of the depressive position is the realisation that the drive towards integration is experienced as love for an object, that is, as the experience of cherishing the welfare of an object above one's own comfort. It is also implicit in these theories that, for an object to be loved, it must

be unique and it must have qualities of beauty and goodness which are able to evoke in the self the feelings of love and devotion. The corresponding inner object that undergoes a development parallel with the self's integration, achieves those qualities as it becomes fully human in complexity.

(Meltzer and Williams 1988: 208)

Meltzer here is wrestling with the paradox that love is to do *both* with qualities in the object *and* with a development in the self which allows it to appreciate and respond to these qualities. Unfortunately, the language of 'objects', though traditional in psychoanalysis, inevitably Platonises the psychological world, and re-emphasises a division between 'inner' and 'outer' worlds precisely as a process is occurring which might diminish that division. (To clarify: an 'object' in the psychoanalytic sense cannot be unique because, as an object, it is defined in terms of its function for me, who am the subject, and in this relationship it can be substituted. If we see the other as a 'subject', however, then he is indeed unique, because all subjects necessarily are, and therefore I can have a unique relationship with him as a result of 'sympathy sense one', the faculty that gives me access to the other as subject. Meltzer and Williams (1988: 208) were perhaps glimpsing something of all this when they said, just before the passage I have quoted: 'There is no such thing as safety in object-relationships to be found in the quality of the object itself'.)

Jonathan Lear (1990) has also written of responsibility from a psychoanalytic point of view. He approached the issue using a less Kleinian vocabulary. He was discussing the significance of Freud's suggesting, late in his life (Freud 1937, 1940), that the great overarching drive Freud called Eros may be present, not just in human beings, not even just in living beings, but throughout the universe. (Freud was clearly pleased with this idea, which has come up at several points in these essays; to most psychoanalysts, I suspect, it has seemed extravagant and in fact it is rarely mentioned in psychoanalytic circles.) Like Meltzer, Lear (1990) also talks about 'accepting responsibility' for one's drives, but, he then asks, how can I do that? If my drives are merely forces beyond my control, which determine my fate, how can I, and why should I, 'accept responsibility' for them? Some thinkers, he says (and he clearly has thinkers like Meltzer in mind), have found a solution by saying I should 'stay within an internal perspective'. From the external perspective of science my drives may appear to be brute forces determining my fate, but if I can stay in the internal perspective, in which I see myself as an agent, then to accept responsibility makes sense. Lear continues:

This solution is thin and unsatisfying. As soon as one divides up perspectives into internal and external *and places natural science within the external*, one has presupposed that the external perspective gives us the way things *really* are. And in so far as philosophy equates the objective with the external perspective, it exerts an inhibiting influence on the process of accepting responsibility. . . . For it is small comfort to be told that around issues of responsibility we should stay within the internal perspective. All the exhortation to stay within the internal perspective cannot finally quell the sceptical doubt that, *really*, there is no reason to accept responsibility.

The significance of Freud's putting love [Eros] *in* the world is to challenge the distinction between internal and external perspectives. There is, for Freud, no external perspective from which love disappears. Love is a basic natural force, and so the perspective of natural science must be a perspective that includes love. And since love is manifest in my own psychological activity, there is no perspective from which one can 'look down' on the drives as brute natural forces, determined for me but other than me.

(Lear 1990: 180–181, original emphases)

If Lear's argument is correct, its implications are very far-reaching, and in two directions. One is to do with our perception of the universe: a step is taken in the direction of some version of panpsychism (already discussed here in Chapters 2 and 6). For the moment, I think it worth noting how many theoretical arguments currently point in this direction, although the arguments against panpsychism, in any obvious meaning of that word, remain to my mind compelling. (To adapt one of my earlier arguments to the present context: if Eros exists throughout the universe, what can be his *vis-à-vis*, his 'object'? Love without an object is unintelligible.)

The other implication of Lear's argument is more persuasive. It is to do with our embeddedness in the body, and here his thought is very much in tune with many recent thinkers, starting perhaps with Nietzsche and William James but now including many psychoanalysts and neuroscientists such as, for example, Gerald Edelman and Antonio Damasio, and among philosophers very emphatically recently Lakoff and Johnson. To 'accept responsibility' for my drives – and, we could add, for my phantasies and my behaviours – requires accepting my reality as a complex psychosomatic unit; it is to shift my sense of self from the various parts of me that have been its fluctuating location hitherto, to the whole psychosomatic unity of the person. That is no doubt more easily said than done, but it seems intuitively right and it gives a sense of a direction for development.

Here Meltzer's emphasis on a specific 'object' for love (a notion which I want to supplement by saying it must be also perceived as a 'subject') becomes important. To 'accept responsibility' for my drives (etc.) entails doing so in a context of a relationship with another, who needs to be sheltered from some of my drives and thoughts, and sponsored by other drives and thoughts, and who needs also to be able to act spontaneously and feel secure in the expectation that I will try to respond lovingly and non-destructively. If it appears to be done in the absence of such a relationship, it will be found to be done in relation to an 'internal object' (again: also a subject) which has or has had a reality for others as well as for me – a remembered person or a figure such as a god who plays a part in a public narrative, or a 'great' man or woman who plays a part in history. Meltzer's sentence ('The corresponding inner object that undergoes a development parallel with the self's integration, achieves these qualities as it becomes fully human in complexity') is perhaps too brief to be entirely comprehensible: the point is not so much that the inner object accrues complexity – though it does – as that it is found to possess more qualities that differentiate it from the self: it becomes more unmistakably 'another'. And to call it an inner object (as, following Meltzer, I have just done), multiplies entities beyond necessity: we are talking about our perception of a real object, existent for others as well as for ourselves. We do not know a cat by perceiving an internal cat (Velmans 2000). It is a real other, a stranger, that we are coming to know, as love deepens. This in turn gives rise to a developing internal object, which plays a part in the mind's internal dramas, but which in health remains continually subject to modification as a result of experience of the 'real object', the other person.

What is responsibility a response to?

Having got this far, that responsibility is something to be 'accepted' in relation to a loved object-who-is-also-perceived-as-a-subject, the central questions open up: what is the nature of this responsibility? To what or to whom is the implied 'response'? What is the sanction upon maintaining it? Why should our values involve 'response' at all, and why should they not be (or, are they not) in reality purely reactive, in the sense in which someone in a society of consumers might say: 'When I am hungry food has a value for me; when I'm not, it doesn't'?

What psychoanalysis has contributed to our understanding of these questions is the fact that the I cannot develop satisfactorily in isolation from others, who not only are to be conceived as objects, understood by empathy and able to fulfil my wishes in relation to them, but also must be perceived as subjects, recognised by sympathy and loved (as well as arousing whatever other emotions they may create in me). Understanding of this sort, of course, could risk self-stultification: I might start looking around for 'subjects to love', turning them in the process into objects to fulfil my alleged need to develop satisfactorily. But this would be a confusion.

In the light of the necessity of others, the instrumental question about values might now be formulated differently. Why should values not be, in reality, instrumental, but now for 'us' rather than for 'me'? (I'm not hungry, so food has no value for *me*, but you are, so it has value for *you*, and therefore for *us*.) This is an important difference, and we should not be too quick to dismiss it as merely an enlargement of narcissism. A great deal of the difference between moral value-systems has to do with how we set the boundaries of the 'us': the individual, the couple, the family, class, nation, racial group and so on. It is an interesting if controversial exercise to think, for example, of political differences in terms of such boundaries: radicals typically emphasising the individual, conservatives emphasising family, class, nation, perhaps racial group, liberals the whole of humanity, greens the ecosystem or some version of it. The psychoanalyst Erik Erikson (1970) spoke of Gandhi's struggle to attempt to overcome the tendency to create what Erikson called a pseudo-species, some group smaller than the human species as a whole, usually one to which we belong ourselves, that will have greater importance than all the rest.

By changing the boundaries of the 'us', therefore, I may accommodate a utilitarian challenge. I may say with seeming virtue that I am aiming not merely for my own happiness but for 'the happiness of the greatest number'. (Utilitarian arguments are in my view very confused, as I shall discuss in a moment.) But I cannot in this way answer the much more difficult challenge of the cynic, who denies the existence of intrinsic value outright. 'A plague of opinion!' says Thersites in *Troilus and Cressida*: 'A man may wear it both sides like a leather jerkin' (III, iii, 265–266). By opinion he means valuation, and in the exhausted world of the unending Trojan War Shakespeare sets his bitter play, in which all the publicly approved values of heroism, hierarchy and fidelity have been subverted and the coward and cynic Thersites comes nearer than anyone else to speaking the truth. 'When you really get down to it', says the cynic, all apparent values are held hypocritically: the only motives are the drives, meaning not Freud's gigantic 'mythological' drives, Eros and Thanatos, but the ordinary list of self-interested motives, self-protection, greed, lust, dominance and so on.

The cynic nowadays can draw on both evolutionary theory and psychoanalysis to support his position: on the arguments that say, for example, that our perception of beauty is at base a perception of health and therefore of a sound breeding-partner in the competition for our DNA to survive; or that the capacity to compose music derives from a primitive recognition that rhythmic movement, or a lively speaking-voice, are indications of various sorts of muscular competence or courage, and therefore, once again, good indicators when choosing a breeding-partner or deciding whether to avoid or provoke a fight. Such arguments do not have to be cynical, and they probably contain a great deal of truth (there must be *some* evolutionary background to all our capacities), but when they are presented with the insertion of a 'merely' or a 'nothing but' they are readily enrolled in the service of cynicism.

What characterises cynicism, as it does utilitarianism as well, is the elimination of intrinsic value in favour of instrumental value; the joke that the cynic is the person who knows the price of everything and the value of nothing is acute. The true cynic lives in a state of despair, because he can find no worth in his own love or his own self, or indeed in his own cynicism. His persistent mockery and devaluation of other people's beliefs may be seen from a psychoanalytic point of view as a projective identification technique: he seeks to create in others the despair he refuses to experience and take seriously in himself (and thus to off-load it). Cynicism needs to be distinguished from healthy forms of 'disillusion' which result in a more realistic perception of reality but not one from which value has been removed.

But the power of the cynic is that he is not wholly wrong. 'Opinion' (valuation) can indeed be worn on both sides 'like a leather jerkin'. Our love for others has its self-interested aspects, and our brave intentions to be faithful may come to nothing, defeated by circumstances or by the emergence of alternative selves as was so miserably the case for Shakespeare's Trojan couple. If we want to defend responsible commitment, it is not because we take it for granted it puts us on the winning side. In fact, one of its markers is that it entails the risk of failure. Thersites, the cynic, has come through nine years of war better than heroes such as Achilles because he had no values to start with: he was not in a position to become 'demoralised'.

It is when we reach the notion of 'intrinsic value' that we can no longer avoid circularity. Intrinsic value claims that the object is unique and has a value in its own right (that is what 'intrinsic' means), but it cannot avoid acknowledging that someone, perhaps a Thersites, may deny that value or just plain be blind to it. And there is no objective criterion, as there is say in the case of colour-blindness, by which we can show that his perception is defective. In other words, lame as it can only sound, the person who perceives intrinsic value is not just anyone, but someone who is capable of perceiving it.

I doubt if we can grasp this further without using words from the lexicon of religion. The emotional recognition of worth is traditionally called *worship* (worth-ship); the willingness to entrust oneself to one's perception of worth is traditionally called *faith*. Faith has become confused with *belief*, as if it necessarily involves assent to some given set of verbal propositions, but it need not involve propositions, as when we say that someone 'keeps faith' with someone else. The word *worship* has become almost unusable today outside a religious context, but in its root meaning it is of value to us because it conveys the *power* of a perceived value (more strongly than *respect*, which is perhaps the nearest secular equivalent).

It is curious that psychologists have not been more interested in this question, of what the affect is that holds us to our values. Immanuel Kant (1788), however, saw its importance, and he described the affective response to moral worth using the word *Achtung* (which is usually translated as *respect*). Here is his vivid account of *Achtung* in action:

> Fontenelle says: 'I bow before a great man, but my mind does not bow'. I would add, before an humble plain man, in whom I perceive uprightness of character in a higher degree than I am conscious of in myself, my mind bows whether I choose it or not, and though I bear my head never so high that he may not forget my superior rank. Why is this? Because his example exhibits to me a law that humbles my self-conceit when I compare it with my conduct: a law, the practicability of obedience to which I see proved by fact before my eyes. . . . Respect is a tribute which we cannot refuse to merit, whether we will or not; we may indeed outwardly withhold it, but we cannot help feeling it inwardly.
>
> (Kant 1788: 48)

Kant's *Achtung* is inspired specifically by the perception of the freedom and autonomy of the other, manifested by his having the capacity to make (even if he does not in fact make) the supremely rational choice to obey what Kant called the categorical imperative. (The categorical imperative is to act only on a maxim which one can will that everyone would choose to be governed by in like circumstances.) Such an intense emphasis on rationality no longer seems to us quite right. Our more 'embedded' and embodied, evolutionary and developmental picture of the human being no longer allows us to separate out rationality from emotionality in this way, and we recognise that our decisions are inevitably influenced by our own bodily state, our history of relationships, and so on. Nevertheless, what Kant was addressing, in his account of *Achtung*, was the question that confronts us now, namely, what is it in our perception of value that makes it influential for us, and (despite the extreme rationality of his formulation) he rightly saw that if value is to be 'intrinsic' it must entail an emotional response that we 'cannot help' feeling. And since, it seems, some people do manage to be quite uninfluenced by values that others find compelling, we have to accept that the 'we' we are talking about is not everybody.

Using this vocabulary, then, we may say that the circular system on which responsible commitment can be based is one in which a subject capable of appreciating a value feels respect or 'worship' for a valuable object which does indeed embody the perceived value. If the subject takes his feeling fully seriously (which will include making it conscious, scanning it for possible illusion or delusion, comparing it with other things he knows or believes about the object, and so on), then this experience may result in *faith* or commitment as a continuing valuation of the object. A continuing valuation implies that the value of the object continues to influence the subject's behaviour. Faith is never immune to doubt and its maintenance requires repeated renewals. (And the cynic, of course, is present as an internal voice, not only an external one.)

What I am doing in spelling things out in this way is a variant of Charles Taylor's (1989) important notion of a 'moral ontology' implicit in all our judgements of value, which (unless it is made explicit in religious or philosophical belief) can be seen as a specific instance of what psychoanalysis recognises as 'unconscious phantasy'. The way Taylor puts it is to say that we have in effect three options. One is to turn to some accepted teaching, such as a religion, which will provide us with an externally given moral ontology. Another is to dismiss all such thinking as not supportable by empirical evidence and therefore unscientific and unworthy of a modern thinker. But a third is to take up 'the challenge of making sense of one's own moral horizon' (Taylor 1989: 341): to accept that one does have responses that recognise value (of which Kant's account of 'respect' is a particularly persuasive example) and to take these with full seriousness.

My present argument adds that if we do take up this challenge, we discover that our moral ontology is dialogically grounded; that is, we discover that it depends on both the evaluative competence of the subject, and on the actual qualities of the object in reality. Any further move, to lift the qualities away from the object and into a Platonic realm of non-natural 'forms' or Ideas, or into a metaphysical realm of abstractions, goes beyond what this argument justifies.

What has intrinsic value?

We are left then with the question of what has these actual qualities? What has intrinsic value, and what does it look like?

I want to start by drawing attention to the interesting fact that utilitarianism, although it is clearly inadequate because it describes all values as to do with 'utility', that is, as instrumental, is nevertheless often quite a good guide in practice to moral action. The reason is that a utilitarian theory is bound to entail an element of intrinsic value which it cannot on its own premises explain. Something is said to be good because it leads to x, where x is happiness, or social welfare, or something of the sort. The theory can be restated in conditional terms: 'If you want x, then what leads to x we will agree to call "good"'. The intrinsic value resides in x, and it is not explained or even addressed by the utilitarian theory as such.

As a preliminary marker of intrinsic value, we may say that it is something that draws us, consciously or unconsciously, to seek ways to approach it. Consciously or unconsciously, we are 'attracted' to intrinsic value; it is 'attractive'. We need to include the familiar psychoanalytic qualifier, 'consciously or unconsciously', because psychoanalysis knows only too well how ignorant we often are of our own goals, and any adequate account of values will have to include a recognition of the fact that we often believe, for example, that our goal is one thing, say 'success', when our inner motives may be causing us to take very sure aim at something else, say sabotaging our success. We believe we love and wish to enhance, for example, when in fact we envy and undermine. We believe we wish to please our boss, when in fact we relate to her in carping and competitive ways which are very unlikely to make her feel pleased to have us around. The negative behaviour, with its predictably damaging impact, must be in service of some 'value' that consciousness has not yet fully appraised. Perhaps dependence seems intolerable to me, so I really do want to destroy my love-relationship; or perhaps I feel so crushed by my boss's excellence and superior position that, to feel I exist at all, I have to 'put her down'. Perhaps both these (apparently and actually) destructive behaviours are secretly in the service of survival – possibly misconstrued in the present circumstances, but nevertheless, once one has perceived it, a true and comprehensible value.

It is only intrinsic value that evokes the emotion of 'worth-ship', worship, though in this too mistakes are possible and can be assessed retrospectively. People who have lost their faith disparage their former worship, though at the time it was perfectly genuine, just as those who have fallen out of love may disparage their former partner. We may say that the emotion was genuine even if the object turned out to be or to seem unworthy of it. And, just as with other emotions, the emotion of worship cannot be induced by thinking or wishing. One cannot fall in love with someone by enumerating to oneself his or her excellences, and so too worship, the emotional recognition of value, cannot be compelled: it is something that arises spontaneously in response to the object, and carries its own conviction at least for so long as the emotion endures. Valuing another person in friendship is a good example.

This may be clearer in relation to aesthetic values, where we tend to feel less constrained than we do when considering moral values. With aesthetic values, at least initially, less seems to be at stake, and we feel more at liberty to acknowledge that we differ from other people's judgement, or that we feel passionately about what other people consider a sideshow. Nevertheless, beauty too draws us to approach it (is 'attractive'); it can be so overwhelming as to be terrifying; we can feel enslaved by it; it can make the world seem a joyful place, that we are delighted to inhabit and be alive in; and it can exist at lesser degrees of power, at which it gives pleasure or comfort. There is also the important fact that we do not always appreciate beauty without going through a learning process: what is enjoyed at first encounter may in retrospect seem kitschy or facile, and often the objects we admire most on deeper acquaintance – Beethoven's quartets, perhaps, or Cézanne's paintings – take time and attention before we can appreciate them fully.

Out of the huge range of themes beauty suggests to us, I want to single out one in particular: that the encounter with beauty gives rise to joy or, at its lower levels, pleasure. The psychoanalyst is of course very aware it may give rise to many other emotions, including envy and (Meltzer's term) apprehension. But these are complications in our response, and I am wanting to stay here with what is elementary and, in a sense, diagnostic. I know I am encountering beauty *because* I feel joyful, beholding it. (I am echoing here Aquinas's famous saying: 'the beautiful is what, when seen, pleases'.)

With beauty, and its subjective reciprocal, joy, we meet the aesthetic analogues of intrinsic moral value and its subjective reciprocal, worship. Of the two vocabularies, the aesthetic one is simpler and, I think, more immediately persuasive to the modern ear. The word 'axiology' is some-times used as an overarching term for the study of values, including both moral and aesthetic, but it has hardly become a household term and we lack a vocabulary at present to unite these two great related discourses or departments of thought. They do, however, belong together, and when one attempts to clarify the notion of 'intrinsic value' it is difficult to do so without reaching for the idea of an appraising faculty that perceives moral qualities as the aesthetic response perceives beauty (with similar allowances of reasonable reliability, intersubjective validation, and the need for educa-tion and the possibility of mistakes and revisions of judgement in the light of further experience). When Kant says: 'respect (*Achtung*) is a tribute which we cannot refuse to merit' he is clearly implying the existence of such a faculty. Trying to think on the 'axiological' level, I want to suggest that the two faculties that appraise aesthetic and moral qualities are parallel and perhaps ultimately spring from a single root.

The idea that beauty characterises the moral world as well as that of perception is far from new. St Augustine spoke of God as *pulchritudo tam antiqua et tam nova* ('beauty so ancient and so new'), and Christian writings speak conventionally of 'the beauty of holiness'. For neo-Platonic thought, earthly beauty was the mortal veil through which we may glimpse divine grace, a theory echoed by Romantics and summarised by Keats when he derived as the ultimate message of his Grecian urn that 'beauty is truth, truth beauty'. Freud approached beauty in one of his more diminishing moods – it 'has no obvious use', he said, 'nor is there any clear cultural necessity for it' (Freud 1930: 82–83) – but later psychoanalysts, in par-ticular Kenneth Wright (2000) and Donald Meltzer, have recognised the huge power and importance of the experience of beauty, and find its origins, above all, in joyful episodes in babyhood when the baby can perceive the mother's face and breast as conveying an experience of lovable safety and beauty.

The psychoanalytic discussion of beauty has so far been mainly in relation to visual experiences. The work of Colwyn Trevarthen and his colleagues, which I have several times referred to (Malloch and Trevarthen 2009), marks a major extension of this work into the area of musicality, and the recognition of the deep roots of human conversation in the dance-like, musical and rhythmic qualities that suffuse the 'protoconversation' of mother and baby. There can be no doubt that this will be an immensely fertile area for research in the future.

'Liveliness' is a useful concept that brings together the ideas of visual and musical beauty. We can already see that 'liveliness' in later life, the capacity to be delighted by the world and deeply engaged with it, the capacity to find things 'meaningful', is intimately connected with such early experience. Meltzer and Williams (1988: 8–9) remark: 'It has probably escaped no-one's attention that the percentage of "beautiful" mothers recorded in the course of psychoanalysis far exceeds the national average' and if this is true, it no doubts reflects the fact that babies find beauty in many sorts of joyful, playful and loving interaction that might not meet the requirements of adult aesthetic criteria. (Even in adult experience we know that 'beauty' in persons is not a mere matter of looks.) The distress of the baby on encountering a lack of liveliness in the mother, for example the 'still-face' experiment (Tronick et al. 1978) in which the baby reacts to the mother's sudden loss of responsiveness by working very hard to re-engage her, then becomes intensely wary and then breaks down in desperate misery and uncoordination – or, in psychoanalytic experience, the long-term effect on children of maternal depression and mourning, and the work such children do to bring a smile to the mother's face – all these things point to the huge importance of beauty and joy in early development.

The notion of 'axiology', which may seem rather abstract when one is imagining adult experience, becomes much more convincing when one thinks of the protoconversation. In this realm, the word 'lovely' is used very naturally, both of mothers and babies, and carries an idea in which moral and physical beauty can hardly be separated, and are inseparable too from the reciprocal subjective response of love, which they evoke and by which they are recognised. This is perhaps the most striking example of an everyday use of language that bridges the axiological divide. In more adult realms, the divide is inescapable: there is often a carry-over of vocabulary between aesthetic and moral discourses, but as a rule the language appears to be at home in one and used metaphorically in the other. This is true of such words as harmony, balance, justice, concord and proportion. Metaphors of light, perceived as beautiful, often also provide bridges: 'Bliss was it in that dawn', said Wordsworth of the heady hopeful early days of the French Revolution; or we say playfully of something that it 'shines like a good deed in a naughty world'. The Dark Ages were those in which the 'light' of classical civilisation had been quenched by invading barbarians.

Nevertheless, the absence of an effective axiology is very striking. It means that in speaking of values in modern English, we lack a necessary deck of vocabulary. To cope with this, I shall use 'beauty' in inverted commas as a term of art, to mean something carried by aesthetic beauty that is also carried by what is experienced as having intrinsic moral worth. 'Beauty' in this expanded sense gives rise to joy and 'worship' (which in inverted commas is another term of art, meaning the emotional recognition of value, not necessarily in a designated religious context).

The pervasively instrumental cast of mind in a materialist scientific and consumerist culture is pernicious when it seems to assert that there are no values other than those of human welfare, defined in terms of possessions, consumption, status (power, celebrity) and freedom from injury. A critic might concede that this vision of human welfare has a degree of beauty in its own right, but it is a restricted one because the vision comes to a stop in a solely human outcome. The criticism of idolatry and the emphasis on the 'infinite' in traditional religions are a way of keeping aspiration and the vision of 'beauty' open and ensuring that it nowhere reaches a stop in this way. The imaginative horizon is always kept open to further possibility. (This open-ness is remarkably important. I know someone who became depressed from contemplating 'the heat-death of the universe', billions of years in the future.) Joy and 'worship' require the exhilarating space of 'infinity' if they are to breathe the oxygen they need.

The circle

I think the basic circularity on which an adequate value-system depends is becoming apparent. For the sake of simplicity, I shall now try to describe it in dogmatic, declarative terms. Intrinsic value is recognised because of the quality I have called 'beauty', a quality transcending the divide between moral and aesthetic discourses: it is a quality present in the object, and to that extent 'objective', but it can be recognised only by a subject capable of perceiving it and in a state of mind to acknowledge it, consciously or unconsciously. In this sense, 'beauty' cannot be described in either purely 'objective' or purely 'subjective' terms.

To recognise 'beauty' is not only a cognitive process but also and more importantly an affective one, involving the experience of joy which gives rise to 'worship', both of which, despite their apparently positive labels, include an element of suffering and subordination of the experiencing subject (who may for this reason try to avoid feeling them). This element of suffering has to do with three things: partly that the perception of 'beauty' entails a diminution of self-regard in the subject as he perceives himself to be by contrast incomplete or insufficient (not having the same 'beauty' as the object), partly that it draws attention poignantly to the absence of 'beauty' in much of the subject's other experience, and partly that it creates a wish that the experience would last 'for ever' and therefore reminds the subject of the transience of all experience and triggers anticipation of the inevitable eventual loss both of the 'worshipped' object and of the self. ('See Naples and die' – the hackneyed saying is a recognition that an experience of beauty may set up such yearning for it that all subsequent life can only be a sad disappointment.) Some people do not dare to fall in love because love brings with it the inescapable painful prospect of, sooner or later, losing the loved person, a connection recognised with sometimes startling explicitness in the traditional Anglican wedding service by the phrase 'till death us do part'. For this reason, faith requires courage. Faith is the determination to accept and give full value to both this joy and this suffering, perceived as the fullest recognition of reality that the subject is capable of. Joy, 'worship' and 'beauty' are irreducible terms in this circle, and it cannot be said which one of them comes first; faith is the determination to take all the terms with full seriousness.

It is important that this circle cannot be confined within one or other of the categories *objective* or *subjective*. It involves – and here I think my thought coincides with Michael Polanyi's – an act of commitment by a *person*, whose being is not adequately described either in subjective or in objective terms, who discovers that he lives, and determines to live, in a world that includes these values, and in which these values will influence, and will often govern, his choices of action. He discovers that, although he is a centre of decision-making, he is not separate from the world, like the isolated Cartesian ego, but is within the world, impinged upon by it, and impinging on it, in a continuing reciprocity. 'The world' is one that includes other people, but that is not all that it is.

Responsible commitment is so-called because it is active in response to a perceived value – it takes fully seriously its own affect of 'worship' in response to perceived 'beauty' – and it involves maintaining, being committed to, a decision made on that basis which, because it cuts off other possibilities, necessarily entails loss of freedom and regret. In this way it is also responsible in the sense that, having committed itself to its perceived values, it will be discovered to hold them when challenged by the environment: the committed person will be discovered to respond as a self that knowingly owes its shape, and has chosen to owe its shape, to those values.

Concluding unscientific postscript

I pause here, because I think what I have outlined above is also a sort of skeleton key to 'religion'. Throughout this book it has been necessary to struggle with a diversity of incompatible vocabularies – both rational ones such as those of psychoanalysis, philosophy, neuroscience and evolutionary biology, and also more intuitive ones such as those of religion and poetry. These vocabularies have been partially inter-translatable but not entirely – hence the need to move between them – and in this final chapter I have succumbed rather reluctantly to the impulse to create new vocabulary, not by creating new words but by putting existing ones into quotation marks. This is unsatisfactory, but less unsatisfactory, I think, than creating new words out of thin air. (Psychoanalysts are already guilty of cathexis and parapraxis, philobat and ocnophile – quite enough guilt for one profession!)

As in my previous summary in Chapter 6 (in which I discussed the effects of distinguishing primary and secondary qualities), I arrive at a vision of a world in which values and 'facts' cannot finally be segregated: there is not a 'real world' of the truths of physics, or of the sciences more generally, and a subjective or 'inner world' of feelings and values. There is only one world, of indescribable complexity – that is to say, we shall never get to the end of attempting to describe it – and the various sciences, like the various religions, each has its own take on this one world. Unsurprisingly, each then develops its own vocabulary and way of thinking, and the result is the intellectual Babel we all have to struggle with. Some thinkers respond to it simplistically, by deciding that one vocabulary or group of vocabularies ('Islam', 'science') conveys the truth and all the rest are redundant or deluded – such thinking leads, for example, to the physicists' fantasy of a 'Theory of Everything', or to fundamentalism or scientism – and others do what I have attempted to do in this book and try to move among languages and take many different views into account.

The attempt to move among languages is paradoxical and doomed to at least partial failure. The sciences, while their vocabularies cannot be reduced to one another (you cannot do biology in the language of quantum physics, or vice versa), accept that they are a provisional construction, always advancing, never completed, whereas religions traditionally have been more ambitious. Religions have often claimed to speak the absolute truth, without leaving any way open to future development. This is partly because they are built on very much more primitive intellectual foundations than modern science. And, of course, as soon as religions become the basis of political structures, that is to say more or less as soon as they are founded, they become shaped like any other grouping by political motives, to become established, to defeat their rivals, to raise funds, and so on. This increases the pressure on them to make claims to certainty and to 'repudiate the feminine' – to appear 'strong' and certain. However, even in this matter it is impossible to generalise: religious mystics have always been powerfully aware of the inadequacy of their language, and some, including the Buddha himself, have made claims with great caution, while with the growing politicisation of science, the increasing costs of research, and so forth, the rewards for dishonest claims to certainty in science, and for increasingly vicious polemics against alternative views, have become very difficult to resist. (At the time of writing, there have recently been examples of this when medical research has been complicit with hugely wealthy pharmaceutical companies.)

When I call what I have written a skeleton key to religion, what I mean is that I think it points to what in essence all religions are (they are ontologies that take 'beauty' and 'worship' seriously). 'Religion' in this sense cannot be simply discarded, as many recent thinkers have claimed to want to discard it, because the values we hold have ontological implications – Charles Taylor's 'moral ontologies' – whether we decide to cash them as mainstream religious teachings or not. Unless we can think about these matters explicitly, we are bound to be left adrift and vulnerable to other thinkers with more one-sided convictions. Such thinkers include extremist politicians, ardent advocates of simplistic solutions (such as the believers in 'market forces' at the start of the twenty-first century), and in general people with a strong motive to seduce us or sell us things (advertisers, ideologues).

When I started writing the papers which became the basis of this book, I was more impressed with 'science' than I am now. That is not because I am less impressed with the wonderful vision that science has given us access to of the development of the universe, from the Big Bang and the generations of the galaxies to the evolution of life on an astonishing and very possibly unique planet. But, as these chapters have I hope shown, the more one contemplates these 'triumphs' of our cognitive and practical faculties, the more devastating seems the failure of the scientific mind to take seriously the valuing and affective side of our capacities. Whether we call it putting Nature 'to the trials and tortures of art' (experimentation), like Francis Bacon (1605: 82), or 'repudiating the feminine', like Freud, the massive, transformative developments called the Scientific Revolution and the Enlightenment have left us with few refuges from the limitless intrusiveness of human greed and power-seeking. I shall not add to the confusion by calling this intrusiveness 'masculine': like love, it is a part of human nature, in all of us, in both sexes, and at all ages.

As I end, I am haunted by the thought of Shakespeare. Shakespeare and Galileo were exact coevals (Shakespeare 1564–1616, Galileo 1564–1642). But Shakespeare seems to belong to the previous age. Galileo was developing his telescope just as Shakespeare was writing his final plays. The man who could write *King Lear* was no denier of the horrors that human beings can visit on themselves. But, at the end of his career, Shakespeare could comfort himself with the thought that, whatever the wickedness and folly of one generation, the next would have the opportunity to do things better. That, I take it, is the message of *A Winter's Tale* and *The Tempest*. Prospero retires to Milan, to meditate on approaching death; Ferdinand and Miranda go forward into a new future. 'Great creating Nature' would always bring forth new possibilities, with the lovely characteristics of youth and hope.

Four centuries later, we have put Nature to the trials and tortures of experiment, following Bacon's recommendation. And as he predicted, she has yielded up her secrets. We now know vastly more than Shakespeare did; we can feed and service gigantic human populations, unimaginable in his day; we can do things – air travel, email, organ transplants, nuclear war – which would undoubtedly have astounded him. He would probably have envied our general physical health and longevity. But the man who wrote about 'great creating Nature' was not a sentimentalist: he knew about 'the repudiation of the feminine', and in his plays he explored again and again the tragedies that follow from human ambition and hubris. Would he feel we are better off, all things considered, for having taken the long road to which we were pointed by his clever contemporaries, Galileo, Bacon, Descartes and the rest?

There is of course no answer to that question, just as, of course, there is no altering the fact that we have taken that road. But the reason why, attempting to think about values, this book has so often gone back to the early seventeenth century, is because it was then that the crucial intellectual moves were made that in the long run shaped, and will very largely continue to shape, the world we live in. The road we are on now is the road we started on then, and if, as seems possible, it is a road that may as it continues become increasingly damaging to the welfare of the planet, including its human population, we need to understand as well as we can how so much attractive intellectual enthusiasm, so much devoted hard work, and so many broadly speaking good intentions, could have resulted in such an outcome. The vivid contrast between Shakespeare's attitude to Nature, and Bacon's, an example of the difference discussed in this book as that between the perception of 'subjects' and the perception of 'objects', gives, I think, an important clue.

References

Auerbach, E. (1953) *Mimesis: The Representation of Reality in Western Literature*, trans. W.R. Trask, Princeton, NJ: Princeton University Press.

Bacon, F. (1605) *The Advancement of Learning*, Book II, Chapter II, edited by W.A. Wright (1891), Oxford: Clarendon Press.

Benson, H. (1976) *The Relaxation Response*, New York: HarperTorch.

Berne, E. (1964) *The Games People Play*, New York: Ballantine.

Bhagavad Gita (1965) Trans. Swami Chidbhavananda, Madras State: Sri Ramakrishna Tupovanam.

Bhagavad Gita (1969) Trans. R.C. Zaehner, Oxford: Oxford University Press.

Bion, W.R. (1962) *Learning from Experience*, London: Karnac.

Bion, W.R. (1970) *Attention and Interpretation*, London: Karnac.

Bion, W.R. (1992) *Cogitations*, London: Karnac.

Bishop, E. (1991) 'In the waiting room', in Bishop, *Complete Poems, 1927–1979*, London: Chatto & Windus.

Black, D.M. (1993) 'What sort of a thing is a religion?', *International Journal of Psychoanalysis* 74: 613–625.

Black, D.M. (2000) 'The functioning of religions from a modern psychoanalytic perspective', *Mental Health, Religion and Culture* 3 (1): 13–26.

Black, D.M. (ed.) (2006) *Psychoanalysis and Religion in the 21st Century: Competitors or Collaborators*, London: Routledge.

Blass, R. (2003) 'The puzzle of Freud's puzzle analogy', *International Journal of Psychoanalysis* 84: 669–682.

Bortoft, H. (1996) *The Wholeness of Nature: Goethe's Way of Science*, Edinburgh: Floris.

Breuer, J. and Freud, S. (1895) *Studies on Hysteria, Standard Edition 2*, pp. 1–309, London: Hogarth.

Brhadaranyaka Upanishad (1953) In S. Radhakrishnan (ed. and trans.) *The Principal Upanishads*, London: George Allen & Unwin.

Britton, R. (1998) 'Belief and psychic reality', in Britton, *Belief and Imagination*, London: Routledge.

Britton, R. (2003a) ' Emancipation from the Superego', in Britton, *Sex, Death, and the Superego*, London: Karnac.

Britton, R. (2003b) 'The concept of the Ego', in Britton, *Sex, Death, and the Superego*, London: Karnac.

Britton, R. (2006) 'Emancipation from the Superego: A clinical study of the Book of Job', in D.M. Black (ed.) *Psychoanalysis and Religion in the 21st Century: Competitors or Collaborators*, London: Routledge.

Brooke, J.H. (1991) *Science and Religion: Some Historical Perspectives*, Cambridge: Cambridge University Press.

Broucek, F. (1982) 'Shame and its relation to early narcissistic developments', *International Journal of Psychoanalysis* 63: 369–378.

Buddhaghosa (1964) *The Path of Purification*, trans. Bhikkhu Nyanamoli, pp. 247–283, Colombo: M.D. Gunasena.

Chalmers, D. (1996) *The Conscious Mind: In Search of a Fundamental Theory*, New York: Oxford University Press.

Churchland, P. (1986) *Neurophilosophy: Toward a Unified Science of the Mind/Brain*, Cambridge, MA: MIT Press.

Conze, E. (1951) *Buddhism*, Oxford: Cassirer.

Crick, F. (1994) *The Astonishing Hypothesis: The Scientific Search for the Soul*, London: Simon & Schuster.

Dalai Lama (1999) *Consciousness at the Cross-roads: Conversations with the Dalai Lama on Brain Science and Buddhism*, edited by Z. Houshmand, R.B. Livingston and B.A. Wallace, New York: Snow Lion.

Dalai Lama (2007) 'Key principles of the Buddhadharma', in Dalai Lama, *Mind in Comfort and Ease*, Somerville, MA: Wisdom.

Damasio, A. (2000) *The Feeling of What Happens: Body, Emotion and the Making of Consciousness*, London: Vintage.

Damasio, A. (2003) *Looking for Spinoza: Joy, Sorrow and the Feeling Brain*, London: Heinemann.

d'Aquili, E. and Newberg, A. (1999) *The Mystical Mind: Probing the Biology of Religious Experience*, Minneapolis, MN: Fortress.

Darwin, C. (1859) *On the Origin of Species*, London: John Murray.

Darwin, C. (1871) *The Descent of Man*, London: John Murray.

Darwin, C. (1887) *The Life and Letters of Charles Darwin, Including an Auto-biographical Chapter*, London: John Murray.

Dawkins, R. (1976) *The Selfish Gene*, Oxford: Oxford University Press.

Dawkins, R. (2006) *The God Delusion*, New York: Houghton Mifflin.

Dennett, D.C. (1991) *Consciousness Explained*, London: Penguin.

Dennett, D.C. (2006) *Breaking the Spell: Religion as a Natural Phenomenon*, London: Allen Lane.

Descartes, R. (1637) *Discourse on the Method*, in Descartes, *Key Philosophical Writings* (1997), trans. E.S. Haldane and G.R.T. Ross, ed. E. Chavez-Arvizo, Ware: Wordsworth Editions.

Dissanayake, E. (2009) 'Root, leaf, blossom or bole: Concerning the origin and adaptive function of music', in S. Malloch and C. Trevarthen (eds) *Communicative Musicality: Exploring the Basis of Human Companionship*, Oxford: Oxford University Press.

Economist (2004) 'Signs of success', *The Economist*, 21 February.

Eddington, A. (1929) *The Nature of the Physical World*, Cambridge: Cambridge University Press.

Edelman, G. (1992) *Bright Air, Brilliant Fire*, New York: Basic Books.

Eliade, M. (1958) *Yoga, Immortality and Freedom*, trans. W.R. Trask, London: Routledge & Kegan Paul.

Ellenberger, H. (1970) *The Discovery of the Unconscious: The History and Evolution of Dynamic Psychiatry*, London: Allen Lane.

Ellmann, R. (1979) *Yeats: The Man and the Masks*, Oxford: Oxford University Press.

Engler, J. (2003) 'Being somebody and being nobody: A reexamination of the understanding of self in psychoanalysis and Buddhism', in J. Safran (ed.) *Psychoanalysis and Buddhism: An Unfolding Dialogue*, Boston, MA: Wisdom.

Erikson, E. (1968) *Identity: Youth and Crisis*, London: Faber & Faber.

Erikson, E. (1970) *Gandhi's Truth: On the Origins of Militant Non-violence*, New York: Norton.

Fairbairn, R. (1944) 'Endopsychic structure considered in terms of object-relationships', in Fairbairn, *Psychoanalytic Studies of the Personality*, London: Tavistock.

Fonagy, P. and Target, M. (1996) 'Playing with reality, I: Theory of mind and the normal development of psychic reality', *International Journal of Psychoanalysis* 77: 217–233.

Fonagy, P. and Target, M. (2000) 'Playing with reality, III: The persistence of dual psychic reality in borderline patients', *International Journal of Psychoanalysis* 81: 853–873.

Fox, G. (1694) *The Journal of George Fox*, edited by J.L. Nickalls (1997), Philadelphia, PA: Religious Society of Friends.

Freud, A. (1936) *The Ego and the Mechanisms of Defence*, London: Hogarth.

Freud, S. (1894) 'The neuro-psychoses of defence', *Standard Edition 3*, pp. 45–61, London: Hogarth.

Freud, S. (1895) *Project for a Scientific Psychology*, *Standard Edition 1*, pp. 295–387, London: Hogarth.

Freud, S. (1900) *The Interpretation of Dreams*, *Standard Edition 4–5*, London: Hogarth.

Freud, S. (1905) *Three Essays on the Theory of Sexuality*, *Standard Edition 7*, pp. 123–243, London: Hogarth.

Freud, S. (1907) 'Obsessive actions and religious practices', *Standard Edition 9*, pp. 115–127, London: Hogarth.

Freud, S. (1911) 'Psycho-analytic notes on an autobiographical account of a case of paranoia', *Standard Edition 12*, pp. 1–82, London: Hogarth.

Freud, S. (1912) 'Recommendations to physicians practising psycho-analysis', *Standard Edition 12*, pp. 109–120, London: Hogarth.

Freud, S. (1912–1913) *Totem and Taboo*, *Standard Edition 13*, pp. 1–161, London: Hogarth.

Freud, S. (1913) 'On beginning the treatment', *Standard Edition 12*, pp. 121–144, London: Hogarth.

Freud, S. (1914) 'On transience', *Standard Edition 14*, pp. 303–307, London: Hogarth.

Freud, S. (1915) 'Instincts and their vicissitudes', *Standard Edition 14*, pp. 117–140, London: Hogarth.

Freud, S. (1917) 'Mourning and melancholia', *Standard Edition 14*, pp. 237–258, London: Hogarth.

Freud, S. (1920) *Beyond the Pleasure Principle, Standard Edition 18*, pp. 1–64, London: Hogarth.

Freud, S. (1921) *Group Psychology and the Analysis of the Ego, Standard Edition 18*, pp. 65–143, London: Hogarth.

Freud, S. (1923) *The Ego and the Id, Standard Edition 19*, pp. 1–59, London: Hogarth.

Freud, S. (1924a) 'The economic problem of masochism', *Standard Edition 19*, pp. 155–170, London: Hogarth.

Freud, S. (1924b) 'Letter to Fritz Wittels', *Standard Edition 19*, pp. 286–288, London: Hogarth.

Freud, S. (1925a) 'Negation', *Standard Edition 19*, pp. 233–239, London: Hogarth.

Freud, S. (1925b) 'An autobiographical study', *Standard Edition 20*, pp. 1–70, London: Hogarth.

Freud, S. (1927a) Postscript to *The Question of Lay Analysis, Standard Edition 20*, pp. 251–258, London: Hogarth.

Freud, S. (1927b) *The Future of an Illusion, Standard Edition 21*, pp. 1–56, London: Hogarth.

Freud, S. (1930) *Civilization and its Discontents, Standard Edition 21*, pp. 57–145, London: Hogarth.

Freud, S. (1933a) *New Introductory Lectures on Psychoanalysis, Standard Edition 22*, pp. 1–182, London: Hogarth.

Freud, S. (1933b) 'The question of a Weltanschauung', *Standard Edition 22*, pp. 158–182, London: Hogarth.

Freud, S. (1937) 'Analysis terminable and interminable', *Standard Edition 23*, pp. 209–253, London: Hogarth.

Freud, S. (1939) *Moses and Monotheism, Standard Edition 23*, pp. 3–140, London: Hogarth.

Freud, S. (1940) *An Outline of Psycho-Analysis, Standard Edition 23*, pp. 139–207, London: Hogarth.

Frosh, S. (2006) 'Psychoanalysis and Judaism', in D.M. Black (ed.) *Psychoanalysis and Religion in the 21st Century: Competitors or Collaborators?* London: Routledge.

Gabbard, G. and Westen, D. (2003) 'Rethinking therapeutic action', *International Journal of Psychoanalysis* 84: 823–841,

Galileo (1615) 'Letter to the Grand Duchess Christina', in S. Drake (ed.) (1957) *Discoveries and Opinions of Galileo: Selected Translated Writings*, New York: Anchor.

Galileo (1623) 'The assayer', in S. Drake (ed.) (1957) *Discoveries and Opinions of Galileo: Selected Translated Writings*, New York: Anchor.

Gay, P. (1988) *Freud: A Life for Our Time*, London: Dent.

Goleman, D. (2003) *Destructive Emotions: A Dialogue with the Dalai Lama*, London: Bloomsbury.

Gould, S.J. (2001) *Rocks of Ages*, London: Jonathan Cape.

Govinda, Lama A. (1966) *The Way of the White Clouds*, London: Hutchinson.

Green, V. (ed.) (2003) *Emotional Development in Psychoanalysis, Attachment Theory and Neuroscience*, Hove: Brunner-Routledge.

Grubrich-Simitis, I. (1996) *Back to Freud's Texts: Making Silent Documents Speak*, trans. P. Slotkin, New Haven, CT: Yale University Press.

Grubrich-Simitis, I. (1997) *Early Freud and Late Freud*, trans. P. Slotkin, London: Routledge.

Hinshelwood, R. (1989) *A Dictionary of Kleinian Thought*, London: Free Association Books.

Hinshelwood, R. (1991) *A Dictionary of Kleinian Thought*, 2nd edn, London: Free Association Books.

Hoffman, E. (1991) *Lost in Translation: Life in a New Language*, London: Minerva.

Hopkins, J. (2000) 'The death drive', paper given at a meeting of the Applied Section of the British Psycho-Analytical Society, 22 November.

Hume, D. (1739) *A Treatise of Human Nature*, edited by D.F. Norton and M.J. Norton (2000) Oxford: Oxford University Press.

Humphrey, N. (1997) 'Response to Mark Solms', *Journal of the American Psychoanalytic Association* 45: 726–731.

James, W. (1882) 'The sentiment of rationality', in James, *The Will to Believe and Other Essays in Popular Philosophy*, published 1897, New York: Longmans Green; reprinted in 1956, New York: Dover.

James, W. (1890) *The Principles of Psychology*, Volume 1, New York: Henry Holt, reprinted in 1956, New York: Dover.

James, W. (1898) *Human Immortality*, bound together with *The Will to Believe and Other Essays in Popular Philosophy*, reprinted in 1956, New York: Dover.

James, W. (1902) *The Varieties of Religious Experience*, London: Penguin.

Jaques, E. (1988) 'Death and the midlife crisis', in E.B. Spillius (ed.) *Melanie Klein Today*, Volume 2, London: Routledge.

Jones, E. (1964) *The Life and Work of Sigmund Freud*, abridged by L. Trilling and S. Marcus, Harmondsworth: Penguin.

Kabat-Zinn, J. (2001) *Full Catastrophe Living: How to Cope with Stress, Pain and Illness Using Mindfulness Meditation*, London: Piatkus.

Kant, I. (1784) 'An answer to the question, "What is Enlightenment?"', in Kant, *Political Writings*, trans. H.B. Nisbet, edited II. Reiss (1991), Cambridge: Cambridge University Press.

Kant, I. (1788) *The Critique of Practical Reason*, trans. T. Kingsmill Abbot (2005), Digireads.com.

Keller, E.F. (1983) *A Feeling for the Organism: The Life and Work of Barbara McClintock*, New York: W.H. Freeman.

Kelman, H. (1987) 'On resonant cognition', *International Review of Psycho-Analysis* 14: 111–123.

Klein, M. (1926) 'The psychological principles of early analysis', in Klein, *Love, Guilt and Reparation and Other Works 1921–1945*, London: Hogarth Press and Institute of Psycho-Analysis.

Klein, M. (1940) 'Mourning and its relation to manic-depressive states', in Klein, *Love, Guilt and Reparation and Other Works 1921–1945*, London: Hogarth Press and Institute of Psycho-Analysis.

Klein, M. (1946) 'Notes on some schizoid mechanisms', in Klein, *Envy and Gratitude and Other Works 1946–1963*, London: Hogarth Press and Institute of Psycho-Analysis.

Koestler, A. (1982) 'The holon', in Koestler, *Bricks to Babel: Selected Writings*, London: Picador.

Kors, A.C. (1990) *Atheism in France, 1650–1729: The Orthodox Sources of Disbelief*, Princeton, NJ: Princeton University Press.

Kuhn, T. (1962) *The Structure of Scientific Revolutions*, Chicago, IL: University of Chicago Press.

Kumar, M. (2008) *Quantum: Einstein, Bohr and the Great Debate about the Nature of Reality*, Cambridge: Icon.

Küng, H. (1974) *On Being a Christian*, trans. E. Quinn, London: SCM Press.

Lakoff, G. and Johnson, M. (1999) *Philosophy in the Flesh: The Embodied Mind and its Challenge to Western Thought*, New York: Basic Books.

Lancaster, B. (2004) *Approaches to Consciousness: The Marriage of Science and Mysticism*, London: Palgrave Macmillan.

Lear, J. (1990) *Love and its Place in Nature*, New York: Farrar, Straus & Giroux.

Lear, J. (2006) *Radical Hope: Ethics in the Face of Cultural Devastation*, Cambridge, MA: Harvard University Press.

Lear, J. (2009) 'Technique and final cause in psychoanalysis', *International Journal of Psychoanalysis* 90: 1299–1317.

Lewis, D. (1972) 'Psychophysical and theoretical identifications', *Australasian Journal of Philosophy* 50: 249–258.

Libet, B. (1996) 'Neural processes in the production of conscious experience', in M. Velmans (ed.) *The Science of Consciousness: Psychological, Neuropsychological, and Clinical Reviews*, London: Routledge.

Locke, J. (1689) *An Essay Concerning Human Understanding*, reprinted in 1997, London: Penguin Classics.

Locke, J. (1924) *An Essay Concerning Human Understanding*, abridged and edited by A.S. Pringle-Pattison, Oxford: Oxford University Press.

Loewald, H. (1978) *Psychoanalysis and the History of the Individual*, New Haven, CT: Yale University Press.

McDougall, W. (1909) *An Introduction to Social Psychology*, London: Methuen.

McGinn, C. (1989) 'Can we solve the mind-body problem?', *Mind* 98 (391): 349–366, reprinted in W. Lyons (ed.) (1995) *Modern Philosophy of Mind*, London: Everyman.

McGinn, C. (2004) 'Consciousness and cosmology: Hyperdualism ventilated', in McGinn, *Consciousness and its Objects*, Oxford: Oxford University Press.

Macquarrie, J. (1966) *Principles of Christian Theology*, London: SCM Press.

Mahfouz, N. (1991) *The Cairo Trilogy, Volume I: Palace Walk*, published in Arabic 1956, trans. W.M. Hutchins and O.E. Kenny, London: Doubleday.

Malloch, S. and Trevarthen, C. (eds) (2009) *Communicative Musicality: Exploring the Basis of Human Companionship*, Oxford: Oxford University Press.

Mayer, E.L. (2001) 'On "Telepathic dreams"? An unpublished paper by Robert J. Stoller', *Journal of the American Psychoanalytic Association* 49: 629–657.

Medawar, P.B. and Medawar J.S. (1984) *Aristotle to Zoos: A Philosophical Dictionary of Biology*, London: Weidenfeld & Nicolson.

Meikle, J. (2004) 'Yoga benefits body, soul and blood vessels', (London) *Guardian*, 8 November, 6.

Meissner, W.W. (1992) *Ignatius Loyola: The Psychology of a Saint*, New Haven, CT: Yale University Press.

Meltzer, D. and Williams, M.H. (1988) *The Apprehension of Beauty: The Role of Aesthetic Conflict in Development, Art and Violence*, Strath Tay: Clunie Press.

Midgley, M. (2001) 'Rationality and rainbows', in Midgley, *Science and Poetry*, London: Routledge.

Mitchell, S.A. (2003) 'Somebodies and nobodies', Commentary on J. Engler, 'Being somebody and being nobody: A reexamination of the understanding of self in psychoanalysis and Buddhism', in J. Safran (ed.) *Psychoanalysis and Buddhism: An Unfolding Dialogue*, Boston, MA: Wisdom.

Nagel, T. (1979a) 'What is it like to be a bat?', in Nagel, *Mortal Questions*, Cambridge: Cambridge University Press.

Nagel, T. (1979b) 'Panpsychism', in Nagel, *Mortal Questions*, Cambridge: Cambridge University Press.

Nagel, T. (1979c) 'Subjective and objective', in Nagel, *Mortal Questions*, Cambridge: Cambridge University Press.

Panikkar, R. (1989) *The Silence of God*, Maryknoll, NY: Orbis.

Parsons, M. (2006) 'Ways of transformation', in D.M. Black (ed.) *Psychoanalysis and Religion in the 21st Century*, London: Routledge.

Peat, F.D. (2002) *From Certainty to Uncertainty: The Story of Science and Ideas in the Twentieth Century*, Washington, DC: Joseph Henry Press.

Phillipson, N. (1983) 'Adam Smith as civic moralist', in I. Hont and M. Ignatieff (eds) *Wealth and Virtue: The Shaping of Political Economy in the Scottish Enlightenment*, Cambridge: Cambridge University Press.

Pigman, G.W. (1995) 'Freud and the history of empathy', *International Journal of Psychoanalysis* 76: 237–256.

Pinker, S. (1997) *How the Mind Works*, London: Allen Lane.

Polanyi, M. (1958) *Personal Knowledge: Towards a Post-Critical Philosophy*, London: Routledge & Kegan Paul.

Pugmire, D. (2005) *Sound Sentiments: Integrity in the Emotions*, Oxford: Oxford University Press.

Pugmire, D. (2006) 'The secular reception of religious music', *Philosophy* 81: 65–79.

Putnam, H. (1960) 'Minds and machines', in S. Hook (ed.) *Dimensions of Mind*, New York: Collier.

Rahula, W. (1967) *What the Buddha Taught*, 2nd edn, Bedford: Gordon Fraser.

Rawls, J. (2000) *Lectures on the History of Moral Philosophy*, Cambridge, MA: Harvard University Press.

Richardson, R.D. (2006) *William James: In the Maelstrom of American Modernism*, Boston, MA: Houghton Mifflin.

Rizzutto, A-M. (1979) *The Birth of the Living God*, Chicago, IL: University of Chicago Press.

Rosenfeld, H. (1988) 'A clinical approach to the psychoanalytic theory of the life and death instincts: An investigation into the aggressive aspects of narcissism', in E.B. Spillius (ed.) *Melanie Klein Today*, Volume 1, London: Routledge.

Safran, J. (ed.) (2003) *Psychoanalysis and Buddhism: An Unfolding Dialogue*, Somerville, MA: Wisdom.

Sandler, J. (1993) 'On communication from patient to analyst: Not everything is projective identification', *International Journal of Psychoanalysis* 74: 1097–1107.

Sandler, J. and Dreher, A.U. (1996) *What Do Psychoanalysts Want?*, London: Routledge.

Santayana, G. (1905) *The Life of Reason*, New York: Charles Scribner's Sons.

Schopenhauer, A. (1819) *The World as Will and Representation*, trans. E.F.J. Payne (1969), New York: Dover.

Schore, A. (1994) *Affect Regulation and the Origin of the Self*, Hillsdale, NJ: Lawrence Erlbaum Associates.

Schore, A. (2003a) 'The human unconscious: The development of the right brain and its role in early emotional life', in V. Green (ed.) *Emotional Development in Psychoanalysis, Attachment Theory and Neuroscience: Creating Connections*, London: Brunner-Routledge.

Schore, A. (2003b) *Affect Regulation and the Repair of the Self*, New York: Norton.

Schrödinger, E. (1958) *Mind and Matter*, reprinted in Schrödinger (1967) *What is Life?*, Cambridge: Cambridge University Press.

Searle, J.R. (1997) 'Consciousness and the philosophers', *New York Review of Books* 44 (4): 43–50.

Segal, Z.V., Williams, J.M.G., and Teasdale, J.D. (2002) *Mindfulness-Based Cognitive Therapy for Depression: A New Approach to Preventing Relapse*, New York: Guilford.

Sereny, G. (1974) *Into that Darkness: From Mercy Killing to Mass Murder*, New York: McGraw-Hill.

Sereny, G. (1995) *Albert Speer: His Battle with Truth*, London: Macmillan.

Share, L. (1994) *If Someone Speaks It Gets Lighter*, London: Analytic Press.

Sherrington, C. (1940) *Man on his Nature*, Cambridge: Cambridge University Press.

Smart, J.J.C. (1962) 'Sensations and brain processes', in V.C. Chappell (ed.) *Philosophy of Mind*, Englewood Cliffs: Prentice-Hall.

Smart, N. (1958) *Reasons and Faiths*, London: Routledge & Kegan Paul.

Smith, A. (1759) *The Theory of Moral Sentiments*, edited by D.D. Raphael and A.L. Macfie (1976), Oxford: Oxford University Press.

Solms, M. (1997) 'What is consciousness?', *Journal of the American Psychoanalytic Association* 45 (3): 681–703.

Solms, M. (1998) 'Preliminaries for an integration of psychoanalysis and neuroscience', paper read to Contemporary Freudian Group, British Psychoanalytical Society, London, 10 June.

Solms, M. and Turnbull, O. (2002) *The Brain and the Inner World: An Introduction to the Neuroscience of Subjective Experience*, London: Karnac.

Steiner, J. (1993) *Psychic Retreats: Pathological Organisations in Psychotic, Neurotic and Borderline Patients*, London: Routledge.

Stern, D. (1985) *The Interpersonal World of the Infant: A View from Psychoanalysis and Developmental Psychology*, New York: Basic Books.

Strachey, J. (1934) 'The nature of the therapeutic action of psychoanalysis', *International Journal of Psychoanalysis* 15: 127–159.

Strachey, J. (1957) 'Editor's note to "Instincts and their vicissitudes"', *Standard Edition 14*, pp. 111–116, London: Hogarth.

Strawson, G. (2006) 'Realistic monism: Why physicalism entails panpsychism', in A. Freeman (ed.) *Consciousness and its Place in Nature*, Exeter: Imprint Academic.

Sulloway, F. (1979) *Freud: Biologist of the Mind*, New York: Basic Books.

Sulloway, F. (1996) *Born to Rebel: Birth Order, Family Dynamics and Creative Lives*, New York: Pantheon.

Symington, N. (1993) *Narcissism: A New Theory*, London: Karnac.

Symington, N. (1994) *Emotion and Spirit*, London: Cassell.

Target, M. and Fonagy, P. (1996) 'Playing with reality, II: The development of psychic reality from a theoretical perspective', *International Journal of Psychoanalysis* 77: 459–479.

Taylor, C. (1989) *Sources of the Self: The Making of the Modern Identity*, Cambridge: Cambridge University Press.

Teilhard de Chardin, P. (1959) *The Phenomenon of Man*, trans. W.R. Trask, London: Collins.

Thomas, E.J. (1949) *The Life of Buddha as Legend and History*, 3rd edn, London: Routledge & Kegan Paul.

Townsend, M., Kladder, V., Ayele, H. and Mulligan, T. (2002) 'Systematic review of clinical trials examining the effects of religion on health', *Southern Medical Journal* 95: 1429–1434.

Trevarthen, C. and Aitken, K. (2001) 'Infant intersubjectivity: Research, theory, and clinical applications', *Journal of Child Psychology and Psychiatry* 42: 3–48.

Tronick, E., Als, H., Adamson, L., Wise, S. and Brazelton, T.B. (1978) 'The infant's response to entrapment between contradictory messages in face-to-face interaction', *Journal of the American Academy of Child Psychiatry* 17: 1–13.

Turnbull, O. and Solms, M. (2003) 'Memory, amnesia and intuition: A neuro-psychoanalytic perspective', in V. Green (ed.) *Emotional Development in Psycho-analysis, Attachment Theory and Neuroscience*, London: Brunner-Routledge.

Varela, F.J. (1996) 'Neurophenomenology: A methodological remedy for the hard problem', *Journal of Consciousness Studies* 3 (4): 330–349.

Varela, F.J., Thompson, E. and Rosch, E. (1993) *The Embodied Mind: Cognitive Science and Human Experience*, Cambridge, MA: MIT Press.

Velmans, M. (2000) *Understanding Consciousness*, London: Routledge.

Vermes, G. (1973) *Jesus the Jew*, London: Collins.

Wallace, B.A. (2000) *The Taboo of Subjectivity*, Oxford: Oxford University Press.

Wallace, B.A. (2007) *Contemplative Science: Where Buddhism and Neuroscience Converge*, New York: Columbia University Press.

Wallace, B.A. (2009) *Mind in the Balance*, New York: Columbia University Press.

Wallace, E. (1991) 'Psychoanalytic perspectives on religion', *International Review of Psychoanalysis* 18: 265–278.

Wegman, C. (1985) *Psychoanalysis and Cognitive Psychology*, London: Academic Press.

Weinberg, S. (1993) *Dreams of a Final Theory: The Search for the Fundamental Laws of Nature*, Santa Fe, NM: Radius.

Wilber, K. (1996) *A Brief History of Everything*, Dublin: Newleaf.

Wilbur, R. (1989) *New and Collected Poems*, London: Faber & Faber.

Winnicott, D.W. (1960) 'Ego distortion in terms of true and false self', in Winnicott (1965) *The Maturational Process and the Facilitating Environment*, London: Hogarth Press and Institute of Psycho-Analysis.

Winnicott, D.W. (1963) 'The development of the capacity for concern', in Winnicott (1965) *The Maturational Process and the Facilitating Environment*, London: Hogarth Press and Institute of Psycho-Analysis.

Winnicott, D.W. (1964) 'Further thoughts on babies as persons', in Winnicott, *The Child, the Family and the Outside World*, Harmondsworth: Penguin.

Winnicott, D.W. (1971) 'Dreaming, fantasying and living', in Winnicott, *Playing and Reality*, London: Routledge.

Wright, K. (2000) *Vision and Separation: Between Mother and Baby*, London: Free Association Books.

Wright, K. (2006) 'Preverbal experience and the intuition of the sacred', in D.M. Black (ed.) *Psychoanalysis and Religion in the 21st Century: Competitors or Collaborators?* London: Routledge.

Wright, R. (1994) *The Moral Animal: The New Science of Evolutionary Psychology*, London: Abacus.

Yeats, W.B. (1951) *Collected Poems*, 2nd edn, London: Macmillan.

Zeman, A. (2002) *Consciousness: A User's Guide*, New Haven, CT: Yale University Press.

Index